# The Handbook for
# Single
# Adoptive
# Parents

Compiled and edited by Hope Marindin

**The National Council for Single Adoptive Parents**
**Washington, District of Columbia**

Hope Marindin
The Handbook for Single Adoptive Parents
ISBN   0-9634045-3-9
p.cm.

# National Council for Single Adoptive Parents

3824 Legation St. N.W.
Washington, D.C., 20015

Cover photographs:
   Cheryl Vichness and her daughter, Gwendolyn Lee
   Madeleine Ryan and  Ariana Fiorello
   Jacob Nestor Borders

As editor, I want to express my gratitude for the advice and information provided by the adoption experts at the National Adoption Information Clearinghouse and the North American Council on Adoptable Children; and to Sharon Kaufman, Director of the Joint Council on International Children's Services; Courteney A. Holden of Voice For Adoption; Susan Freivalds of the Adoption Education Institute and Betsy Burch, Executive Director and Queenpin of Single Parents Adopting Children Everywhere. I hope I have avoided errors in comprehension and transmission.

*All material herein not credited to named authors was written by Hope Marindin*

# Table of Contents

# Chapter I

## Questions Single People Have

### "Is a one-parent family fair to a child?'

"Would I be depriving my child of a necessary role model? Would my child be stigmatized by not having a daddy [or mommy]?" A lot of people, especially those who advocate for "family values" say yes, with the implication that a single person has no business adopting alone. Some social workers agree, and the agencies they work for, and often the sources from which they place children.

That would also apply, then, to parents who are single by the death of their spouse, and to the enormous number of people who are single by divorce. Somehow, most of their children grow up to be healthy adults. According to a March 1995 estimate from the Bureau of the Census, 27% of American children were living with one parent that month. Very often, a divorced or widowed parent remarries, endowing a child with a stepparent and sometimes step-siblings. There is some evidence that losing a parent by death or especially by divorce, and the replacement of that parent by another, can create emotional problems that the adopted child of a single parent does not have.

Most single adoptive parents grew up in two-parent families, and might even agree that the ideal family for a child is one with two loving parents (of different genders)where the mother stays home. The stay-at-home mother is a pretty rare phenomenon in large areas of U.S. culture these days, but a family with two working parents can still be a happy one. The opposite is not true: that a one-parent family is *ipso facto* an unhappy one. Study after study has shown that children in one-parent adoptive families feel secure and loved, and turn out fine. Two such studies are reprinted as Chapter VI of this Handbook.

It might be added that single people are not competing with couples for children and--the corollary--depriving some unlucky infant of a proper family if they "win." In the United States a healthy caucasian, Asian, or Latino infant can be placed in a heartbeat with a couple; there are probably three approved couples for almost every healthy U.S.-born baby. When it comes to "hard-to-place" children, however, the law of supply and demand takes over. A smaller number of couples is willing to adopt children who are waiting than the number who want newborns. Single applicants are accepted, then, for children who have waited for a family because they are older, or siblings, or disabled in some degree, or minorities.

It is possible for single people to adopt healthy U.S.-born infants, but it requires effort and research--and often a lot of money. Single people who want to adopt healthy infants more usually adopt from abroad, in areas where--at present--there are more children, including healthy infants, than there are adoptive families.

### "I'm in my forties . . . can I adopt a child?

Oddly enough, being in your late thirties, or even your forties, appears to be a plus when it comes to single-person adoption. Agencies seem to feel that single people in their thirties are more mature and they are probably right: By his/her upper thirties, a single man or woman is going to have a stable job and be a stable person who knows her/his own mind, and that's part of what agencies look for.

U.S. immigration law requires that a single person be at least 25 in order to adopt from abroad.

China will accept applicants, married or single, up to age 45for children under age one. Peru has an age ceiling of 55. The maximum age in Guatemala is usually 50---to adopt an infant! Single women must be at least 40 to adopt from Bolivia. One agency placing from Russia says the age ceiling is 60; another requires the maximum age difference between parent and child to be 55. Within the U.S., where most agencies prefer that single applicants adopt special-needs children, mature applicants are generally preferred. Maturity, in short, is an advantage.

## "I'm a single man: Can I adopt?"

Yes. With some difficulty, often, because of the unspoken assumption by many agencies, or their sources, that a man who is unmarried in his thirties or higher (a) must be gay, and (b) if he is gay, he is probably a child molester. On the contrary, research has shown no statistical connection between homosexuality and pedophilia. Pedophilia is identifiable by a trained psychologist, and men who suspect that they are meeting barriers related to questions about their sexual orientation should ask the agency to administer a test such as the Minnesota Multiphasic Personality Inventory, or to undergo an interview with a psychologist of the agency's choice, to establish their potential (whether gay or straight) to provide a healthy family for adopted children. In other words, refocus the question to "would this particular man be a good parent?"

Far fewer single men than women try to become parents by adoption, which is a pity, because boys form a definite majority of waiting children in the United States and abroad (except for China). Most single women adopt girls and, oddly enough, most adoptive couples look for girls as well. A single man applying to adopt a boy would have an advantage from the start.

A single man interested in adoption might also have an easier time if he indicated that he wanted to adopt a toddler or school--aged boy, or even a sibling group that could include a girl. As for sources, the United States, Eastern Europe, and Asian countries would be good places to look. Few countries in Central or South America appear to allow single men to adopt.

## "Should I adopt in the United States, or should I look abroad?"

That depends on you, and on the kind of child you want. The basic situation is as follows:

**Adoption of U.S.-born Children:**

In the U.S. there is a shortage of babies aged newborn to a few months old, dating from the early '70's when the pill arrived, abortions became easier, and social attitudes relaxed toward mothers who kept children born out of wedlock. At the same time, there seems to be a decline in fertility---perhaps real, perhaps partly due to the decision of many parents to postpone childbirth (and the pill has given them that option) until their careers are established. Meanwhile, the years of greatest fertility go by.

The upshot is that there may be three approved couples for every newborn, and agencies have an understandable preference for the two-parent family, all else being equal. That goes, according to most but not all agencies, for birth mothers' preferences too, and since birthmothers more and more are being given a voice in selecting the adoptive parents, that can further lower the chances for a single person. Many private adoption agencies will not even accept single people as applicants to adopt an infant, although they may be willing to do a home study that can be sent to another agency for a domestic or foreign placement.

**Waiting Children:** There is no shortage of "waiting" children needing homes, however---children from infancy up who have been taken from abusive or neglectful homes; children who are handicapped in some way, or African-American, or siblings who should not be separated. The Children's Bureau of the Dept. of Health and Human Services Adoption and Foster Care Analysis and Reporting System found that in 1999 a pool of 117,000 children in the custody of public social service agencies were free for adoption or could be quickly freed if a home were found for them.

Additional tens of thousands, by the way, are in custody but are not free for adoption because there is good reason to expect their return to their birthparents, or because the social service staff is overworked or otherwise incapable of beginning the necessary steps, or because the court system that makes the decision to terminate the birthparents' rights is still thinking of children as property rather than human beings at the most vulnerable time of their lives, with rights of their own to a permanent family. In recent years, especially in 1997, federal laws have been enacted that strongly encourage public agencies to place children in permanent families rather than leaving them in foster care for years.

The majority of couples and single prospective parents want babies, and one can entirely sympathize with this desire. But although a minority of waiting children (in the U.S. and abroad) have been so traumatized by separations and several kinds of abuse that they are unable to be part of a family, most older waiting children are hungry for love and perfectly capable of becoming loving sons and daughters and successful, happy adults. And those children can be adopted, in most cases, by single people. In fact, they are often better off with a single parent, who does not have to persuade a less-enthusiastic spouse, and who can go on making future decisions on her or his own as well. As a bonus, there are usually concrete financial benefits--- subsidies for the adoption process, maintainance subsidies until the child reaches majority, health care through Medicaid, and many social services. Still other advantages of adopting school age or older children are that you have a better idea of the child, and lower costs for child care.

**Infant Adoption:** A single person determined to adopt a healthy caucasian U.S. newborn does face a more uphill battle. If she/he is prepared to spend quite a lot of money---we are talking $30,000-$50,000 and up---it is possible to find an agency working directly with birthmothers that will accept their application. Alternatively, she (these are mostly women) can try adopting privately---advertising for a birthmother or working through an individual. It is likely to be a long haul, with some disappointments on the way, but some have succeeded by this route. A single black applicant will have an easier time looking for a black infant but again, a black couple will generally have first choice. A 1996 law sets penalties, incidentally, for restricting the placement of African-American children to African-American parents only, but taking all factors into consideration, a black applicant will still have a better chance to adopt a black baby.

**Adopting from Abroad:**

Adoption from abroad has been a successful alternative for many thousands of single individuals for twenty-odd years, since a federal law opened it to single people. (Before the passage of P.L. 94-155 on December 16, 1975, single people could not use the INS process that allows adoptors to bring foreign-born children into the U.S. as their "immediate relatives") Subsidies are not available for foreign adoptions (except for the tax credit described in Chapter II) and it is usually more expensive than a domestic adoption; from $12,000 to $30,000 total, including travel, depending on the country of origin.

Single people must approach foreign adoption with realism. Many adoptable children have spent most of their lives in orphanages, and institutional life can have a crippling effect on the emotional growth of some children. There are some health conditions that may affect children adopted from abroad, such as Fetal Alcohol Syndrome in countries where there is heavy use of alcohol by both men and women. There are the kind of scams that can occur in any activity where the desire for the goal---drugs for some people, children for others---is intense and the monetary return is high. People who want to adopt from abroad should do some research into the conditions of the country where they are looking, into the agency or other source with which they propose to work, and into the kinds of problems previous adoptors have encountered, if any (as recommended by Kathryn Creedy, in Chapter II). That said, the great majority of adoptions from abroad are entirely successful, and in fact blissful.

To find a source that will work with a single women or man, the individual who lives in a metropolitan area can find agencies in the yellow pages under Adoption. An agency that has a connection with a foreign source of children may or may not be willing to accept a single applicant for that source--- Korea, for example, will not place a child with a single applicant through any of the licensed organizations there---but may have a source in another country that will accept a single person. Failing that, the agency will probably be willing to do a home study on the applicant to be sent to an agency elsewhere that will place with her or him. Or there may be another local agency that will work with the applicant. Even in more rural areas, an applicant may locate foreign-source agencies in the Report on Foreign Adoption, a listing of licensed agencies in good standing with their state authorities, with no record of major litigation. It's available for a $25 donation from International Concerns for Children, 911 Cypress Drive, Boulder, CO 80303-2821; (303) 494-8333 Mountain Time. ICC's website is www.iccadopt.org; e-mail, icc@boulder.net.

## "How much income should a single parent have?"

There is no fixed answer, because it depends so much on the life style that the family will have. From time to time the U.S. Department of Agriculture publishes estimates on what it costs to raise an only child to age 18 for families of various socio-economic levels. In 1999, this estimate was $145,564 for a child in a low-to-middle income family, $198,574 in a middle-income family, and $289,974 for a high income family---and this is just through high school!

**Costs for the Adoption:**

A single person looking for a healthy infant or toddler needs enough money for the home study and the miscellaneous lesser fees involved in preparing a dossier, and the administrative fee charged by the agency: probably totalling around $4,500. If she or he is looking abroad, the foreign costs probably range between $8,000 and $22,000 depending on the country, including travel. If she/he is adopting a healthy U.S. infant, the costs for searching, paying an intermediary, or paying an adoption agency can range from $5,000 to $50,000 depending on the approach. Most of these costs must be paid within about a year. Most of them will rise from year to year.

If the single person is looking in the United States for the "special-need" or hard to place or waiting child, the adoption costs can be almost zero. Subsidies of several kinds have been enacted, starting in 1980, that not only pay for the adoption but provide financial, medical, and counseling assistance until the child reaches majority. This help is outlined in Chapter II, Mechanics of Adopting.

**How can you afford to raise a child?**

Once the adoption is paid for, your budget will rise, but not sharply. If you have a steady job, that is half the battle. Once you become a parent, you become rather aggressive about working to increase income through raises, promotions, or shifts to a better-paying job---although, as the answer to the next question makes clear, parenthood also leads to limits on the degree of involvement in work. The major expenses for a younger child are child care and, to some degree, health insurance, and there is a wide range in both areas. There are ways to cut

clothing costs (before your child becomes aware of the popular brands of jeans, sneakers etc.) and furniture; a move from one-bedroom to two-bedroom housing costs more but there are ways to be inventive there too. Share rent or mortgage costs with another, buy or rent a residence and sublet a room or two; move in with a relative.

As your children reach the upper elememtary grades through high school, child care costs decrease and spending on clothing, food, and such equipment as bicycles/cars rises, as does education if a private school is desired. The most expensive years are the college years and, with some effort, the parent can locate educational loans and perhaps grants from the institution itself, or loans from or guaranteed by the government. You do not have to assemble the whole $145,564--$289,974 before the adoption.

## "How can I manage both a child and a job?"

There will be difficult moments: plan for them ahead. The two most frequent challenges come with child care and job demands; next comes health care in some cases.

**Child care:**

You need care for your child that is both reliable and kind. Various alternatives are described in more detail in Chapter III. The real tests will come in emergencies, when you can't get home or day care because of one or more of the following crises: Your child has come down with a contagious disease, your child bit another child or another child bit her, he or she has head lice, the caregiver is sick, the center closed because the pipes burst, you are too sick to take your child there . . . etc. For these memorable occasions you need back-up care. Line it up ahead, through contacts in your support group, your relatives, your best friend, a stay-at-home neighbor. (A neighbor may be iffy; you may know her least of all, or she might suspect you of planning to take regular advantage of her---without paying.)

**Health Insurance**

This is likely to be a lesser problem because most people are already enrolled in a plan through their employers. Your only question will be whether or not your child can be enrolled before you pick him or her up from the agency, the other state, or the other country. For the long run, health plans vary (and are discussed in more detail in Chapter III). Employers vary---some let you choose from several plans; most offer only one.

In the event that you are self-employed, and the unlikely event that you have not considered this need well before you actually adopt, find out if you can obtain health insurance through your professional or trade association. Purchase of health insurance as an individual is very expensive, and you may have decided to forgo it because of your rugged constitution . . . but for a child, you will need it. A child can have lots of health problems that are not life-threatening but that cost money---more money, in the end, than you will save by not having health insurance: Your child, roughhousing, breaks a bone in his foot. Her tonsils need to come out. One of his little friends sticks a bean in his ear. She gets strep throat, or needs tubes in her ears. Your beautiful healthy child, adopted from abroad, turns out to have a touch of TB, or Hepatitis-B. It can happen.

**Conflicting demands of your job:**

Many single people feel that this presents the more serious challenge. Teachers are expected to be present for late afternoon parent conferences, shifts of medical personnel change, middle-management staff members are sent out of town on business. This means that you not only have to find back-up or flexible child care, but you aren't home with your child on a regular schedule. Or you are called at work to come pick up your child when the babysitter reports a temperature of 101, and your boss is annoyed. You aren't available any more for overtime and Saturday work. In short, your job no longer comes first.

For most of the difficulties in combining a job and a child, part of the answer can be found in greater economy and part in more income, but a good part will be expressed in compromise. A dull job that offers security for you and your child over anexciting job that means you aren't there in an emergency; a lower-paying job with a considerate employer over a fulfilling job working for a supervisor who thinks your need to put your child before your work opportunities is incomprehensible.

# *"I'm homosexual. Can I adopt?"*

A gay man, or a lesbian woman, almost certainly can adopt. The period between decision and success can be more difficult, particularly for a gay man, than for straight singles, but it can be done. A gay man might want to take the suggestions for pre-empting agency fears of pedophilia mentioned above in "Can a man adopt?" Certain countries (China, definitely); and some agencies, particularly religiously-oriented ones, may be strongly opposed to placement of a child with a lesbian or gay individual. Sometimes sources within other countries, used by agencies otherwise sympathetic to non-traditional applicants, may oppose placements with gays or lesbians.

Placement of a waiting U.S.-born child can be a good option. Gays have adopted infants privately as well as through agencies. One of the keys is a local home study agency that believes in the applicant's capacity to be a good parent to an adopted child. There are sources that work with non-traditional adopters, and counseling is available from individuals and groups on where to look and how to adopt the child you want.

Many gay people are in committed relationships, and thus are not "single" in realistic terms. As of Year 2000 laws in two states, Connecticut and Vermont, allow both partners to adopt a child, and second-parent adoption has been granted in individual jurisdictions in several other states. In most states, however, the court will require adoption by one partner, as a single parent. Using the agency's home study, the court will expect the partner who is most involved in working to adopt, to be the adoptive parent.

Family Pride Coalition, the source of the above information, noted that, regrettably, Florida bans gay people from adopting (in Florida), Utah bans adoption by "unmarried cohabiting people" and Mississippi forbids adoption by same-gender couples. The ACLU is challenging Florida's law as unconstitutional, and we can expect challenges to the others. An essay on gay or lesbian adoption appears in Chapter II: The Mechanics of Adopting.

## *What about open adoption? Suppose she changes her mind?*

Open adoption is still in an emerging, fluid situation, varying somewhat from state to state. More and more often, the birthmother is being given a voice in the selection of the adoptive parents, even in agency adoptions, and this sometimes includes meeting them. In private adoptions there can be quite a lot of contact. Following the adoption, and varying in degree, there may be ongoing contact between the birth and the adoptive parents. To say that this makes many prospective adoptive parents uneasy is an understatement.

**Revoking the decision to surrender a newborn:**

Few agencies will place a U.S. newborn with a single person, unless the baby has a marked problem of some kind, but single people do adopt privately on occasion, directly from the birthmother or through an intermediary. The only way to deal with the possibility of a revocation is to anticipate it, by checking the statutes in your state and the state in which the birthparents will surrender the baby, to see the length of time within which the birthparents may revoke the surrender. The wisest course probably is to work with a lawyer who is familiar with adoption. For example, the lawyer might recommend DNA testing of the birthfather, and know how to go about it.

It is better to face and deal with the problem before the adoption, than to go through the hell endured by the adoptive parents of Baby Jessica and Baby Richard--and to put another baby through it too. Without losing sympathy for the parents of Baby Jessica, it has to be pointed out that when they realized the situation that the birthmother had placed everyone in, they tried to avoid complying with the laws of their state, and ended up making things worse.

If you are adopting from an agency, ask the agency early on whether they notify you of the baby's birth before or after the birthmother has formally surrendered him or her. And check the statutes in the agency's state to verify what they tell you, although an agency's word is likely to be safer than the information provided in an independent adoption, if only because the publicity in such cases can be devastating for an agency.

If you are adopting a child from abroad through a U.S.-licensed agency, the surrender takes place under the rules of the other country. Before this edition of the Handbook is out of date, many countries--and possibly the U.S. too--will have ratified and implemented the international treaty on adoption across national borders, formally known as the **Hague Convention on Protection of Children and Cooperation in Respect of Intercountry Adoption**. Among other things, that treaty calls for members to enact regulations pertaining to child placement, probably including the surrender of the child. At present we know of no international situation comparable to the Baby Jessica/Baby Richard cases, but there have been international scandals involving alleged kidnapping of children for adoption.

**Long-lasting relationships with birth parents:**

At present, this appears to pertain mostly to adoption of newborns, and when the birthmother is involved to some degree in selection of the adoptive parents--rare, for single person adoptions. It can develop, however, following successful search and reunion. When adoptive parents consider this possibility their feelings are apt to run the gamut from furious to accepting. Consciously, they may know that they are their children's psychological parents and that the love between them is solid as a rock. Speaking as one who has lived through this, however, I know that the parent will still sweat out the first reunion and wonder what comes next. In the great, great majority of cases, that turns out to be no big deal--on the surface. Under the surface, however, it greatly benefits the adopted child--as well as the birth parent--to answer questions, and undo what had seemed a complete cut-off from the child's culture and history.

When a parent has adopted an older child, this child knows that he or she started out in another family, and in many cases knows why he or she is no longer living with that family. Sometimes the child knows where that family lives. This situation can be complicated, and the resumption of a relationship may be questionable or downright injurious for the child--alternatively, it might have a healing effect. There are too many variables here to be discussed in a brief note.

# Chapter II
## The Mechanics of Adoption

### The First Step in the Process:  The Home Study

Before any adoption, domestic or foreign, can take place, the applicant must obtain a home study--a report by a licensed social worker on the character, history, health, financial ability to support a child, neighborhood, and housing of the person who wants to adopt, culminating in a recommendation for approval or disapproval of the application. Any public or private agency will require a home study before proceeding with a domestic or foreign adoption.  If the agency will not place a child with the applicant, or if none of the children that the agency is able to place interests the applicant, the agency can--if it agrees--send the home study to another agency, elsewhere in the U.S., that can locate a child whom the applicant would like to adopt. Even if an adoption is conducted without the help of a public or private agency---through a lawyer, say, or a brother in law, or even directly with a birth-parent, the court will require an approved home study before allowing the legal adoption of the child.

Some states permit an accredited social worker to conduct a home study independently, sometimes requiring the study to be submitted for approval to a licensed agency.  The way to find out state law in this case is to call the family division of the state court that approves adoptions. In the great majority of cases, however, the single applicant must obtain a home study through an adoption agency-- and an agency operating in her or his own state, so that after the child is placed in the new parent's home, the original source can receive periodic post-placement reports to be assured that the adoption will be successful.  Here is where the single appli-cant faces the first hurdle.

You, the applicant, should not be discour-aged by the first apparent refusal of an agency to accept you.  Ask the agency if it will conduct a home study and send it to another adoption source. A public agency may well refuse, on the grounds of insufficient staff time, unless you apply to adopt one of the children in its custody, but a private agency will often agree to conduct the home study which,

after all, provides some income, although not as much as the fee for actual placement.

A home study culminates, as mentioned above, in approval or disapproval of the subject as a candidate for adoption.  Sometimes, however, approval comes with a condition such as  "approved for the adoption of a child over the age of . . . "  or "approved for the adoption of one child only," if the social worker or the agency believes that an indi-vidual applicant is too old, or that she or he could not or should not cope with more than one child.  If you don't want such a restriction attached to your home study, the time to discover and discuss this attitude is before the completion of the study.

**Locating an agency for the home study:**  In an urban area, a single person beginning the adoption process looks in the telephone book in the state or local government section for a department of social services (or similar title), or in the yellow pages under "Adoption" or "Social Services"for a private adoption agency.  The resident of a small town, or a state with relatively small population, however, may have a more difficult situation. There are some states that contain few private agencies, and those may be at some distance from the applicant.  At the same time, the public agency may be limited by small staff in its ability to conduct a home study on an applicant who is not interested in any of "its" children, or the agency may disapprove of single-person adoption. Legally, no state forbids placement of children with single persons, but converting that into an adoption can be an uphill battle.

Two possible alternatives:  Check to see if the state permits a home study by a social worker not affiliated with an agency, and any conditions attached to that, such as certification of the finished study  by a licensed agency.  As a long shot, it might be pos-sible to work with an agency in a neighboring state, that would also be able to make post-placement visits--since that is one of the main reasons for a local home study.

# Where to Look for a Child

## Adopting a U.S. Child from an Agency

A single woman or man who asks an adoption agency about adopting a U.S.-born child is usually told that there are almost no healthy white infants available for placement with a single person, although whether the applicant is white or Afro-American it might be possible to adopt a black or biracial infant. The agency will almost never have older children to place, unless the agency contracts with the state to care for or place a "waiting" child from public custody, as described below.

**Locating a child:** Once you have an approved home study, if the local public agency does not have a child to place in whom you are interested, you can look anywhere in the United States (and even Canada) for an agency able to place a child of the age, sex, state of health etc. you are hoping to find. There are various lists of agencies from several sources:

The National Adoption Information Clearinghouse publishes a list of public and private agencies by state. Only the name, address and telephone number of the agency are listed. The NAIC address is 330 C St. SW, Washington, DC 20005; the telephone is 1-888-251-0075 Eastern time. Their home page website is www.calib.com/naic. They have basic information and advice for adopters, and a list of state statutes pertaining to adoption.

The North American Conference on Adoptable Children has agencies and parent support groups as members. NACAC is an excellent source of information on registries of hard-to-place children from every state and many Canadian provinces. It holds an annual conference, the site of which rotates among the East, Midwest, and Western parts of the U.S. and Canada. NACAC's address is 970 Raymond Ave. Suite 106, St. Paul, MN 55114-1149; telephone (612) 644-3036 Central Time. The **Internet** plays a large and growing role in offering information about adoptable children. On the web, agencies, facilitators and perhaps also individuals go on line with their programs for foreign adoption and perhaps domestic as well, often with photographs and brief descriptions of particular available children. Considerable caution should be used in this information source, because of the difficulty in checking.

One impeccable source of information on waiting children is the photo-listing website of the National Adoption Center/Children Awaiting Parents, at http://www.adopt.org. The National Adoption Center has another website, www.adoptnet.org, described by Rita Laws in <u>Adoptive Families</u> as a "web-based chat room with regulatly scheduled topic chats, "Guest Expert" chats, and open forums. There is a message board where visitors can leave comments and questions and return later to read replies left by others. There are chat transcripts and articles that can be downloaded, read online, or printed out for later use, and links to other helpful adoption web pages." There is a free e-mail mailing list called AdoptNetUpdate to notify subscribers of upcoming events, and readers can buy adoption-related books through Adoptnet's secure book-buying service. Topics in the scheduled chats include adoption tax credits, negotiating adoption assistance contracts, or finalizing adoptions.

## Adopting a Newborn from an Agency

The single applicant gets a home study, which will be forwarded to the agency working with the birthmother (if that is a different agency). It would be sensible to include as much supplementary persuasive information as possible--such as a personal letter from the applicant to the unknown birth-mother, photographs, and anything else appropriate.

The cost is high, probably higher even than adopting from abroad. There seem to be two reasons for this: A good agency brings the birthmother to its own area (many of these agencies advertise for birthmothers in other states), and supervises her for the last few months of her pregnancy. The agency makes sure that she is eating properly, keeping her prenatal doctor appointments, and not drinking or doing any kind of drugs; probably finds her a place to live and even gets clothing for her. She can, and some do, change her mind about placing the baby, after the baby is born, and the agency must eat this cost--- which is passed on in client fees. The second reason, frankly, is the law of supply and demand as it applies to healthy US-born babies. Healthy caucasian babies draw the highest placement fees; next come biracial babies (either African-American or hispanic); and last, babies with two black parents. That is the reality, and one hopes that it is changing.

## Adopting a Newborn, Privately

Single women and men have a long history of private, or "independent" adoption of newborns. Considerable effort is involved, and often a "fall-through" occurs when the birthmother changes her mind after seeing her newborn. There are several variants of this approach: perhaps an individual knows of a pregnant woman who cannot keep her baby, or has a friend who knows of such a birthmother; sometimes s/he conducts a search involving advertising in likely publications, perhaps with a special postoffice box and even a special telephone number (both probably not giving the full name of the searcher); or works with the help of a professional such as a doctor or a lawyer to locate a birthmother and to carry through the process.

There is a long-established parent support group in the Maryland-D.C.-Virginia area, "Families for Private Adoption," that offers seminars twice a year in locating an infant directly. More importantly for people not in that geographic area, FPA publishes a 170-page manual, for $30, titled "Successful Private Adoption!" The manual is oriented toward MD/DC/VA with respect to state laws and names of attorneys but otherwise provides information very applicable to a searching individual anywhere. It discusses advertising, using resumes, obtaining background and medical information, coping with problems, and financial information. FPA's telephone number is (202) 722-0338, EST or EDT.

**CAUTION!** The desire for a child comes right after the need for air, water, and food in the emotions of many or most people, and there are people who see this as a wonderful opportunity for a scam. While not excluding the occasional adoption agency, it must be said that it seems to happen most frequently when dealing with individuals. Watch out for: the woman who stresses the overwhelming joy she had in her own adoption, and how much she wants to share this happiness with others ----before she talks about anything else.

Beware of the individual facilitator, birthmother, or agency who or which needs large sums of money up front, and then asks for more large sums before the adoption is complete. The article by Kathryn Creedy later in this chapter spells out steps to check on sources and individuals. The same care should be taken with internet as with word-of-mouth individuals you do not personally know.

In recent years a second issue has come front and center with potential adoptive families: The consent of the birthfather (or possibly the birthfather's family). Any individual contemplating an independent adoption must acquaint him/herself with the state law pertaining to consent of both natural parents. State laws differ on parental consent! The best way to do this is to locate a lawyer in that state, preferably one who is familiar with adoption (there are lawyers and lawyers).

A comparable but much less frequent situation involves a child who has/might have American Indian heritage. Adoption by a non-Indian **must** be approved by the child's tribe. Check it out FIRST.

Your information on the birthfather and on any ethnic heritage must come from the birthmother, however, and unfortunately, we all have heard of cases where she did not tell the truth.

A third factor that may or may not affect your situation is that nowadays independent adoptions seem in the great majority of cases to call for a greater or lesser degree of openness. This can range from simply meeting the birthmother face to face before the adoption, to agreements on contact afterwards, with degrees of communication in between. Our belief is that not only is this becoming a common requirement in both agency and private adoptions, in the long run it benefits the child enormously. This is discussed more fully Later.

## Foster Parenting, or Adopting from Foster Care

One third of all people who have adopted children from foster care are single---31% are women and 2% are men.

The children in foster care are there because they have been abandoned as infants (usually by birthmothers with substance abuse problems) or, much more often, removed from abusive or neglectful families. A very small number is there because they were orphaned and no relative stepped up to care for them. According to Fall 1999 figures from the U.S. Department of Health and Human Services's Children's Bureau, the average age at which these childen entered foster care was 8.6 years. Any infants may be in sibling groups. Nearly half were caucasian, 30% were Afro-American, and 15% were hispanic.

In past years, child protection agencies aimed to return children to their families, after working with the families to improve their parenting abilities, and in the meantime children were placed in foster homes. The number of children taken from their families rose steadily for decades, and as the child protection agencies became overburdened, and the birth parents' problems weremore frequently intractable, sometimes children were simply forgotten, and remained in foster care for years, perhaps moving from one foster family to another.

In recent years, however, there has been a push to force a decision for the child within a definite time span---to return the child to the birth family or, if that was unlikely, to terminate the parents' rights (TPR) and place the child with relatives if possible. Unrelated adoption was the third choice. The Adoption and Safe Families Act of 1997 backed this push with grant money to help staff the public agencies. Now, two-thirds of adoptable children are adopted by the foster parents with whom they have been living, 15% by relatives, and only 20% by families whom the children had not known before.

There is still a need for foster parents! In the fall of 1999 there were an estimated 555,000 children in public care, and the number adopted was only in the mid-40,000s---about 7%.

All foster children are in the legal custody of the state government, but the parental rights are still retained by the birthparents. A foster parent has no legal right to the child, so that if the birthparents improve their parenting skills enough, the county or state office can and does take the child back, sometimes with very little warning. That's the downside of foster parenting, and if the foster parent has bonded with the child the separation can be very painful. The upside is that a good foster parent can be a source of strength and comfort for a child who has been at least emotionally battered, and who may have been taught by his or her previous experience that adults can't be trusted. Such a foster parent can give the child a legacy of love and the knowledge that a parent can be strong, consistent, and reliable.

There is another upside: these days, if the custodial body decides that the child cannot return to the birthparent, and placement with a relative is not appropriate, the foster parent usually is given first consideration to adopt, sparing the child another loss. Accordingly, the type of people sought for foster care and the type sought for adoption are becoming very similar, and the process for both kinds is almost the same. Applicants for either will go through a process designed to evaluate them and will then get training in what to expect.

Although foster children are the responsibility of the state, the local foster care offices are often overburdened, especially in larger urban areas. So the state (or county) contracts out the care of many of their foster children, although not the legal custody, with private adoption agencies. Thus, the applicant may be directed to one or more private agencies, which operate under generally the same rules, with perhaps a little more flexibility than the official bodies. Many private agencies, for instance, are open to somewhat older applicants, to single men, to gay or lesbian couples---if the agency sees a particular such applicant as able to meet the needs of a particular child.

The single applicant may face slightly more stringent requirements than does a couple. The agency will want an unmarried applicant to show a support system, such a family, close friends, church, or community. The agency will want to know, for example, how the single parent will cope with having to take off work if the child is ill, or needs to be taken to a therapist regularly; or when the parent must negotiate special education services.

A person interested in fostering or adopting should contact the nearest branch of the State department of human services, usually in the person's own county (look in the State Government section of the phone book) and ask to talk to the office in charge of foster care. Usually you don't have actually to become a foster parent to adopt a foster child, but you may have to get a foster care license.

The office will put you on the schedule for the next group orientation session. This may be followed by more intensive training---thirty hours is not uncommon---in which the future parent gets a candid picture of the children, most of whom (88%, according to the Children's Bureau) will have some kind of special need. S/He hears about HIV infections in some; drugs or alcohol passed to a few fetuses before birth; a history of physical abuse, sexual abuse, neglect; or just the fact that there were too many children and their mother couldn't cope.

The applicant will learn that the foster child gets a lot of help from the State and federal governments. The foster parent gets a monthly base sum as reimbursement for clothing, food, and housing. The child is entitled, as needed, to slots for day care, mental health therapy, managed care from doctors and nurses, advocacy for special education---the foster parent is not hanging out there alone. In some states, however, the applicant must fight for this help against a reluctant bureaucracy, even though the funding comes from the federal government for some purposes, such as home study costs and some subsidies; and for other subsidies from the state and federal governments jointly, specifically to help foster children stay healthy and happy in a relatively normal childhood. There are complaints from child advocates that state legislatures, which must approve the state's part of a matching grant, can skimp on their share---or fail to approve matching funds at all, and lose the grant.

The foster parent and the custodial agency sign a "subsidy agreement" tailored to the particuar child's needs, before the child is placed in the foster parent's home. This agreement is renewed periodically.

"Emancipation" occurs when the foster child reaches 18 and/or graduates from high school, depending on the state. A more accurate term would be dumping. When foster children "age out," they are no longer the responsibility of the state, which ceases to fund them and their foster "parents." Some states provide programs that teach the child to cook and write checks but apparently none provide vocational training. The Independent Living law, passed in 1986, funded "life skills workshops" for emancipating teens and some states have set up splendid programs, probably augmenting them with state funds. A recent amendment to this law provided funding to teens to pay for housing through age 21 if they were attending academic or vocational education programs, and some states waive tuition for aging-out foster children at state universities. The funding is limited, however, and usually only the most motivated young people take advantage of these opportunities.

As a result, most foster children are dropped off to the world without jobs, skills, health insurance, or a place to live. According to a May 1999 report by the US.General Accounting Office, in the year following emancipation between 27% and 35% of ex-foster children had been arrested or jailed. Between 12% and 35% had been homeless. Between 32% and 44% were on public assistance. The common thread with all these youth is that they don't have parents or parent-figures on whom they can rely for help. Adoption, by related or unrelated families, would provide that permanent support.

**Adoption.** In the past, however, adopting a foster child meant a considerable financial sacrifice. After the adoption is finalized, the adopted child is not entitled to the same kind of support that he or she used to get as a foster child. That is one reason that foster parents sometimes refuse to adopt the children in their care, when they get the chance.

This is unfortunate for several reasons. First, a foster child does not have the emotional feeling of

permanence that the legally adopted child learns to acquire. Second, the U.S. Government has enacted subsidies in the last several years for adoptive parents of special-needs children, and incentives to states to move children into permanent families--- described later in this chapter. Third, adoption is a legal commitment from the parent to the child that is permanent in all but the most serious cases. Unlike the foster care rule, it means that when the child reaches the age of majority he or she is not abruptly chopped off from the foster family and all subsidized programs, and left to fend alone for jobs, housing, and health care.

Age is the greatest handicap to a child's adoption. A child over the age of six is considered "special needs" on age alone. Next is medical or emotional disability, followed by the presence of siblings, and last his or her race. These are the factors, in order, that make a child "special needs."

Both foster and adoptive parents can have children placed with them who live in other states. That means that the applicants can go to the internet for photo-listings of waiting children anywhere in the U.S. and have the public or private agency send their home study to the social worker for the child whose listing appealed to them. In such a case, the home study would not be subsidized. The placement would require the approval of the respective administrators of the Interstate Compact on the Placement of Children in the "sending" and "receiving" states.

**Choosing an agency:** Jim Weires, coordinator for foster care and adoption for Youth and Shelter Services in Ames, IA., lists the keys to adoption success: (1) Get as much information on the child as possible; then ask for more! (2) Communicate with the child! Exchange expectations and feelings---try to forestall surprises. (3) The ideal agency for a person adopting a waiting child has a realistic and thorough pre-placement training process, and supports you after placement well past the "honeymoon" and into the testing period---for as long as necessary. (4) Collect names, addresses, and phone numbers of people and organizations to call for help, advice, and suggestions.

The third key should be incorporated into the Adoption Agreement between you and the state, outlined on page 21. If the agency staff is not willing to do this, and you want to adopt a ward of the state, look for an agency that has subcontracted with the county, and that is prepared to undertake these responsibilities in order to help achieve a successful placement of a foster child.

# Adoption from Abroad

**Choosing a country.** For a single person, adoption from abroad can be a quicker way to find a presumably healthy child than domestic adoption. For individuals hoping to adopt a baby, infant girls from Chinese orphanages can be as young as six months; babies under a year can be adopted from certain Eastern European and Latin American countries. Children from most of the Eastern European countries resemble the majority of Americans.

Foreign adoption can be expensive, when the expenses for travel, document processing, legal fees, agency fees, and fees for the facilitator and visiting a foreign country are added up. At that it might be less costly than applying to a private agency to adopt a healthy newborn.

**Choosing an Agency:** A person looking abroad for a child needs a home study from an agency that is nearby or at least in the same state, that can also conduct postplacement observation of how the child and the parent are adjusting to one another. This local agency may or may not have a connection in one or more foreign countries through which it can place orphans, or, even if it does, it may not be able to offer a child in which the client is interested. In that case the applicant can look to another agency, quite often in another state, which does have such a "source," and the local agency sends the home study to that agency.

So, the client can pay a fee to the local agency for the home study and postplacement reports, to another agency for the administrative costs for its "foreign program," and to that agency's foreign connection for its work in actually locating and placing the child. That "facilitator" is usually an individual, often a lawyer, who in turn contacts an orphanage or hospital, or directly finds pregnant women. In several countries, as indicated earlier, the contact must be made directly with the government agency of the other country, responsible for approving (sometimes assigning) the placement of its children.

Ethical U.S. agencies are careful about the foreign facilitators with whom they work, because improper activities involving placements have taken place in various countries at different times over the past twenty or so years. In response, many Central and South American countries have established centralized control over placements, as have Romania and China, with varying impact on foreign adoptions. Check the reputation of a foreign-source agency, as discussed in the Creedy article, below.

The charitable organization and information service International Concern for Children publishes on its website and in its <u>Report on Intercountry Adoption</u> a list of agencies working to place children from abroad. For each agency the <u>Report</u> lists the kinds of children available for adoption (age, ethnicity, etc.), an estimate of the time invoved, and the estimated cost to the applicant. Agencies are grouped by area: Asia, Latin America, (Eastern) Europe, and the Pacific Islands. A large amount of information accompanies the listings, on preparing for adoption, working with agencies, parent-child adjustment, medical concerns and much else. The ICC website is www.iccadopt.org, and the e-mail address is ICC@Boulder.net.

Adoptive parent support groups can also identify new agencies, or agencies too small to have come to the attention of ICC. Support group members also often use private facilitators who are not connected with a licensed U.S. adoption agency and are not listed with an information source such as ICC or the National Adoption Information Clearinghouse. Support group members often express great satisfaction with such private contractors.

**Preparing the necessary documents**: Once you have chosen a country from which you want to adopt, and an agency with which you want to work-- which has accepted you as a client--you will be sent a packet of instructions listing materials you must assemble as your "dossier." As with domestic adoption, you must produce your birth certificate, naturalization certificate if you were born abroad, divorce certificate if you were formerly married, death certificate of spouse if you are a widow(er), record of recent physical examination, and proofs of health insurance, life insurance, and employment.

As the source agency will instruct you, these documents must be certified as originals, or at least true copies. Usually every document in the whole dossier is notarized, then the notary's license is certified by the local government agency that granted it, then the secretary of state of the state in which you reside certifies the licensing agency, the U.S. Department of State certifies the dossier again, and finally the nearest consulate of the foreign country certifies it. Naturally, there is a fee at each step, and the consumption of several weeks of time all told.

The completed dossier (of which you have made a complete photocopy in case it is lost in the mail) is sent to the source agency. Your local agency sends a completely certified copy of the home study direct to the source agency. After several weeks or even months, you will be sent a picture, description, and hopefully a videotape of a child who has been assigned, or "referred" to you, and you will have a few days to decide whether or not you accept this child. Among the information accompanying the video will be, or should be, a medical report and a background report ("child abandoned at police station" or "mother died and father unable to support children . . . ") **All this material should be reviewed by a pediatrician, preferably one familiar with international adoption!**

If you accept the child, the source agency will give you a rough idea of the length of time before you travel to the other country to adopt and bring your child home. Some countries permit the child to be escorted, and instead of buying plane tickets you will pay the travel costs of the escort and the child. The U.S. Immigration and Naturalization Service (INS) prefers that you visit the other country and see your child before adopting him or her, as a safeguard against disruption of the placement.

It really is a good idea on several counts. It allows you to see the culture from which your child is coming, which usually has fascinating and beautiful aspects, as well as sharp differences from our own. You can take photographs to show your child later, and can purchase examples of crafts or art created in that country. Along with meeting your child, you can usually get an idea of the circumstances in which thechild has spent her life before coming to you. Even a brief visit will stay in your mind for years.

If the source agency has not given you advice on how to behave in a country and a culture that is quite different from ours, you should make an effort to learn something about the country as it is now. In almost all cases, the source country is not as comfortable to live in as America. The water may not be safe to drink, there may be political reasons for not venturing out on your own, in some countries you may see poverty that will shock you to the heart. It is important not to be an "ugly American," demand

ing and critical. In the annual <u>ICC Report on Intercountry Adoption</u>, mentioned earlier, are excellent articles including one on "Guidelines for Behavior While Visiting Another Culture."

Accommodations abroad vary; in China and Latin America visitors seem to stay in pretty good hotels. Hotels exist in Russia, but they sound bleak, isolating, and high-priced, with unappealing food. Most adopters are put up with Russian families in their apartments. Not only does this cost less, but it generally provides a warm, friendly atmosphere and much better cuisine.

**Applying for a visa from the INS:** Before you leave to pick up your child (or before the child can be proxy-adopted) you must apply to the INS for advance approval of a visa for your child to enter the U.S. as your immediate relative. First, you file Form I-600-A with the INS office for your state. With it you send a fee and many of the same documents that you send abroad, and your agency sends your approved home study. Also accompanying Form I-600-A is Form 864, an Affidavit of Support, contractually binding you to support the child financially, and to reimburse any government agency or private entity that provides the child with any means-tested public benefit (welfare, food stamps, etc.) Your last three Federal income tax forms must accompany the new Form. All these IRS forms can be obtained by calling 1-800-375-5283. The webside is www.ins.usdoj.gov.

If the INS approves your application, it will cable the U.S. Embassy in the country from which you are adopting. You must not leave until you know this cable has been sent.

After your child has been adopted, you visit the U.S. Embassy abroad. The consulate will require that the child be given a physical examination at a recommended clinic in the capital city, and you will file INS form I-600-A for the actual visa, after which you and your child leave for home!

---

**Significant Websites:**

**http://travel.state.gov/** U.S. State Department: links to related sites with information on international adoption, source-country briefings, travel conditions, forms and fees.

**www.embassy.org.** Foreign embassies in D.C.

**www.ins.usdoj.gov** Immigration and Naturalization Service; information, fees, download forms

**www.rainbowkids.com** International adoption newsletter.

**www.lapa.com** Latin America Parents Association; chapters all over the U.S.

**www.frua.org** Families for Russian and Ukrainian

# The Future of Foreign Adoption

## by Susan Freivalds

*The major good news . . . is that intercountry adoption will remain open as a way for children overseas to find new homes in the U.S.*

*An international treaty has been signed in the City of The Hague in the Netherlands that will make the process of intercountry adoption somewhat different, probably safer for all parties, and perhaps a little slower. Susan Freivalds describes the likely next steps after U.S. ratification of the treaty, and its impact on the intercountry adoption process.*

### Origins of the Treaty:

A birthmother thinks the child she released for adoption is going to the U.S. to be educated and will then return. A financially struggling agency folds, taking all its clients' funds with it, when an overseas program temporarily closes. Prospective adoptive parents are pressured to make an immediate decision to adopt a child for whom no medical information is available. Another round of stories circulates regarding the international adoption of children to serve as organ donors (which, of course, is medically impossible). Scenarios like these are part of the reason the Hague Convention on Intercountry Adoption was drafted and is currently under consideration for ratification by countries around the globe.

### Treaty Requirements:

Safeguards include mandated home studies for adoptive parents, prohibitions on inducements to birthparents, and prior approval for children to immigrate into their new countries before their adoptions are finalized. A Central Authority in each country will oversee the application of the treaty and serve as a single identified source of reliable information, but will delegate all the case-specific duties and responsibilities in an intercountry adoption to "accredited bodies" or to other "approved" service providers.

Accredited bodies in the U.S. will be non-profit, licensed adoption agencies which must "be directed and staffed by persons qualified by their ethical standards and by training or experience." Approved bodies and persons (attorneys, for-profit agencies, and others) must also meet standards of "integrity, professional competence, experience and accountability" and be "qualified by their ethical standards and by training or experience."

The Convention requires that home studies and child reports be prepared, in every case, under the responsibility of accredited bodies. It does not disallow either independent adoption or parent-initiated adoption. For most families, the process would be much the same as it has always been: Contact an adoption service provider, who then proceeds with the adoption by directly contacting counterparts overseas.

### U.S. Prospects for the Treaty:

For a treaty to take effect in the U.S., the Senate must give its "advice and consent" to ratification. Before that consent is given, however, Congress must pass legislation to ensure uniform implementation throughout the U.S. This has now taken place, and the President has signed the law.

The State Department will now take approximately two years to set up the Central Authority and to finalize the rules and regulations that will govern its operations and responsibilities. This work includes identifying one or more entities to accredit agencies and approve individuals to work under the treaty, approving the standards by which agencies and individuals will be considered, and overseeing the accreditation and approval of the initial cadre of agencies and individuals.

### Effects on agencies:

Only agencies that want to handle the actual child referral tasks in another Hague country will need to secure Hague accreditation. While the treaty requires that home studies be done "under the responsibility" of an accredited agency, U.S. implementing legislation specifically exempts from accreditation agencies providing only home study and post placement services. It will be the responsibility of the accredited agencies to ensure the quality of the home studies that they accept for child placement. In this regard, nothing will change for home study agencies; currently their work must be acceptable to the agency that actually refers the child. This way of implementing the treaty minimizes the burden on small agencies that provide home study services for international adoptions and maintains the nation-wide wide network of such agencies that currently exists. Agencies that choose not to seek Hague accreditation may continue to work in countries that are not party to the treaty and/or to provide home studies and post placement services for adoptions from other Hague countries. Individuals who want to provide services in Hague adoptions will need to seek "approved" status from the Central Authority.

The implementing legislation allows individual states to set up accreditation functions, as well as providing for the Central Authority to designate one or more "accrediting entities" to provide this service on a national basis. Most likely, states will not opt to provide Hague accreditation, and agencies will be accredited by an accrediting entity chosen and overseen by the Central Authority. The Council on Accreditation of Services for Children and Families (COA) will undoubtedly be one of the accrediting entities, as it is the only organization currently providing voluntary accreditation for intercountry adoption services. The standards and process it uses and the fees it charges will be mandated by the Central Authority. COA officials state that they recognize that the process to accredit agencies to work under the Hague treaty will be less rigorous and less expensive than their current "full accreditation" process. Smaller agencies will be able to meet the standards and afford the cost.

### Effects on Families

Prospective adoptors should not notice much change in the way their adoption proceeds. Because any licensed agency or individual can prepare a home study under the treaty, access to adoption services should not be affected by U.S. ratification. For child referral, families will need to select an agency that is accredited to work in the country they choose, just as they currently must select an agency with a program in their country of choice.

Since the U.S. Central Authority will delegate its case-specific duties to the accredited agencies, families will continue to work directly and almost exclusively with their agencies, not with the Central Authority. The State Department plans to retain much of the current visa application process, with families applying directly to the INS for a new "Hague visa." In-country procedures will also not need to change; families will still visit the consulate to receive their child's visa after the adoption is finalized or guardianship transferred.

### Changes for the Better:

Accreditation of agencies and approval of individuals will bring national accountability to intercountry adoption services. Service providers will have been examined in regard to their experience, knowledge, ethics, and financial stability. Families will have a centralized place to go with their complaints and demands for improved service and for current information about intercountry adoption. The Central Authority will also be authorized to intervene in adoptions where complications arise.

The treaty requires that children be preapproved for immigration into their new countries before their adoptions are finalized. This will eliminate the current annoying possibility that a child can be legally adopted overseas and then denied entry into the U.S. Most likely, the current "orphan definition" will not apply to children adopted under the Hague treaty. This means that two married birthparents may place their child for adoption to the U.S., as long as the adoption meets the laws of the country of origin and takes place under the treaty.

The major good news, however, is that intercountry adoption will remain open as a way for children overseas to find new homes in the U.S. As of August 2000, forty countries had adopted the treaty through ratification or accession. (For an upto-date status report, consult the website of the Hague Conference on Private International Law at hcch.net.)

Some countries (Paraguay, Lithuania, Brazil, and Venezuela among them) have threatened or actually closed adoptions to countries that have not ratified the treaty. Conducting adoptions under the Hague treaty will allow intercountry adoption to remain feasible in countries where it is not politically popular. Additionally, with an agreed-upon framework for completing adoptions, countries should not feel it necessary to suspend adoptions as they rework their laws from time to time. The goal of the treaty is to provide a smooth, expeditious, and transparent adoption process, in the best interest of the children.

*Long-time adoption expert Susan Freivalds was a member of the small team representing the United States in the five-year process of drafting the Hague Convention. She is Executive Director of the Adoption Education Institute, serving adoptive and prospective adoptive families with a network of expert advisors and resources at sfreivalds @adoptioneducation.org.*

# B.  How to Afford Your Adoption

The process of adoption is expensive, unless you are adopting a "hard to place" child from a U.S. source.  In 2000, total costs for foreign adoption ran from $20,000 to $30,000, depending on the country.  Adoption costs for a healthy U.S. newborn range from $12,000 to $50,000+. depending on the method.  Only the adoption of special-needs children is free or nearly so, reflecting the desire of the President and Congress to encourage and support the placement of waiting children in permanent homes.

## Strategies for Paying Adoption Expenses
by Norman Hecht

For some years I have been fortunate to bring together my professional background in banking and my passion about adoption.  In working with adopters in their attempts to meet the some-times extraordinary financial demands of adoptions today, I have found their acceptance of the "boxes" banks and other lending institutions force clients into quite troublesome.  This article is designed to broaden the scope of possibilities by suggesting a variety of approaches to meeting adoption expenses.

**TAX CREDITS:**

Help for paying adoption expenses is now available from the U.S. Government in the form of the Federal Tax Credit for Adoption Expenses.  Passed in 1996 and in effect for expenses after December 31, 1996, this law provides for up to a $5,000 tax credit per child for payment of qualified adoption expenses.  The credit is increased to $6,000 per child for special needs domestic adoptions. This credit is discussed at greater length on page 19,

Of course, you still have to pay the expenses first and while you may get some cash back from your taxes, it may only begin to cover the costs of the adoption.  So, what do you do to cover the initial outlay and the remainder?

**FAMILY:**

Gifts or loans from family members have been the most traditional sources of funds to pay adoption expenses.  Family members oftentimes are more than willing to help with a gift or an interest-free loan.  But, oftentimes the strings that come attached to the "gift" are harder to swallow than interest.  Family members often feel a right to give their input as to the kind of adoption and the sort of child one should adopt.  When they are the funding source, adopting parents are put in the awkward position of having to listen to them (or at least of appearing to listen).  A "poor" choice can result in a lot of hurt feelings.  Also, in some families it can add to the tension between family members and can be an ongoing source of irritation when "the loan" is brought up again and again.

**COMPANY  BENEFITS:**

Investigate your employer for grants, reim-bursements and other benefits that may be available to help with adoption expenses.  Many companies offer benefits for the birth of a child, but have never considered an adoption benefit.  Here's a chance to raise corporate awareness and seek equality with those giving birth.  It isn't always easy, but I know of several individuals whose businesses now offer a reimbursement plan for adoption expenses where, prior to the employee's inquiries, such arrangements had not been considered.

Employer support in this area is far from unusual.  Wendy's International, as part of its com-mitment to adoption, issues a report annually, which last year listed close to 200 companies among the Fortune 1000 that offered adoption benefits.  Hence there is some chance your employer has such a program.  If not, it could prove useful to let your company know of this trend and, of course, to point out the user and public relations value of supporting adoption.  Another persuasive argument to make:  It is unlikely that the introduction of these programs will bring on a rash of  adoptions by employees!

To learn more, call the **National Adoption Center** in Philadelphia at **(215) 738-9988,** or visit their web page at **http://nac.adopt.org/.** Together with the Dave Thomas Foundation they have put together some wonderful information to help convince employers what a great idea adoption benefits are.

SAVINGS, PART 1:

The most wonderful option would be to tap your savings account. No interest to pay. No "permission" needed from a loan officer. No family pressure to choose the option they feel is best for you. But, also a fairly unlikely source given the cost of infertility treatments you may have had. I haven't seen a lot of people able to go this route in the past ten years. Few have the resources left by the time they get to the adoption question.

SAVINGS, PART 2:

A variation on the above has one borrowing to create a savings account to secure a loan. This works well if done in advance of the adoption, as it creates a pool of funds to be used at the time of the adoption. For instance, a $5,000 loan paid back over a year's time has a payment of under $500 a month, but after a year, if you borrowed the money, put it in a savings account, and used the savings as collateral for the loan, the $5,000 is yours. No bank should have a problem doing such a loan. It is about as safe as can be for them and a great way to "force" savings for a borrower.

The down side? You have to have enough time in advance of the need to get the loan in place and paid off, if you are planning on using the savings you have pledged as collateral to pay for the adoption. Also, a $500 monthly payment is not small. But if you have child one and are planning on child two in three years, this is a way to force yourself to save.

**401K AND PENSION PLANS:**

Many people have asked me about dipping into their retirement plans to pay for adoption expenses. Outright withdrawals often come with stiff penalties and have tax consequences which may make them a poor choice to turn to for paying adoption expenses. Some plans allow you to borrow at very favorable rates compared to other loan rates. These along with insurance policies with cash values can be great sources. However, it is best to check out the penalties and tax consequences before dipping into retirement plans. If the costs are high, look at other alternatives first.

**GRANTS AND LOANS:**

Some small grants are available from the **National Adoption Foundation,** a national non-profit organization providing financial support to adoptive and prospective adoptive parents. It was created by Norman Goldberg, an adoptive parent. The grants range from $1,500 to $2,500. Interested adopters may contact NAF at 1-203-791-3811 EST. . The grant itself is sent to the adoption agency doing the applicant's home study.

NAF also works with **MBNA** America in Delaware, the third-largest banking institution in the U.S., to offer a line of credit to creditworthy applicants that can be used for adoption or other expenses. The line can range from $2,500 to $25,000; as of August 2000 the top interest rate was 13.99%. The loan is unsecured and there are no points, no application fee, no pre-payment penalty and no annual fee. Borrowers' applications are submitted to MBNA, which considers the applicant's past and present credit history, income, and debts when deciding whether and how much to lend. There are several payment options: one available is a long-term payment period that means low monthly payments (although more interest cost in the long run). MBNA can be reached at **1-800-626-2760.** The bank makes a donation to the foundation for each loan approved. MBNA also offers a home equity line of credit (see next page) for which you would call 1-800-841-1982.

Other good resources in this area have been churches, synagogues, and the like. Congregations have commonly pitched in to support families in this work in the past and it is a great way to spread the word about adoption, raise consciousness in the community, and gain the support to get the job done. Being too proud to ask for help denies the community an opportunity to express its concern and support. In other words, it is worth a try.

**CREDIT CARDS:**

A quick way to cover the expenses is to use all the fine-looking credit cards that we all seem to collect in our wallets these days. A brief trip to the bank and bingo, the money is there to pay the expenses for many people. Of course, credit cards do not come cheaply. With rates anywhere from 12% to 22% a year, they are an expensive way to cover the adoption's expense. Also, the relatively small minimum payment required tends to string out the repayment a lot longer than a traditional loan, increasing the overall cost of borrowing significantly.

## HOME EQUITY LOANS:

Home equity loans use the equity in your home as collateral for the bank to lend you money. They generally come as either fixed term second mortgage loans, which will pay back over a period of time and go away, or as revolving credit lines, which can be repaid and used again for a period of time and later turned into a fixed-term loan. Both offer the advantage that the interest might be tax-deductible. The revolving line of credit also has the advantage of being available to be used again to finance a second or third adoption, without asking for a bank's permission. Because you are using the equity in your home, you may often be able to borrow more than you could without collateral. If you own a home, this can be an excellent choice.

## UNSECURED/PERSONAL OR OTHER LOANS:

I consistently recommend that people considering these expenses talk to their bank about what options are available. It is not uncommon, however, for bankers to have a very narrow view and almost no knowledge of adoption, except what finds its way into the evening news. Don't be surprised if they have a negative stereotype of adoption in general. Here's an opportunity to practice educating the public on adoption issues. If you can get beyond the idea stuck in the banker's mind that this is an "adoption" loan , and help her to see that this is just like any other personal loan, car loan, boat loan, or home improvement loan that she is used to seeing, she may be able to look at it that way. Having some other collateral, like a car or boat, can help change the rate on the loan as well.

There are some rules to observe when dealing with banks. Make an appointment with a **lender**, not just the local manager or customer service person. Many banks staff their offices with people whose job is to collect and process paper, not help borrowers design loans. Ask for the person who actually makes loan decisions and spend a little time with him or her explaining your situation. Bring along a Personal Financial Statement (bank jargon for a listing of your assets and liabilities: the things you own and the money you owe) Expect a good banker to ask some questions about your income, monthly payments, plans for the future, and tax situation. He can then provide options that might meet your needs.

Avoid the trap of simply filling out an application for a specific loan and term and letting someone you never see run the loan through their mill and come back with a "no" answer or a loan that doesn't meet

your needs. Banks love you to do the work for them and make it easy for them to say either yes or no. Instead, ask for options. Ask why they think one type of loan would suit you better than another. For example, maybe you ought to use a Home Equity Line of Credit because your tax situation makes sense to do it this way. But, maybe you ought to have a five-year second trust loan instead. Why? Generally, most people pay the minimum payment monthly. But, if you want to adopt again in five years, the banker may tell you that you would have a difficult time paying down the line of credit enough because the minimum payment would make the loan last eight years! If you ask some questions and are dealing with a professional, they'll explain it to you. Listen to them.

Conventional wisdom says that it makes sense to shop around for the best rate. I think it makes more sense to shop for a banker you can work with. A difference of 1% on $10,000 is $100 a year. The cost of working with the wrong banker may be a lot higher. Having the wrong type of loan may mean you are not financially ready for your next adoption when you are emotionally ready. A banker who will take the time to work with you means you have someone to help design the right loan for you now and later. What's more, they can help with planning for the next 20 years of raising your child. (Paying the expenses to bring a child home is a drop in the bucket compared to what it costs to raise them to adulthood.)

Shop for a banker, not a bank or a rate. Ask questions. Be prepared for questions. Know why. You are embarking on an expensive journey. Be prepared. If they don't know what you are talking about, or don't feel comfortable discussing options, try my email, **normhecht@netscape.net**, or give me a call at (301) 807-6635 and I will be happy to help.

Norman and Leslee Hecht and their children, Kelly and Trip, whom the Hechts adopted from South Korea.

# Other Financial Assistance: The Adoption Tax Credit

The Minimum Wage Law of 1996 included a tax credit to encourage adoption (briefly mentioned on p. 16). This is at present a credit against income tax of $5,000 for families who adopt a US- or foreign-born child; and $6,000 for families who adopt a US-born child with special needs, from either a public or a private agency. This means that a single taxpayer can deduct the amount of the credit directly from the tax calculated on the adopter's income.

## Who Can Apply for the Credit?

The adoptive parent(s) of a child who is under age 18, or under age 21 if physically or mentally incapable of caring for him/herself.

Certain adopters cannot get the credit: stepfather adoptions are ruled out, as are adoptions involving surrogacy. The adoptors' income(s) also matters: Reductions from the tax credit start at $75,000 adjusted gross income, and are phased out completely for adopters with an AGI of $115,000.

## Current deadlines:

The credit for adoption of any foreign-born children, or healthy US-born children, ends on December 31, 2001. The $6,000 tax credit for the adoption of a US-born special-needs child, adopted from a public or private agency, continues without a termination date.

## What Adoption Expenses Qualify?:

"Double dipping" is not permitted: If the adoptive family's employer is providing financial assistance toward adoption expenses, or if the family is receiving financial aid for adoption costs from a federal, state, or local program, this dollar aid is deducted from the tax credit.

Adoption expenses under this bill mean "reasonable and necessary" adoption fees, court costs, attorney fees and other expenditures directly related to the adoption of a child, including foreign travel costs for transportation, food, and lodging.

## Special Rule for Foreign-born Children:

The $5000 tax credit may not be taken until the foreign-born child has been adopted. Most adoptions of foreign-born children take place before the child comes home to the U.S., but some countries--Korea and India are examples--grant only guardianship to the adoptive parent(s), and the legal adoption must be completed in the U.S. Certain Latin American countries, also, grant what is called a "simple adoption," in which the parental rights of the birth parents are not completely severed. Families adopting under such a decree often choose to re-adopt in the United States.

Such adoption-completions, or re-adopting a foreign-born child in the U.S. after adoption in the native country, do not entitle a special needs child from abroad to the $6000 tax credit.

## When to Claim the Tax:

The rules as to when the parent can begin to claim the tax are complicated, and best explained by a tax accountant. The rules are different for foreign adoptions, as well.

On the plus side, expenses can be carried over for up to five years, which could be useful if the credit exceeds the calculated tax. The "leftover" credit can be applied to the following year's taxes.

## Is an Extension Possible?

As of the fall of 2000, there was a bill in Congress to extend the credit for healthy US- born, or healthy or special-needs foreign-born children. The U.S. Treasury must file a report on the effect of the present adoption tax credit before Congress decides to act. The law was originally intended to stimulate special-needs adoptions, but since those adoptions can be essentially free (if the adopters know what subsidies they are entitled to and how to push for them), the Treasury may conclude that the act was unnecessary.

The adoption tax credit was part of Public Law 104-188, signed August 20, 1996. The regulations implementing it are located at Section 23, Adoption Expenses, of the Code of Federal Regulations. For more information, go to www.irs.ustreas.gov.

# Financial Aid for the Adoption of a Hard to Place Child

A person adopting a special-needs child can, under current laws, receive financial aid of various kinds for the child until he/she reaches the age of majority--18 for the federally-funded programs. Benefits may include one-time payment of adoption expenses, monthly subsidy, medical care, and many social services.

A. **Assistance for non-recurring adoption expenses:** Parents adopting special-needs children from the U.S. may apply for **reimbursement** of some of the expenses of adoption. The amount ranges from $250 to $2,000, depending on the state (half from federal funds, half from state). It may cover the home study or update, your pre-adoptive medical examination, attorney and court costs, travel expenses, and post-placement supervision. Parents should apply for this reimbursement before finalizing the adoption. Most states limit this payment to US-adopted children, but some states may provide non-recurring reimbursement to foreign-born children.

The $6,000 **tax credit** for special-needs adoption was described on the previous page. This tax credit, it might be noted, is available to US-born special-needs children adopted privately, in the U.S.

B. **Long-term subsidy for adopting a special-needs child:** The "Adoption Assistance and Child Welfare Act of 1980" added Title IV-E to the Social Security Act to help place children considered hard to place for adoption because of one or more special factors or conditions: age, membership in a minority ethnic or racial group or in a sibling group, medical conditions, or physical, mental, or emotional handicaps.

Parents adopting a child from abroad may not receive IV-E assistance no matter how handicapped the child may be. The money comes jointly from the federal government and the state. The U.S. Department of Health and Human Services sets the matching rate, varying from state to state depending on the number of children involved and the economic situation there. The monthly subsidy varies from about $250 to $1200, depending on the state and the needs of the child. As mentioned, this part-federal subsidy ends when the child turns 18; states can, and some do, continue financial assistance beyond that age.

The income of the adopting parents cannot be used to decide the eligibility of the child, but it can affect the amount that the state pays the parent. Once the child is declared eligible, the payments will follow the child to the state where the adoptive parents reside, and if the parents later move to still another state, the state from which the child came will send its payments to the child's new state. The payment may vary from child to child, and can also change over time for various reasons, some having nothing to do with the particular child.

C. **Medical assistance:** Children eligible for the IV-E subsidy are also automatically eligible for Medicaid, the federal program that provides basic coverage for many medical expenses, IF their IV-E status is based on medical needs. The state and the federal government cooperate in the funding, but the states may design their own programs and thus Medicaid coverage varies from state to state. A certain minimum level of service must be provided: in-patient hospital services (except for mental disease institutionalization), outpatient hospital services (except for mental disease), laboratory and X-ray services, screening and diagnosis to identify physical or mental defects, and physicians' & dental services.

Also, IV-E children are entitled to many additional Medicaid services when these are needed to correct or ameliorate defects, illnesses, or conditions found during screening. Among a long list we might note clinic services, physical therapy, prescription drugs, prostheses, eyeglasses, inpatient psychiatric services, respiratory care and many more.

The problem, however, is that many physicians will not participate in Medicaid because the allowed fees are lower than they will accept, so that many parents rely on their private insurance. It is still worth enrolling the child and getting a "Medicaid card," however, because not only may the parents' health insurance situation change, but a private health plan may not cover adopted children or treatment for certain extensive medical problems. When parents move from job to job, however, the 1996 Kennedy-Kassebaum health act, P.L. 104-191, requires "portability" of the parents' health plans.

If the family lives in a different state from the one placing the child, and also if the family should then move to still another state, the Medicaid Card must be issued by whatever state the child is in, at the level of services developed by that state. Parents may rely on the Adoption Assistance Agreement for this rule, and on the Interstate Compact on Adoption and Medical Assistance, ICAMA (effective in states that are party to it). The American Public Human Services Association (see Resources) can tell you if your state is a party.

**D. Social Services:** The child may be eligible for Title XX (of the Social Security Act), the social services block grant to states, under the plan that the particular state has drawn up. The parent must *ask* to have the child covered. Depending on the state plan, Title XX can provide post-placement services that may make the difference between an adoption that works and one that fails: examples are regular or specialized day care, respite services, counselling and assistance on obtaining help, and even in-home supportive services such as housekeeping and personal care. Again the ICAMA can help to assure continued services in other states than the original one.

**E. SSI:** Under the Social Security Act the Federal Government's Social Security Administration pays monthly disability checks (Supplemental Security Income, or SSI) to---among others---some individuals, including children, who were disabled before age 22, and whose adoptive parents' family incomes are below certain ceilings. No state funds go into SSI. If a child's eligibility for SSI has not already been established, a prospective parent should check with the SSA to see if their special-needs child will be eligible under SSI regulations. Obtaining SSI qualifies the child for IV-E aid, so many families aim to obtain SSI for that reason and then let it drop after they secure IV-E eligibility.

**F. State-only Subsidies** Some special-needs children who don't qualify under Title IV-E may still be eligible for a subsidy paid for by state funds only. These subsidies can include medical assistance, but this coverage is not guaranteed to follow families who move out of state. State laws, and especially state regulations, can change. The best source for updated information is the North American Council on Adoptable Children (see p. 63 for address).

**How Do You Get This Help?** The parent may have located the child through a private adoption agency that has a contract with the state (or another private agency networking with the first), but the parent must negotiate an Adoption Assistance Agreement

with the state itself, which has custody of the child. The parent should begin this process at the time she or he applies to adopt the particular child, because the law specifies that if the policy of the particular state permits, assistance can begin when the child is actually placed, even before court finalization. The parent needs to spell out in the agreement what s/he wants and anticipates needing for the child. Some parents of special needs children have stated that they must often fight, and keep on fighting, for this assistance. Perhaps some of the programs partially funded by the state face a reluctant state legislature. In the long run, however, there is no doubt that the funding benefits not only the individual child but the state itself. So fight!

It is possible to change an Adoption Assistance Agreement after finalization. A parent would have to prove the existence of a condition that the parent was not told about, or that a misdiagnosis was made somewhere, or that a condition that made the child hard to place has worsened. Again, check with NACAC.

It would be wise for the parent to identify not only predictable needs but also potential needs; to do this the parent must obtain all possible information from the state, the private agency, the foster parents or other caretakers, medical records, etc. The family and the state can renegotiate the amount of the payments as circumstances change, including the family's financial situation, an increase in the cost of living, or a change in the needs of the child.

With respect to all assistance, it will pay to become familiar with all the programs, because you may have to fight for this help. Despite the existence of the laws cited in this Handbook, it must be stated that many, many parents of special needs children have found it very difficult actually to obtain help for their children. Ignorance or misinterpretation of the law may cause some of this, but it does appear that many state social service agencies and school systems simply resist providing services to children because they will be expensive, and perhaps complicated if a child has multiple needs.

This is especially true for mental health assistance. In Adopting the Older Child the author, Claudia Jewett, states, "The fact that all children adopted when they are older need therapy is one of the few absolutes in this book. If one thing [could] lower the risk for families adopting older children, improve their quality of life, and lower the cost for society, it would be to guarantee these families free and appropriate mental health care."

# Choosing an adoption agency . . .

# What to look for--and what to look out for

**by Kathryn Creedy**

*There is no such thing as consumer protection for adoptive parents*

Choosing a source for adopting your child is, perhaps, the single most important decision you will make as you begin your your journey to parenthood. Indeed, your choice does not merely rest on interviewing agencies, reading their materials, interviewing their happy clients and going with your gut reaction. It is, in fact, a matter of research since there is no such thing as consumer protection for adoptive parents. Thankfully, prospective parents have an entire array of sources to help them make that choice.

**First there is information you need to know.** Parent training/preparation and post-adoption services are considered to be critical to successful adoptions by most adoption professionals. This is especially important for parents considering orphanage adoptions or the adoption of waiting children in the United States. Such training should go beyond general parenting tips to include a full and frank discussion of the health and development issues that children from institutions or foster care encounter and for which their parents must be prepared. It should also include discussions on resources for parents and how to get the services your child needs.

You should also seriously study the general information they provide on health. Does it say that all these children need is tender loving care or does it seriously discuss the impacts of poverty or institutionalization?

If an agency or source indicates that all these children need is the former, move on. It is crucial today to obtain a full accounting of health information. You are not, after all, looking for a guarantee of the perfect child since even birth children do not come with such guarantees. What you are doing, however, is making a decision that will affect not only you but the life of a child. You need to know everything possible for two reasons: Accurate and complete information is necessary for you to make your decision *and* it is also necessary for the best interest

of the child. It will ensure placement in the right family as well as the swift delivery of important services as early as possible.

Recently, an agency that places many children from Russia stated on one network television broadcast that parents are obligated to seek out any health information that has not been provided by the agency when they are at the orphanage---*after* they have made the emotional and fiscal investment in traveling to adopt a child. This is also well after the prospective parents have made their supposedly informed decision about the acceptance of a referral. To make such an incredible statement is negligence and ignores the agency's own responsibility to the children and its clients. It neglects the best interests of the children placed in its care as well as the interest of the client seeking to make an informed decision.

The source is obligated by law to provide complete health information to you at the earliest consideration of a specific child. Many of the children in orphanages abroad or in foster care in the United States have been there since birth, making any gaps or lack of information questionable. As your representative, the agency is the only source of this information and any suggestion that parents can only get this information when they are at the orphanage is absurd in the extreme. If it is available at the orphanage at that time, it is available to the agency personnel when you are trying to make your decision.

**First and foremost is networking.** Join and attend the meetings of a local parent support group, which is *not* affiliated with an agency. Its members will give you leads to agencies and other sources to check. They can help explain agency or foreign country procedures. They can give you confidence in questioning procedures. Adoptive parents can recommend agencies or sources and compare notes with you as you go through the adoption process.

Many agencies have parties or picnics; attend them and compare notes with the other parents. Bear in mind, however, that there is an element of theatre in these social functions. The agency is showing off happy parents with these new parents, however, can lead you to new programs or prepare you for problem areas.

Perhaps the best source to find a support group is the *Adoption Resource Guide*, produced by New Hope Communications (www.adoptivefam.org or 1-800-372-3300) which updates its geographical listing of parent-support groups annually. It also lists adoption attorneys and has a good section on agencies and their programs. You could also contact your local department of social services to see if it knows of any adoption support groups. While you are at it, check into the adoption of the waiting children. Today, most local DSSs welcome single parents.

In addition, the National Adoption Information Clearinghouse (www.calib.com/naic or 1-888-251-0075 ) is a comprehensive site for all aspects of adoption including a geographic listing of support groups (www.calib.com/naic/databases/nadd/naddatabase.htm). Some groups hold classes or even conferences on adoption and if they offer such a class, take it. Similarly, the National Adoption Center (www.adopt.org) is a link both to children available for adoption as well as information on adoption.

Network with people featured in newspaper coverage of adoption such as local couples bringing a new baby home from abroad. Many parent suppot groups newsletters and magazines have listings of homecomings---network with these families as well. Check out local parenting magazines for listings of adoption activities.

Some of the best parent support groups are on line with the dozens of listserves geared toward different areas of adoption through which you can get first-hand reports on any source you may be considering. Posting to one of these listservces and asking members to e-mail you privately is, perhaps, one of the best ways to gather intelligence on various agencies. The number of e-mails asking about particular agencies clearly suggests that "problem" agencies, lawyers, and facilitators are being discussed. The National Adoption Center also has an on-line chat center for support and information at www.adoptnet.org. On AOL just plug in the keyword "adoption" or access one of the sites dedicated to providing a wide range of adoption information.

Many parent support groups also have their own web sites with both basic and detailed information on adoption from their source countries along with geographical chapter listings. These include Families with Children from China (www.fwcc.org), Families for Russian and Ukrainian Adoption (www.frua.org), Families with Children from Vietnam (www.fcvn.org), Stars of David International (www.starsofdavid.org), Adoption Resource Network (www.arni.org) or International Adoption Alliance (www.i-a-a.org). There are also sites completely dedicated to adoption including listing prospective parents' resumes and adoption registries, including Adopting.org; Adoption.com; www.adoption.org; and Rainbow Kids.com. These sites have many other links, including agencies which have their own web sites that include pictures of available children.

Finally, there are the adoption publications including *Adoptive Families Magazine* (www.adoptivefam.org), *Adoption Today* (www.adoptinfo.net) and *Roots and Wings* (www.rootsandwingsmagazine.com). *Adoptive Families Magazine* has a parent-to-parent column that has proved very useful to those seeking information on good agencies or parent support groups.

## Questioning Parents Who Have Already Adopted about Their Agency

When agencies interest you, ask them to give you names of recent clients who have adopted through them. If an agency refuses to give references, move on to a different agency. The following questions represent good adoption practice plus actual experiences. Use adoption etiquette when querying adoptive parents: First ask if it is a convenient time. If not, ask when you may call back or give them permission to call you back collect. After asking them their adoption story:

Ask whether they would use this agency again, but don't stop there: their comfort level with frustration may not match yours.

Ask how agency personnel dealt with questions or problems. How forthcoming were they about explaining what was going on? How receptive are they to holding hands during the process? How are they with sticking to schedules, promises and statements made?

If they complained, did the agency take reprisals such as ceasing to work on their case, failing o return calls, or being generally cold and uncooperative?

When they voiced concerns or complaints did the agency question their ability to continue with the adoption or to parent? (Your ability to parent was resolved with the home study and thus should never be used in this way. Unfortunately, it has been.) Alternatively, if they peppered the agency with compliments or gifts, did their paperwork miraculously move faster?

How did the agency communicate? Was it thorough? Were there updates from agency personnel? Did they check in with the client or did the client do all the calling? Did the agency return phone calls and, if so, how long did it take?

What kind of information on the child's health did they get? Was a medical dossier available for review by a pediatrician prior to acceptance of referral?

How seriously did the agency take health questions or provide health information, especially regarding getting blood tests in a developing country?

Were there any unexpected costs?

How respectful was the agency toward the choices the parents made about the type of child they wanted? (You, not the agency, are adopting the child.)

When they were overseas, how helpful was the agency representative? What did he/she do in completing the adoption? How accessible were these in-country contacts?

## Checking Out the Agency

Several parents have suggested doing a local computer search on agencies you may be considering. Checking the newspapers in the city/county/ state in which the agency is located may reveal information about bad cases or shady owners.

Checking with state licensing authorities is a must, just to ssure that the agency and/or facilitator is licensed. A list of state licensing agencies can be found at the NAIC webside given above.

Once you have your short list of agencies, contact them and ask to have their general information sent to you. Once you have reviewed the mater-

ial, call each agency and ask about its policies. (The following questions, with a few additions, are reprinted from the former AFA's adaptation of Shopping for an Adoption Agency, published by The Adoption Information Service, Seattle, Washington.)

Is the agency licensed to do business? How long has it operated?

Have the owners/directors ever run another agency? If so, what became of it?

Is the program in which you are interested the agency's own program or do they contract it out to a contractor who is working in a given country? Ask whether they have checked out this contractor with local, state, or federal authorities as well as with the authorities in the country in question. Just in case, check him/her and the agency out yourself, through the networking mentioned above.

Will the agency accept a home study done by a licensed home study agency?

What kinds of support, training/parent preparation services, or post-placement services does it offer?

If a given adoption is disrupted before placement, what are their policies for refunding your money or arranging another adoption?

If you are not approved, can you find out why?

**Questions on a Particular Program**:

What types of children do they place (age, nationality, special needs)?

What are the restrictions for adoptive parents (age, income, marital status)? Do these restrictions vary by program or type of child?

Are these restrictions agency policy, the law of the other country, or the preference of the particular source in the other country?

What are the fees for the programs in which you are interested, and what do they cover and what do they leave out? Do they cover the home study (and will they deduct this fee if you already have a study), all post-placement services, the placing agency's fee (foreign or domestic), international processing costs, travel for you and the child, travel within the foreign country?

How much time is expected to be spent in-country? Do the foreign costs include living accommodations, meals, and transportation to the orphanage, government offices? What are estimated costs for miscellaneous fees for visa applications, dossier preparations, translations, all authentication steps, medical exams, exit taxes? If any of these items is not covered by the agency fees, what are your estimated out-of-pocket costs? (Clients have been blindsided by unexpected costs after arrival in the other country.) Agencies with any experience in a given program should be able to give you a fairly good assessment of travel costs, based on the latest client informtion. Understand, however, that these are estimates.

How long does it generally take from home study approval to assignment?

What kind of written medical information does the agency provide at referral? Can you get a complete medical dossier **and video tape** to give to your pediatrician in order to make your decision whether or not to accept a referral?

What happens if you feel that you cannot accept a referral? How long do you get to decide?

Once you accept the child, generally how long will it take until the homecoming?

What are the travel, document, and and authentication requirements? Do you take care of authenticating documents and making travel arrangements or does the agency?

What happens if the adoption does not work out? Does the agency have programs for disrupted adoptions among its postplacement services?

Is it possible to talk with families who have adopted through this agency and through the program in which you are interested?

Remember there is no such thing as a perfect agency. Every agency will have both happy and unhappy customers. Every agency will have both dream and nightmare adoptions. At the beginning of every adoption process, the prospective parent is told that adoption is a leap of faith. That is true. But that leap of faith should not include whether or not your source or agency is a reputable one. Only good consumerism, networking and communications will resolve that issue.

---

Kathryn B. Creedy is on the executive board of Celebrate Adoption, a non-profit organization dedicated to enhancing the understanding of adoption through education and media advocacy (www.celebrateadoption.org). She was active in the writing, publishing and promotion of *An Educator's Guide to Adoption,* published by Celebrate Adoption. She is a regular contributor to adoption publications such as *Adoptive Families,* and is also the media columnist for *Adoption Quarterly.* She is the single mother of two girls---Alexis, born in 1990 in Romania and Brooks, born in 1993 in Bolivia. They were adopted in 1991 and 1993, respectively. She continues to be concerned about the lack of consumer protection in adoption.

---

## Four Adoption Terms Defined:

Natural Child:  any child who is not artificial

Real Parent:  any parent who is not imaginary

Your Own Child:  any child who is not someone else's child

Adopted child:  a natural child, with a real parent, who is my own

(with thanks to author Rita Laws)

# Gay and Lesbian Parenting: Meeting the Challenge of Adoption

by Rosio Gonzalez, MSW and Jill Jacobs, MA, Executive Director, Family Builders by Adoption.

*It has been found that gay and lesbian parents have many unique strengths that make them exceptional parents.*

An increasing number of gay and lesbian individuals is choosing to become parents through adoption. In 1990, an estimated 6 to 14 million children were being raised in gay and lesbian households, through step-parenting, birthparenting, donor insemination, foster parenting or adoption.[1] Thus, the visibility of gay and lesbian parenting has brought many issues of adoption to the forefront. At present, there have been openly gay adoptions in a number of states including the District of Columbia, Ohio, New Mexico, and California[2]. Although adopting as a gay or lesbian couple is still rare, single parent adoption is often a viable avenue for gay or lesbian individuals.

The ability of gay and lesbian individuals to adopt is affected independently by each state's adoption statutes. In many cases, final decisions are made by judges at the local level.[3] As a result, many sympathetic judges have overturned negative rulings on local gay and lesbian adoptions. Recently, New Jersey became the first state in the nation to allow legal adoption by gay and lesbian partners. However, Florida prohibits this type of adoption and several other states have legislation pending also to prohibit adoption and foster care by gay and lesbian families.

Gay men and lesbians continually face the possibility of resistance from adoption and placement agencies, causing many individuals to be cautious and often reticent about contacting an agency directly. Families are encouraged to seek existing adoption agencies in the community, and to inquire about their experience and approach when working with gay and lesbian families. However, it is important to note that agencies, like people, have differing personalities and views about non-traditional adoptions. It is also likely that within an agency social workers may differ in their views. Consequently, choosing the right agency involves extensive research by the prospective parent. He or she can accomplish this by calling a local gay and lesbian community center, a well-known national gay and lesbian organization, or by searching the internet for other available resources.

Once prospective parents have identified an agency, they should consider speaking directly with a social worker who can provide information on the agency's policies, methods of handling the home study and placement process, procedures on disclosure or non-disclosure, number of gay and lesbian placements made per year, and resources available to gay and lesbian families within their community. This information will enable the prospective parent(s) to make a well-informed decision.

Depending on local policy and prevailing norms, some agencies or adoption workers may dissuade the applicant from disclosing his/her sexual orientation. This does not necessarily imply that they are not supportive of gay and lesbian adoptions. Ultimately, the prospective parent(s) must make a decision based on their own comfort level. However, it must be noted that the falsification of information is a basis for denial of an adoption application.

The home study evaluation can be a very intrusive and difficult process. However, if a sense of trust, honesty, and openness is established between social worker and applicant, the process can be very positive, allowing both parties to assess the applicant's ability to care, nurture, and meet the challenges involved in parenting a child.

There are many standard issues discussed in the homestudy process, which includes a comprehensive individual history, important relationships, health history, parenting style and experience, problem solving, and various other subjects. For gay and lesbian applicants, the homestudy may also include: how the single gay or lesbian parent will provide opposite gender role models for the child; where the applicant is with regard to issues of individual development and self-image as a gay or lesbian person; what kind of family and community support exists, and how the applicant might deal with issues of discrimination or homophobia against the child or the parent(s).

The wording of the home study will depend on the atmosphere of the local community. In situations where the worker is less experienced, the prospective parent(s) might take a proactive role in assisting the worker to understand the issues specific to gay and lesbian families. For example, this may include how a social worker might describe the commitment in a relationship where there has been no legal marriage.

The prospective parent may not easily find a social worker sensitive to gay or lesbian issues, in either a private domestic, international, or public agency. The task may be less difficult in a large urban area where there is a strong gay presence. It should be noted that many rural areas serve gay and lesbian individuals too. Nevertheless, prospective parents may still be confronted with the choice, at the recommendation of an adoption worker, to avoid talking about or disclosing information about sexual orientation.

The rising number of children in the foster care system who need safe, nurturing, and permanent families is encouraging many agencies to welcome gay and lesbian applicants. Overall, many agencies are finding that non-traditional families are an excellent resource for children who are waiting to be adopted. It has been found that gay and lesbian parents have many unique strengths that make them exceptional parents. These consist of having the ability to accept differences, the experience of being in the minority, being open about sexuality with children who have been sexually abused, and having an understanding of the special needs of gay and lesbian children.[4]

In order to survive parenting, finding a support system is crucial for any individual. Some gay and lesbian families may locate support more easily than others, whether it consists of family, friends, neighbors, or organized bodies. If the prospective parent(s) cannot find resources for support from the adoption agency, the local gay and lesbian community center, by word of mouth, or through a national gay or lesbian organization, they might think about starting a group, or asking the agency's help in starting one.

The opportunities for adoption vary depending on the applicant's preference for adopting domestically or internationally, infant or older child. Undoubtedly, far more children are available in the U.S. than elsewhere. Often, however, adopting an infant domestically means that the birthmother is involved in choosing a parent for her child, and her attitudes and beliefs about gay and lesbian parenting may influence her decision. International adoptions vary by country, and many countries forbid gay and lesbian adoption. Thus, it is crucial for prospective parents to gather specific information from international adoption agencies regarding each country.

As national and international views about gay and lesbian parenting unfold and change, so will attitudes toward adoption. Currently, many successful gay and lesbian families are meeting the challenges of parenting. Although adoption is a growing and viable avenue to parenting for gay and lesbian families, it takes perseverance to get through the process.

---

Endnotes

1

National Adoption Information Clearinghouse, *Working with Gay and Lesbian Parents.* Washington, DC 1966

2

National Adoption Information Clearinghouse, 6-8

3

National Adoption Information Clearinghouse, 7

4

Adoption Resource Exchange for Single Parents, Inc., *Gay Men and Lesbians; Building Loving Families* Allison Beers. Springfield, VA 1997.

# Laws and Legal Processes that Affect Adoption

## Laws Affecting Domestic Adoption

### Notification:

In almost all states the birth father must be notified if the birth mother plans to surrender her baby for adoption. The laws vary from state to state with respect to the amount of time the father has to contest the mother's decision, and to file for custody of the baby. A request to the court for custody of the child is not automatically granted, but depends not only on the law in that state but on the ability of the father to demonstrate to the court's satisfaction that he can provide good care and a good home for the child.

To check the state law for the state from which you are adopting, ask the agency if you are going through an agency; a lawyer if you are working privately through a lawyer, or the National Adoption Information Clearinghouse (see p. 63).

### Revocation:

Laws vary from state to state governing the amount of time a birthmother, and sometimes the birthfather too, have to change her/their mind about surrendering the child for adoption. In Texas, for example, the birthmother has two days; in Maryland she has thirty. An adoptive parent can take custody of the baby before the revocation deadline is up, at the risk of becoming bonded to the baby. Check the agency, the NAIC, or the AAAA.

### Transfer of Custody

At birth, the birthmother and/or an involved birthfather have/has custody. If the birthmother decides to surrender the baby for adoption she may do so at any time after birth, but has a varying amount of time, from days to months depending on the state, in which she can change her mind about parenting the child. After the deadline has passed, the custody transfer is permanent, although there are some states where custody can be challenged if fraud or coercion can be proved.

In some independent or "private" adoptions, custody is transferred directly to the adoptors according to the law of the state in which the baby is born. For this a lawyer's help is needed, to make sure that the wording complies with state law. In agency adoptions custody is transferred to the agency. The agency then transfers custody to the adoptors, when the placement is agreed upon between the applicant(s) and the agency---and the applicant pays a fee for this. Naturally, the adoptive parent must produce this custody statement in court when he/she/they are formally adopting.

### Interstate Compact on the Placement of Children

All fifty states and the District of Columbia adhere to the Interstate Compact on the Placement of Children, drawn up to prevent abuses including the casual transfer of children from one state to another. For example, parents can no longer take a child from one state to another and just abandon him or her if they change their minds. The states' interest is to prevent having such children simply dumped on the State to support.

Under ICPC, both the state in which the child was born, referred to as the "sending state"; and the state to which the parents take the child to live, called the "receiving state"; must approve the transfer of jurisdiction. This approval must be gained by presenting the adoptive parents' paperwork, including the home study and some indication of ability to pay for the expense of raising the child, to the ICPC Administrators in both states. In most cases this adds only a few days to the process. An adoptive parent working through an agency or a lawyer will be told how to comply with the ICPC. There is no fee.

### Adoption of a Waiting Child:

Three decades ago widespread criticism began that State child protection offices refused to place minority children with parents who were not of the same racial or ethnic background, and took too long to terminate the parental rights (TPR) of parents even when return to those parents was not possible. The result was that children waited so long in out-of-home care that they became unadoptable. Responding to this criticism, Congress passed a series of laws aimed at ensuring safety, permanence, and child and family well-being. People interested in adopting a child from public custody should know these laws, which could help them if they meet resistance.

The Adoption Assistance and Child Welfare Act of 1960, Public Law 96-272, gave states financial assistance to increase protection of children in their care. The Omnibus Budget Reconciliation Act of 1993, P.L. 103-66, increased services both to support retention of children in their original homes and if that was impossible, in their out of home care. Third was the Multi-Ethnic Placement Act of 1994, P.L. 104-188, aimed at reducing long stays of children in foster care when parents of the same racial or ethnic groups could not be found. The law forbade discrimination on that account, while requiring that States increase their efforts to find foster or adoptive parents who do reflect the racial and ethnic diversity of waiting children. The fourth law, the Adoption and Safe Families Act of 29997, P.L. 105-89, increased incentives to states. Stressing safety, the law shortened the time allowed for decisions on TPR and increased pressure on states to finalize permanent placements for waiting children. Licensing requirements were made uniform for foster parents, kinship placements, and adoptive parents.

### Adoption:

In domestic adoptions, the actual legal adoption does not usually happen until a certain period of months has passed--usually specified under state law. During this period, state adoption law usually specifies a certain number of postplacement visits by the agency social worker (in independent adoptions, a worker in private practice or working for an agency), usually three, sometimes more. The worker wants to see if each party is adjusting well and that the adoptee is getting the appropriate

health checkups plus whatever health care is required, as well as any additional matters appropriate to the age and special requirements of the child. The worker's reports are passed on to the source agency, in an agency adoption; and to the court with jurisdiction over the case.

At the end of the postplacement report period the parent files for adoption in the county court. Usually the parent hires a lawyer to file the petition but in many states it is possible to call the family division of the court, ask for the required forms, and do it yourself. Among the documents that the court will require will be the postplacement reports, the home study, and of course proof of transfer of custody from the birthparent(s) to the adoptive parent, either directly or through an intermediary.

### Disruption or Dissolution:

Rarely, an adoption does not work out, for any of a variety of powerful reasons. If the parents realize this before the formal adoption, ending the

planned adoption by legally giving up custody is called a **Disruption.** It is likely to be messy. The adoption agency, if one was involved, and/or the public social services agency will be required to find substitute care for the child; the source agency will be involved if the child crossed state lines.

Sometimes a parent decides after formally adopting that she, he, or they cannot parent the child, and petitions for **dissolution** of the adoption. A major change may have taken place in the parent's life, such as a serious disease. Perhaps the parent has come to believe that the child has been so damaged by abuse or neglect in earlier life that he or she is incapable of bonding with the parent, possibly to the point of violence. In this case the agency(ies), or the state, will be involved in providing short- or long-term care, depending on the circumstances. Dissolution, like adoption, takes place in court.

## Laws Affecting Inter-country Adoption

There are special requirements for a foreign placement. In most cases, the prospective parent uses a U.S. adoption agency that has a contact with a foreign source, rather than going independently. In every case, the adoption must comply with the regulations of the U.S. Immigration and Naturalization Service of the Department of Justice.

### INS Permission to Enter the United States:

Since 1975, as mentioned in Chapter I, single people have been able to use the "I-600" process, named after the INS form used to request an entry visa to bring their adopted child into the United States as a member of the family. If the adoption agency does not provide the applicant with a set of forms, fingerprint cards, and instructions, the applicant may call the INS information number, 1-800-375-5283, press several buttons, and have a set mailed directly to her or him. The documentation that must accompany the form is spelled out in the instructions.

In early 1997 the INS introduced a new form, I-864, Affidavit of Support. The applicant(s) must contractually agree to provide for the financial support of the child, and must accompany the form with copies of the last three federal income tax returns. The parent must also agree to reimburse any government agency or private agency that provides the child with any means-tested public benefit.

In most foreign adoptions, the parent visits the other country and adopts the child there, then goes to the U.S. Embassy in the capital of the country to secure the child's entry visa. The U.S. Embassy has the final say on the eligibility of the child for adoption, and on a few occasions has declined to grant a visa when it felt the adoption was not legal under U.S. law, stranding the parents and children. If the visa is granted, the family then leaves for the U.S. The child will enter the U.S. carrying a passport from the home country.

Some countries do not lelgalize adoption; instead they grant guardianship to the adoptive parents---India is an example. If the children's status complies with U.S. law, they too are admitted to the U.S. as family members.

When Congress wrote the immigration laws, they applied slightly easier standards in some areas than are required in the U.S. If the birthfather has disappeared, abandoned the mother, or is unknown, it is not necessary to try to track him down, as it is in the U.S. On the other hand, if the birthmother is married, whether the husband is the child's father or not, the child is not considered an orphan, and istherefore ineligible for entry into the U.S. unless . .

. . . both parents have abandoned the child or disappeared or died; then the child can qualify as an orphan. This might be an issue in an independent adoption from Central or South America. Any child, no matter what the marital status of his parents, who is unconditionally and permanently released to anauthorized third party may be considered abandoned. An authorized third party may be a government agency, a court, an adoption agency, or an orphanage that is authorized by the government to accept children for placement with a U.S. citizen.

U.S. consulates in some South American countries that appear to have had some unethical placement practices now require DNA testing of the child and the mother, to confirm that it is in fact the child's mother who is giving him or her up for adoption.

### Re-adoption in the United States:

It is a good idea, even for those parents who have already adopted their child in the foreign country, to adopt the child again in an American court. This is not because of doubt by the U.S. government of the legality of the foreign court's action; rather it safeguards the child against vagaries of American customs and laws. Some U.S. states do not recognize the decisions of foreign courts, and thus would not recognize adopted children as the legal "issue" of parents; adoptive parents must specifically identify their adopted children as inheritors of their estates to head off challenges.

Your child with a foreign adoption decree might not be recognized as your child for other purposes as well---permissions for hospital procedures, for instance. It is handier to carry around an adoption decree from a U.S. court than a birth certificate or adoption decree in a language unknown to the school admissions office. Lastly, some South American countries grant what is called a "simple" adoption, where the birthparents do not lose all parental rights to the child--in the eyes of *that* court. U.S. readoption would confer complete parental rights on the adoptive parent.

Where the adoptive parent has not seen the child before the adoption---the child having been adopted by proxy and then escorted to the United States---the INS insists on re-adoption in the U.S. Several countries in Asia, Europe, or Africa insist on escorting for the child, or provide that as an option.

### Naturalization:

The last step, for children born abroad, is naturalization as a U.S. citizen. As of Fall 2000, adoption, abroad or here, does <u>not</u> automatically confer U.S. citizenship upon the U.S. parent's new child. Incredibly, many parents who legally adopt children from abroad do not bother to go on to get them naturalized---a fairly simply step. The consequences of this range from moderate to serious:

Some government loans and scholarships are not available to non-citizens. Recently-enacted legislation restricts still further the government benefits available even to legally-resident aliens. A young person traveling abroad who got into some trouble would lack the protection of U.S. citizenship.

Worst of all, if a young person who is legally still an alien commits any kind of felony in the U.S., present law mandates deportation to his/her native country. A recent example of this involved an 18-year-old, adopted from Thailand as a toddler, who had "borrowed" a car for a joyride with some friends. In spite of his parents' frantic appeals, he is back in Thailand, where he knows no one and no word of Thai. An adoptee who is over 18, or who has been deported, cannot apply for immigration again.

A bill now awaiting action in Congress would confer citizenship on a child adopted from abroad as soon as he/she arrived in the U.S. Children who were adopted after their arrival would become citizens on completion of the adoption. It would not be retroactive, however, nor change the over-18 rule.

# Connecting with the Birthmother

*It's not that they want a mother's love--they have it. They want their identities, and they want to know <u>why.</u>*

We all know that in the last few years "open adoption" has arrived in various degrees, both before and after adoption. You haven't yet adopted. You want a child, and you want this child to be <u>yours</u>--by law, and by love. Where does the child's original family fit in here? After several years' experience with open adoption, two things seem to have become clear: First, you don't need to fear the birthmother, and second, connecting the child and his or her original family--from just knowing who they are and how it happened that he/she is no longer with them, up to direct contact--is very good for your child.

**Where are you looking for your child?. . .** Abroad? Undoubtedly the reason a number of couples and single people adopt from abroad is the belief that the biological parents won't or can't attempt to contact their children later.

The majority of single women and men adopt U.S.-born children now in public custody, who have lost their original families through death, abandonment, or termination of parental rights for neglect or abuse. These children range from infants to young teenagers, and the majority of them know their original parents. The social service agency may or may not know how to reach the parents. Adoption records are confidential in all states, but some states will provide non-identifying information to each party, and perhaps a letter from the birthmother to the child she surrendered.

A smaller number of you will adopt infants privately or through private agencies. If you are able to do so--through luck, persistence, acceptance of a special needs child, or willingness to spend a good deal of money--you may already have found that today, the birthmother often gets to choose, and you and she learn a great deal about each other.

**Who is the birthmother?** There is no way to draw a picture of the typical woman who loses her kids. If she has lost them to "the state" because addiction or dependence led her to neglect them or to allow a friend to abuse them, she still does not voluntarily "give them away." She may be a wife in a South American village who just can't feed one more child. She doesn't want to "give this child away," but she must, or the baby will die. Or maybe she is a girl in college, intent on a better life, who decides with her boyfriend that they can't stop their future in its tracks, but she doesn't casually "give her child away." She may be a child terrified of her parents' fury, or a woman terrified of her boyfriend or husband's rage-- and denial or unwillingness has made it too late for an abortion--so that surrender is a relief but never a joy.

Agencies often call her decision to place her baby "making an adoption plan for her child," which sounds rational and businesslike, but I doubt that it is ever quite so cool. Very seldom is she going to try to undo this decision--often the original reasons remain--but in most cases it leaves a hole in her heart. One birthmother told me, on what information I don't know, that most birthmothers who sign over parental rights never bear another child, which seems terribly sad.

**Who is the child?** In almost every case, even if the child is in a wheelchair, he/she is basically a normal kid (we are probably not talking about profoundly retarded children, or children so damaged by abuse that they can't bear to love or be loved), and he can give and and respond to love. You will be the mother or father in her life, the one who changes her baby diaper, tends him when he gets a tummyache, goes to her soccer games, pushes his wheelchair, argues with her about her clothes/hair/chores/messy room, worries when he starts to drive, and so on.

But in many of these children there is a wide hole in their identities, if not their hearts. Where did he come from? Did she just materialize from a lamp? And why didn't his first mother want to keep him? What was the <u>reason</u>? Logic plays no part in this. They can't put themselves in her place, yet. Most of their friends may have biological kin, not all of whom may be completely respectable, but they know who these people are. It's not that they want a mother's love--they have it. They want their identities, and they want to know <u>why</u>.

**Why might you fear connecting with the birth-mother?** One fear is that your child, even after years of perfectly secure parent-child relationships, still loves her birthmother best; that the loss of the birthmother is a "primal wound" from which the child will never recover. Current attachment theory, however, is that infants can form attachments to foster or adoptive parents just as well as to birthmothers. Researchers cited by Lois Melina in the May 1997 issue of her widely-read newsletter Adopted Child (psychologist Robert Karen; Alan Sroufe, psychology professor at the University of Minnesota Institute of Child Development; and Charles H. Zeanah, M.D., professor of psychology at Louisiana State University) say there is no evidence that the birthmother has a bond with the fetus that gives her an advantage in forming an attachment with the infant.

Adoptive parents also fear that a birthparent will surface years later and seek to reclaim her child. If the adoptive parent follows the law and the regulations of her state, or of the Immigration and Naturalization Service, there is next to no chance of that happening. The adoptive parent is in a very strong position.

Sometimes an adoptive parent fears that the child would be disappointed when a reunion occurred. Perhaps the birthparents were poor and uneducated, or the parents want to protect the child from painful information about the birth family. To quote adoption writer Melina again, "It is not our job as parents to protect our children from the realities of life--especially from the realities of their own lives." She adds that a parent should obtain information and provide it to the child because "it is his story and we are all entitled to our own stories . . . of course, a commitment to telling a child her story does not require full disclosure to the child from infancy," but rather providing it as and when the child can handle it.

**How does this information benefit the child?** Undoubtedly, not all children seek information about their birthfamilies. If they were older when they were adopted they already have information, and some of it may be painful.

A child adopted as a newborn may sense that the new caregiver is not the one whose heartbeat he or she knew for nine months, but as indicated above, there is no evidence of a prenatal bond between birthmother and fetus that gives her a permanent edge in the child's heart. But children, however securely attached to their adoptive families, still may

feel like the ghost at the banquet when they are old enough to realize that most of their friends are seated solidly in blood kinships and histories of place and family, and they are not. They may have no history, and no resemblance to their adoptive families.

Children who were older when they were taken from their original families, and who know much of their histories, may grieve for this loss, even if their early lives were painful. This may seem incomprehensible to the family and friends of the new parents, and even to the new parents themselves, but it does happen. The abuse may have been random, with good times interspersed among painful ones. The child may have positive memories, even in abusive situations, of one or both birthparents or other relatives, friends, or siblings in the original family.

Starting in their teens, many adoptees begin to wonder about their biological parents. Perhaps in combination with the normal teenage urge to rebel, or at least to achieve individuation, some adoptees may even want to search for and contact their birthparent(s). If their mothers (adoptive) have made no attempt to communicate with the birthparent before, this is apt to be unsettling.

Histories are one thing; contact is another, and it usually seems as if actual contact is needed more by the birthmother than the child--until the child becomes an adult, and especially when he or she becomes a parent in turn. Then the desire to know more about blood relatives kicks in strongly. Still this does not, repeat not, mean that the love and experience with the adoptive family take second place in the child's heart.

**How and what kind of connection should be sought?** This depends greatly on how the child came into the adoptive family. If this was an independent adoption directly arranged by the prospective parent, a great deal of information is likely to have been exchanged, and quite possibly a promise of continuing contact to varying degrees. If the adoption was facilitated through an agency where the birthmother chooses the adoptive families from dossiers and letters prepared by the prospective adoptors, there will probably be direct contact before the adoption. Continuing contact seems to depend on the good will and perseverance of one or both parties.

If the adoption has been arranged through a more conservative private agency, it may be quite difficult to achieve any connection, even when the adopted child is older. Some older agencies tend to have a more restrictive approach to adoption in general--not allowing the clients to read their own home studies, not placing infants with single people-- and revealing almost no information to each party about the other. It was for situations like this that adoptee-birthparent search groups developed almost guerrilla techniques to uncover documentation.

Public social service agencies were equally rigid in the old days when there was a surplus of babies. Now that they are chiefly working with older children, sibling groups, and special-needs children, prospective parents are likely to be given a great deal of information about the waiting children, and the adoptive parents have some discretion as to the use of this data, once the adoption decree is final.

Lastly, for children adopted from abroad, obtaining information several years after adoption could be very difficult. As far as I know, only Korea (which no longer permits single people to adopt)

maintains records of children placed for adoption through any of its four approved semi-governmental placement organizations.

It is likely that in countries where orphan placements receive considerable government over- sight, at least--Viet Nam, perhaps, or India; certain Central and South American countries, and Eastern European countries--varying degrees of record- keeping exist with a potential for access. Some Colombian and Guatemalan orphanages have helped adopted adults locate parents or relatives, or at least to visit the area where they had been abandoned. Inter-country adoptions arranged through indepen- dent "facilitators" operating directly with prospective adoptors or by contract with a licensed U.S. agencies may present a spongier, less likely source of infor- mation, especially as the years go by.

It should be noted that when the Hague Convention on Intercountry Adoption takes full effect, participating countries will be required to collect and keep information on the child, who presumably can eventually gain access (see p. 14).

---

## Characteristics of birthmothers, and of foster children waiting for adoption

The **National Adoption Information Clearinghouse** has assembled information from various sources on the changing trends over the last four decades in women who placed their children from adoption. The findings and their sources are summarized below:

Overall, the number of unmarried women placing their children for adoption dropped steadily between 1952 and 1988 (the most recent year studied). Among black women the percentage has always been small; in 1988 it was 1.1%. In the 50's up to 1972, by contrast, 19.7% of unmarried white women placed children for adoption; by the end of the 80's it was 3.2%. The drop was especially sharp among unmarried teenagers.

The decline among white women initially reflected the legalization of abortion; it has contin- ued as the stigma of unwed motherhood has lessened. (Bachrach, Stolley, London, "Relinquish- ment of Premarital Births; Evidence from the Na- tional Survey Data," Family Planning Perspectives, vol. 24, Jan-Feb. 1992.)

Women who voluntarily place their children for adoption tend to have higher educational and jobgoals than those who keep their children, and

often come from higher socio-economic backgrounds (Stolley, Kathy S., "Statistics on Adoption in the U.S.," The Future of Children, vol. 3 No. 1 Spring 1993.) Birthmothers who place their children privately tend to be 17-30 years old, with no more than a high school education, and most are not related to the adoptive parents. (Barth, Brooks & Iyer, "Adoption in California . . . Child Welfare Research Center, 1995.)

The **DHHS Children's Bureau** compiled data in 2000 from the Adoption and Foster Care Analysis and Reporting System on children in foster care: At the end of 1999, 52% of children in foster care were boys. Forty percent of the children adopted that year were white non-hispanic, 43% were black non-hispanic, and 15% were hispanic.

What factors discourage adoption most? **Age** held back 22% of the 1-5 year cohort, rising steadily to 65% of the 16-18 year-olds. **Medical, mental, physical, or emotional disabilities** came next, but declined from a high of 43% of under-age- one babies to 18% of children aged 11-18. **Siblings** were next in significance, declining from 20% for under-age-five children to 10 % of ages 16-18. **Race** was least important, peaking at 14% of 1-5-year olds, declining to 3% of foster children aged 16-18.

# Chapter III

## Managing Once You've Adopted

## Practical Aspects

### Adoption Costs

The cost of an adoption varies tremendously from place to place and child to child, and it is simply impossible even to hazard an average estimate. Instead, we shall list the kinds of expenses an adoptive parent can run into, depending on the kind of adoption she or he undertakes.

**Home Study:** Most public agencies now charge no fee, and agencies supported by community funds are apt not to charge. Private agencies may charge a flat fee or, sometimes, a sliding scale related to the income and perhaps the other expenses of the applicant. The fee can be as low as $25 for the adoption of a hard to place child, to many hundreds for a high-income parent with no other children to support. It may be paid in installments. If you can adopt a child through the same agency, there may be an additional "placement" or "program" charge.

**International Placement Agency Fee:** If the prospective parent uses a placement agency, there will be a "program" fee of several hundred dollars, representing the agency's overhead, staffing, and intangibles such as risks assumed.

**Independent Adoption Fee:** Legal private sources, such as attorneys, charge regular legal and/or medical fees, which can still amount to $15,000 or quite a bit more. We have heard of domestic black market fees of $80,000 up. Internationally, the independent facilitator will charge in the middle thousands, sometimes including a donation to the orphanage.

If you are working with an independent facilitator for a foreign adoption you will need a lawyer in the foreign country to handle whatever action takes place there--adoption or merely transfer of custody; his fee is likely to be in the hundreds to several thousands.

**Travel Costs:** If you are adopting a child from abroad, there will be a one-way cost for the child-- and an escort, if you do not pick up the child yourself; if you travel, you will pay your round trip fare plus one way for the child. To economize, consult the agency, or other parents who have recently gone the same route; they may know ways to lower the cost to a fraction of the quoted fare. Several travel agencies now specialize in foreign travel for adoption, and advertise in adopted-related publications and at adoption conferences.

**Legal Costs:** Your local lawyer's fee to handle the actual legal adoption or re-adoption will be one of the lesser expenses you face--certainly in the lower hundreds, depending on where you live. Even here, adoptive parent support groups can put you in touch with lawyers who charge low fees for adoptions, particularly for waiting children. In fact, some support groups have provided do-it-yourself adoption kits. There will be minor court costs, either way; perhaps another $50-$100.

**Miscellaneous Fees:** For a foreign adoption, you should budget several hundred dollars, to be safe, for extra fees and unanticipated costs. Items required are original certificates of birth, divorce, or spouse's death and the like; plus the fees for the several steps required to "authenticate" these already-certified documents (the notary, the body that licensed the notary, the secretary of state for your state, the U.S. State Department visa office, and the consulate of the foreign country). Also included may be telephone cables and long distance calls between you and the agency in the U.S. and abroad, postage, and filing fees for Immigration and Naturalization Service applications for the entry visa for your child.

# Child Care

Costs for the several methods of care outlined below ran about as follows in the Mid-Atlantic area in the late 1990's:

Live-in: $200-$250 a week, including light house
    keeping work, room and board $50-$75
Live-out: $250-$350 a week, including light house-
    keeping.
Day Care Center: $550 a month for a preschooler;
    $650 for infants; many have a sliding scale.
Take-to: $100 a week, minimum
Before & After-school: $300.
    Afterschool every day, $240 per month
    Three days a week, $180 per month
    Before-school only, $60 per month.

It should be noted that domestic employees are now covered under the U.S. minimum wage law. This applies to both live-in and live-out child care, provided you employ the person more than eight hours a week and pay her at least $50 a calendar quarter (any consecutive three months). The federal minimum wage in 2000 is $5.15/hour. Some states mandate a higher minimum.

**U.S. Social Security:** When you hire someone to come into your house to look after your child, you are that person's employer and, legally, you ought to see that Social Security and Medicare contributions are made for that person. (When you take your child to another person's home for day care, that caregiver is legally regarded as a "self-employed person" who should pay her own Social Security contributions.)

Customarily, both the employer and the employee contribute to the social security payment, each at the rate of .062 times the paycheck for social security, and .0145 for Medicare. For instance, if you pay a caregiver $250 a week, the employee would contribute a total of $19.13 (deducted from her wage) for social security plus Medicare and you, the employer, another $19.13. Alternatively, the employer can contribute the whole amount. This contribution is totalled and paid only at the end of the calendar year, along with the employer's tax return.

It should be added that many daytime caregivers flatly refuse to make social security contributions, or to let you make them on their behalf, for reasons that may or may not be obvious. But the point must be made that if these caregivers change their minds, even twenty years later, and decide that they would like to receive Social Security and Medicare benefits, and if they can prove that you paid them for child care and did not make Social Security and Medicare contributions, you are liable for not only the back taxes but a penalty for non-payment!

The matters of health care and subsidies were outlined in Chapter II, but we remind the prospective parent here that there are many specialized organizations that can give considerable assistance to the parent of a child with, for example, cerebral palsy, hearing problems, physical crippling, or mental retardation; and it is absolutely vital that the prospective parent investigate these sources first before settling on a child who will need long-term medical attention of any kind. A source of information on these organizations, as well as on support groups of parents whose children have one or another of these conditions is the National Adoption Information Clearinghouse at 330 C Street N.W., Washington, DC 20447; (703) 352-3488 EST. Another good person to contact is Dr. Dana Johnson of the International Adoption Clinic at the University of Minnesota,(612) 626-1164, or Dr. Jerri Jenista, (313) 668-0419.

Many parents of "special needs" children have found that a good health plan can help them to absorb medical costs without undue pain, even for necessary operations and repeated therapy.

## DAY CARE ARRANGEMENTS:

When the child arrives, single parents usually take time off from their jobs, from a few weeks to a few months, in order to help the child establish herself or himself in the new home. If this is the first child, such a shake-down period is also vital to the new parent, to permit her or him to become acquainted with the joys and responsibilities of parenthood. If your child is under ten, however, and unless you have a live-in relative, eventually you will have to arrange for all-day or part-day care. Schools end at 3 o'clock, and not only do they close for two and a half summer months but they shut their doors for half a day to several days at a time for "professional development," snow, local and national holidays, and Christmas and spring vacations.

Single adoptive parents--and two-parent working families too--often feel defensive against the charge that, because they work all day, they deprive their children of a happy and psychologically healthy childhood. It might be interesting to take a look sometime at how long and how widely the ideal two-parent, mother-at-home family has existed. What about the millions of families who immigrated to this country, where both parents worked long hours in shops, on farms, or in factories?  We might find that the "nonworking" mother was a phenomenon limited to the upper middle classes and above, and only for the last two or three generations.

Even with respect to small children, it is interesting to note that that one of the foremost students of early childhood, Dr. Jerome Kagan of Harvard University, concluded after careful study that "Attendance at a day care center staffed by conscientious and nurturant adults during the first two and a half years does not seem to sculpt a psychological profile very much different from the one created by total home rearing . . . the effects of the home appear to have a salience that is not easily altered by the group care context.  The family has a mysterious power, which is perhaps one reason why it has been the basic and most stable social unit in this and other societies for so long a time."  ["The Effects of Infant Day Care on Psychological Development," by Jerome Kagan, Reichard B. Kearsley, and Philip R. Zelazo; Symposium of the American Association for the Advancement of Science, February 19, 1976.]

Even those single people who are able to adopt babies will need in time to deal with the after-school hours and even more, with the days and weeks when school is closed.  Here are some of the solutions that parents have used:

1. "Live-in,"  A live-in housekeeper/babysitter is given room and board plus a salary.  This is probably the closest approximation of the mother-at-home, and assures that someone will be there at all times.  You can also get the bonus of help with cooking and cleaning, depending on the rate and the arrangement.

Locating live-in help is not easy, however.  In many cases parents look for individuals who are not native to the U.S.  The most common methods are to advertise in daily and, if available, neighborhood newspapers (asking for references) and to ask friends who have live-in help.  Some employment agencies handle live-in help  and often there are non-profit agencies established specifically to assist Latin-American or other immigrants and visitors.

Legally, you are the employer of this person, and you should declare her wages to the U.S. Internal Revenue Service, filling out a W-2 form for her and deducting for Social Security and Medicare (see previous section).  Consult the IRS on income tax matters.  Also, it is not only a humane but a sensible policy to provide health insurance for your live-in help.  The rate is higher for an individual, of course, but if it helps you to hire a really good caregiver, and

helps to keep her healthy, it might well be a saving in the long run.

Lucky is the single parent who lives with relatives to share the burden of child care and house care.  This is not uncommon, and it is something to celebrate.

2. "Live-Out" care:  Daytime care by someone who comes to your house is another possibility for all-day or after-school care.  Sometimes teen-agers in the neighborhood or college students working their way through can be hired; usually, however, you locate an individual who does this for her living, either through a neighborhood or daily newspaper advertisement (by you or by the caregiver) or through an agency.  You have the worry of whether or not the sitter will arrive each day on time, or whether she may call in sick, forcing you perhaps to use annual leave.  The advantages are that this approximates the mother-in-the-home almost as closely as the live-in arrangement, and as with that situation the child remains in his or her familiar home surroundings.  You can also often arrange for cleaning and cooking help from the caregiver.

You should treat this person as any regular employer does his employee--and that means allowing vacation time and sick leave.  This, of course, means that you may well have to take off from work yourself if the caregiver is ill, and that her (paid!) vacation will probably coincide with yours. Again, as the employer of this person, you should withhold the required taxes and contributions.

3. Nursery School/Day Care Center for young children):  Day care centers will sometimes take children as young as two and a half (and some rare ones will take infants), although in almost all cases they prefer children to be toilet-trained, which can be chancy at that age in the case of boys.  The child generally attends until he or she enters kindergarten or, less often, first grade.  Take time off from work and visit several such centers--well before you need to enroll your child because, especially in the fall, the good centers fill up early.

These centers can be superb, with wonderful equipment, lots of exercise, educational value, and loving adults.  These days, many large corporations and governmental bodies are opening centers on or near the job site.  There is usually a nursery school program in the morning and supervised play in the afternoon, when the children have begun to flag. They usually run from 7:30 a.m. to 6:00 p.m. all year round, with only the legal holidays observed--real day care centers for the working parent.  Meals provided sometimes include breakfast, and always lunch as well as a mid-morning and mid-afternoon snack, and the good centers use the advice of a nutritionist in staying away from junk foods. Note, however, that if your child is sick, you must make other arrangements until he or she recovers.

4. **"Take-to":** Often the least expensive is the system under which you ferry your child to a caregiver who looks after the child in her own home. She has no travel time and can do her housework and cooking during the day. She is legally regarded as a "self-employed person" who should pay her own Social Security contributions and income tax. Naturally you want someone near where you live or work. You can look for a caregiver who has children of her own around the age of yours, or one who looks after other children as well. To locate such a person, advertise in your local or neighborhood newspaper. Consult your local department of public welfare: They may license caregivers and keep a list of them, which will give you at least a floor on quality. Ask friends.

The disadvantages here reveal the advantage of the at-home systems. Avoid the woman who "keeps" a horde of children and uses television as a pacifier. Some studies have indicated that prolonged television-watching, even of the best children's programs, dulls creativity in a child because the communication between the child and the screen is not two-way. Other drawbacks of take-to: the transportation time lengthens your day, cutting into your time for playing with and caring for your children yourself. You have less control over what your child takes in. But the take-to system can work very well if you take the time and trouble and perhaps expense of locating a good caregiver. And some can be very, very good indeed.

5. **After-school programs:** In some places, parents have combined to set up after-school programs, using space in a public school or church. Often a non-profit corporation with a parent board of directors operates the program, hiring professionally-trained staff and young "counselors," setting policy, and charging fees. It usually runs from 7:30-9:00 a.m. and again at 3:00 to 6:00 p.m., but operates all day on days when the school is closed. The children start at age five and continue to around ten or eleven, and the staff-to-child ratio is around one to ten. The program includes games and crafts, sports, and occasional field trips and movies. Apply early.

# Health Care Plans

By and large, children are healthy, but they need innumerable shots and boosters and they can have allergies that require lots of laboratory work. Susan Freivalds of the Adoption Education Institute reminds parents to investigate the extent and type of health coverage for a newly-adopted child. She says:

Section 609 of ERISA, the Employee Retirement Income Security Act, which became effective in 1993, applies to group health plans provided by private employers, including "self-insure" plans or coverage by a third party. It requires that any group plan that covers dependent children **born to** plan participants must also apply to children **placed with** participants,, with the same terms and conditions. Additionally, the plan may not restrict or deny coverage on the basis of a pre-existing condition! The definition of "placement" is that the adoptive parents have assumed a legal obligation for partial or total financial support of the child, whether or not the child is physically in the adoptive home or whether or not the adoption has been finalized.

Plans not subject to ERISA include individual policies and those of employers that are governmental agencies (including schools) or churches and church-affiliated hospitals, schools and organizations.

Children adopted from disadvantaged countries sometimes arrive with parasitic or other stubborn or chronic infections. Adoptive parents have found that most pediatricians are not accustomed to the kinds of diseases, particularly the parasitic infestations, that children very occasionally bring with them, and you must search around for a parasitologist who can test for and treat parasites from that particular area of the world. Associations of parents who have adopted other children from that country are invaluable advisors here. A list of such support groups is found in the Resources section at the end of this chapter.

A list of single adoptive parent support groups is also included under Resources at the end of this chapter, but because support groups are started and maintained by adoptive parents, **addresses and phone numbers are apt to change**. NAIC lists adoptive parent support groups of all kinds, with addresses and phone numbers only.

A list of doctors across the country who work with children adopted domestically or from abroad is also included in the Resources section.

Most single parents can participate in health plans through their jobs. Plans fall into two groups: Health Maintenance Organizations, usually for-profit companies with stockholders; and medical insurance plans.

**Health Maintenance Organizations** are becoming very popular with employers, as they tend to hold down the increasing costs of medical treatment. Under this arrangement a regular fee provides complete health care, usually by the Plan's own group of doctors, who represent a wide range of specializations. It is usually possible to select your own staff members for continuing non-emergency care. One can be sure of consistent handling of emergencies too, and the Plan will refer patients to, and at least partly pay for, specialized medical treatment that the Plan is unable to provide in-house.

The Plan offers a parent two main comforts: (1) You do not need to shop around for needed specialists, in most cases; and (2) one's total medical expenses for expected and unexpected care are known from year to year and are reasonable. Additionally, because group health care is the old Chinese plan of paying your doctor to keep you well and out of the hospital, plans provide preventive health care such as yearly physicals, mammograms, and dental care that health insurance plans are reluctant to pay for. Plans will not support what they consider unnecessary medical treatment, however. Rates will be higher than for insurance only, but because they cover complete health care, they save money over insurance plans by year's end, especially as the number of people in the family grows.

There are some drawbacks. It may take a while to get an appointment for a non-emergency matter such as a general physical. HMO's use a "gatekeeper" whom a patient must first see if he/she wants medical treatment, and there have been complaints that this person's attitude is more oriented to cutting costs than to medical care. HMOs often provide scant mental health therapy on an outpatient basis and almost none on an inpatient basis. It may be hard to get approval for very specialized and/or complex care, such as a major operation. A parent contemplating the adoption of a child with a serious health condition, or one who may have a history of familial or institutional abuse (that can generate emotional problems) should do a lot of research and comparative analysis, and consult other adoptive parents. Federal and state legislation may be proposed to make small changes in HMOs' operations to meet some complaints.

**Medical insurance plans** are now the minority of health care methods. Usually the Plan reimburses the subscriber, or pays the hospital or laboratory directly, for most or all lab fees or hospital care and pays the larger part of outpatient treatment, including mental health outpatient therapy. It is not likely to pay for regular physical examinations, regular dentistry, or cosmetic surgery, unless dental work and plastic surgery is required as a result of an accident. The subscriber must pay a fairly hefty deductible each year before the reimbursements kick in---on the order of $200 or $250 apiece for two or more members of the family. Investigate before you enroll or change your enrollment, because it is sometimes possible to choose among the plans of several insurors at different fees and with different options and methods of obtaining the reimbursements.

For self-employed individuals the rates are steeper than for those who are part of a group insurance plan--if in fact they can obtain private medical insurance at all. The difficulty of finding a replacement insurance plan is a point to keep in mind if you contemplate changing or quitting your job.

When your children are young, it is worth while to take part in a high-option family insurance plan--with higher fees--and use it for all it's worth. This writer has made evening runs to the emergency room when one child broke a bone in his foot roughhousing, another inserted an unpopped kernel in his sister's ear, and one of the three had a false appendicitis scare. Look at your insurance policy to see if it covers your child before adoption, or if it covers all pre-existing conditions your child may have.

## FINANCIAL BENEFITS OF PARENTHOOD

Partly offsetting the expenses listed above are some income tax benefits of becoming a parent, particularly a working parent. Moreover, subsidies of various kinds are sometimes available to assist an adoptive parent.

### Credit for Costs of Child Care

In the federal income tax law there is a "Credit for Child and Dependent Care Expenses." It allows a parent a direct credit against his or her income tax for child care he or she must have in order to work, including expenses for household services, as long as the parent must pay these costs in order to work. There are certain requirements:

o        You must be maintaining a household; that means you must be paying more than half of the cost of your household that is also the home of the child.

o        If you pay a relative to care for your child, you must make contributions (half of which you usually deduct from her wages) to her Social Security and Medicare tax, and this relative may not be your dependent, nor be another of your children who is under age nineteen.

o        Your child must be under age thirteen, and you must be entitled to a dependency exemption for him or her. A child aged thirteen or over who is disabled may continue to be eligible.

o        Your child must have an ID number; usually the Social Security number.

        This credit is non-refundable, meaning that if it exceeds your total tax, the excess cannot be refunded to you.

        You must use Form 1040, not 1040-EZ. There is a maximum credit of 30% of qualifying expenditures (against a maximum credit of $2,400 for the care of one qualifying dependent and a maximum of $4,800 for the care of two or more) paid by a taxpayer with adjusted gross income (AGI) of $10,000 or less. The 30% credit decreases by 1% for each $2,000 (or fraction) of adjusted gross income* over $10,000. This results in a minimum credit of 20% for taxpayers with AGI over $28,000. There may also be prorated reductions in the credit for employer-provided child care benefits. Form 2441 carries the instructions for this credit; Publication 503, Child and Dependent Care Expenses, explains in in greater detail.

        *Adjusted Gross Income is your total income minus adjustments for alimony paid, deposits in IRA or Keogh accounts, interest penalties on early savings withdrawals, self-employed health insurance costs, and half of the self-employment tax.

        Moreover, expenditures for the care of a disabled dependent **of any age** out of your home but not in an institution (if your dependent regularly spends at least eight hours a day in your home) are eligible for the dependent care credit. However, the care centers providing this out-of-the-home care must comply with state and/or local regulations in order for their fees to be deductible. This provision might be helpful to a working single adoptive parent with an older disabled child, or with a disabled dependent relative.

        As an example: A single parent pays a housekeeper $5,000 to take care of her home and her ten-year-old daughter while she works. Her 1996 AGI was $25,000. The maximum credit she can claim is $528 (22% of $2,400). If her disabled mother had moved in with her during the year and cost her $2,400 or more in care, her maximum credit would have been $1,056 (22% of 4,800).

**Lower Income Tax for Head of Household:**

        Simply becoming a parent--and thus, the head of a household--lowers your income tax. Each dependent entitled the head of a household to a $2750 exemption in 1999, likely to rise with inflation in succeeding years. You may claim this exemption even before your child's adoption becomes final, as long as you can show that you provided over half of the child's support during the year (and that no one else claimed the child as a dependent). This exemption is subtracted directly from your income before you compute your tax.

        Again, your child must have an identification number that you use to claim this exemption, as well as the Child Care Credit. If the child is US-born, and the adoption is not yet final, but he doesn't have a Social Security Number yet, you may apply for an Adoption Taxpayer Identification Number (ATIN) instead. Order IRS Publication 501 and Form W-7.

**Tax Credit for Adoption**

        The tax credit for adoption was described at greater length in Chapter II. Its provisions went into effect on January 1, 1997; the (maximum) $5,000 tax credit is available through tax year 2,001 for adoptors of healthy US-born and foreign-born children. The maximum $6,000 credit for adoption of US-born special-needs children has no termination date.

**Adoption Subsidies**

        The subsidies for adoption of of a US-placed special needs child were also described in Chapter II. Persons contemplating adoption of a waiting child in the custody of a U.S. state or local government should check with the agency placing the child (which may be a private agency that has contracted with the public custodial agency) or with their state department of social services for information. You may file for it in Tax Form 8839.

# TEN FINANCIAL COMMANDMENTS FOR SINGLE PARENTS

By Peg Downey, Certified Financial Planner

*The following "Financial Commandments" serve as a checklist and workbook for getting your financial house in order. If you work through each of these ten items and take the necessary actions, you will have a firm financial base for you and your family. You will also have the peace of mind that comes from knowing that you have handled a very important task well and that you have protected yourself and your children.*

|  |  |  |  |
|---|---|---|---|
| I. | Plan! | VI. | Understand and use your employee benefits. |
| II. | Develop a spending plan. | VII. | Invest for the future. |
| III. | Accumulate an emergency fund. | VIII. | Teach your children about money. |
| IV. | Get life insurance. | IX. | Get your estate in order. |
| V. | Get more insurance: disability coverage. | X. | Lastly--seek help if you need it. |

## I. Plan!

Leaving things to chance may have worked when the only person you had to take care of was you, but you can only be carefree now when you know your child or children are well taken care of. But, with the costs of raising a child through age 17 being somewhere between $111,570 and $234,780 for a single parent,* one of the most important things you can do for your family is to plan your financial life: Protect your children in the event of unforeseen circumstances, provide for their college, buy a house if you want, assure your independence during retirement, lay the groundwork for all your life goals.

The Planning Process: The whole point of taking charge of your finances is to help you reach your goals.

1. Take some time to identify these goals: Do a little daydreaming and thinking about all the things that you want for yourself and your children. The rules for daydreaming are the same as those for brainstorming: everything goes; no second-guessing yourself.

2. Write all these dreams down on a piece of paper and don't worry (right now) about how realistic they are. By each dream write down when you want to

have reached that dream and how much it would cost if you wanted to pay for it **now**. In other words, make your dreams specific by attaching dates and dollars. For instance: Dream: I want to buy a new car. Date: I want the car in two years. Dollars: I need $2,000 as a down payment. (The car payments I will fit into my regular "spending Plan--a.k.a. "budget.") If you are able to be this specific about your dreams, they become goals. If you are still vague about something, as in "I want us all to do something special someday," you can keep that in the dream category.

3. For each of the goals, you need to calculate what dollar amount you would have to put aside on a monthly basis to accomplish that goal. For instance, if you want to buy that car in 24 months, and you'll need the $2,000 down payment, you'll need to be putting aside $2,000/24=$83.33 each month. Now that you know how much to save, you need to examine your current spending to see how you can rearrange your spending to allow you to save this $83 a month.

Of course, in order to know what it's going to take to get where you want to go, it takes knowing where you are now. Create a balance sheet (use sample following)--a listing of everything you own and everything you owe. Then be sure you take these assets into account when you're figuring what needs to be accumulated to meet your goals. That is, if you already have saved $1,000 toward the car's downpayment, you only need to accumulate another $1,000. That means this goal requires you to put aside $1,000/24 = $41.67 a month.

Retirement Goals: A somewhat harder goal to calculate is "How much do I need to save for retirement?" This is a complicated question that financial planners use extensive spreadsheets to calculate. What follows is a simplified version that should give you an approximation.

## II. Develop a spending plan:

A spending plan may also be known to you as a "budget." But "spending plan" implies decisions you make about spending choices, as opposed to "rules" that are enforced on you from the outside. Once you have a child there are many new objects that require you to spend money--daycare, increased healthcare costs, etc.

The Family Economic Research Group (USDA) estimated in 1995 that the total annual expenditures on a child by a single-parent family (with an income

---

## *Balance Sheet for Retirement Income*

Years Until Retirement: _____          Expected Return on Investments: _____

o Annual income needed in "today's dollars. Look at the spending plan you have developed and adjust it for how you expect things to change at retirement. No childcare expenses, for instance, but more travel money (to see the grandchildren!). A frequently used rule of thumb suggests you need at least 75% of today's income; 90% might be safer.          $ _____ (1)

o Income need adjusted for inflation: (1) multiplied by Table 1 Factor          $ _____ (2)

o Annual pension, Social Security, other retirement benefits          $ _____ (3)
(Your Benefits Counselor at work can give you an estimate of your future pension, assuming that your salary remains the same until you retire. You can get a "Personalized Benefit Estimate" from the Social Security Administration by calling 1-800-772-1213 and requesting Form SSA-7004.)

o Net future income needed: (2) minus (3)          $ _____ (4)

o Lump sum needed at retirement for Net Future Income:
     (4) multiplied by 17 (if retiring at 65)
     (4) multiplied by 20 (if retiring at 62)          $ _____ (5)

o Total Assets today available for retirement 401(k) and other employer savings plans, IRAs, other investments          $ _____ (6)

o Future value of today's total assets for retirement: (6) multiplied by Table 2 factor.
          $ _____ (7)

o Additional Lump Sum required ("The Retirement Gap") (5) minus (7)          $ _____ (8)

o Annual contribution needed to fill Retirement Gap: (8) divided by Table 3 Factor          $ _____ (9)

o Annual employer contributions to your company savings plans: 401(k)s, ESOPs, SEPs. and profit-sharing plans.          $ _____ (10)

o Annual amount you need to set aside in today's dollars: (9) minus (10)          $ _____ (11)

## CALCULATION FACTORS

| Years until Retirement | Table 1. | Table 2 | | | Table 3 | | |
|---|---|---|---|---|---|---|---|
| | 5% | 7% | 8% | 9% | 7% | 8% | 9% |
| 1 | 1.05 | 1.07 | 1.08 | 1.09 | 1.00 | 1.00 | 1.00 |
| 5 | 1.28 | 1.40 | 1.47 | 1.54 | 5.75 | 5.87 | 5.98 |
| 10 | 1.63 | 1/97 | 2.16 | 2.37 | 13.82 | 14.49 | 5.19 |
| 15 | 2.08 | 2.76 | 3.17 | 3.64 | 25.13 | 27.15 | 29.36 |
| 20 | 2.65 | 3.87 | 4.66 | 5.60 | 41.00 | 45.76 | 51.16 |
| 25 | 3.39 | 5.43 | 6.85 | 8.62 | 63.25 | 73.11 | 84.70 |
| 30 | 4.32 | 7.61 | 10.06 | 13.30 | 94.47 | 113.28 | 136.30 |

above $33,700) started at $7,610 for a child two and under (this includes housing, food, transportation, clothing,health,child care and other)and increased to $8,710 by the time the child was between 15 and 17.

You will want to reconsider your spending so that you can allow for these present expenses as well as to save for future expenditures such as college.

Setting up a spending plan is a four-step process: 1) Plan for your goals, 2) Gather information, 3) Establish target spending goals, and 4) Monitor, revise, and modify.

**1. Plan for your goals.** In Part I, above, you determined what your goals are and how much you must save each month to reach these goals. You will use this information in the third step of this process.

**2. Gather information.** You need to know how much you are spending and on what. Try this experiment: Sit down with the "income statement" (use Appendix I as a model) and fill in the blanks with what you think you are spending. Then total all the expenses. Compare that total to your total income. Chances are that you have identified less spending than income. Does this match with what you know about yourself? If, for example, your income looks to be $500 a month higher than your expenses, have your total savings grown by $6,000 ($500 x 12 months) since last year at this time? If not, you are spending more than you think you are. So, here's how to solve the mystery:

o Go through a year's worth of your checks and charges and identify the amount spent by categories. This is a simple matter with software such as Quicken, but it can be done just as easily with paper and pencil. Use the categories identified on the income statement. Once you've totaled the full amount spent on any one thing for the year, divide it by 12 and enter that number on the income statement.

o This approach creates a totally fictitious month in the sense that expenditures that only come up once or twice a year, such as car insurance, are amortized over the full twelve months. Nonetheless, it allows you to identify total annual expenses--except for the "Great Black Hole." The Great Black Hole is all the mysterious expenses that have leached away your cash--such things as your ATM withdrawals and the extra from the check you wrote in the grocery store. Don't give up hope! These expenditures can be easily identified: carry a small 3" x 5" notebook with you for **one** month. In it jot down everything you spend cash on. At the end of the month you can use this information to determine how much to add to the dollar expenditures identified by your checks and charges. You will now have the answers to how much you are spending and on what.

**3. Establish target spending goals.** Step Two was more than likely full of surprises. Step Three is full of choices. Begin by adding from Step One the monthly savings necessary for accomplishing your goals to the line on your income statement that says saving/investments." Next, look at all the expenses listed on your completed income statement. Do you like what you see? Where would you prefer to spend more? Where less? Remembering the rule that "outgo must not exceed income," go through your numbers and make choices about what you would prefer to spend. You may well find yourself making tradeoffs between current (clothes, entertainment) and future spending (the new car, college, etc. represented by the amount listed after "saving/ investments."

4. "The best laid plans," and all of that. You need to **monitor your spending** in order to honor the decisions you made in Step Three. The same little notebook you used in Step Two comes into play here. Consider each page to represent a mini-checking account. On each page enter the dollar amount you have set as your target spending goal. KEEP THIS NOTEBOOK WITH YOU AT ALL TIMES. Every time you spend money, subtract it on the appropriate page. The constantly declining balance will keep you aware of how much more you have to spend in that category. When there's no money left, you can't spend any more in that category until the next month. The next month you once again add in the amount of your target spending goal into this "mini-checking account."

Remember: You have set these target spending goals, so you can change them. Each month consider if you wish to readjust the amounts in each category.

A word about credit cards. Credit cards should only be used as a convenience; they should not be used to buy things not budgeted for. Charging is JUST THE SAME as spending cash. Be sure you only charge what you actually intend to spend in any given category and then pay off your credit cards each month.

## III. Accumulate an emergency fund

Things happen. And when they do, you want to be prepared. An emergency fund, of 3 to 6 months' living expenses, is a good cushion to have readily available in case the car breaks down, you're temporarily without a job, or the kids need emergency medical attention. With this kind of cushion, your financial plans won't be thrown into turmoil. Rather, you'll be able to take things in stride.

What kind of accounts should this emergency fund be kept in? You need to have the money readily accessible and in a secure place. Often there's the temptation to think of this as money that can be

invested ("I won't need this for a while, so maybe I could buy that stock my Uncle Joe says is guaranteed to make 150% in three months.") Stop right there! Emergency funds should be kept in nothing more adventurous than a money market fund, a savings account, an interest-bearing checking account, or bank certificates of deposit.

## IV. Get life insurance.

Preferably, get term life insurance. Term is pure insurance coverage; if you stop paying the premium, the coverage goes away. Other kinds of insurance (referred to as cash value, whole life, universal, or variable) talk about an investment component and how if you build up cash value (by paying higher premiums than those for term insurance) you'll be able to borrow this money if you ever need it in the future. Actually, you are much more likely to need the cash that would be necessary for higher premiums for other purposes now. And the promise to let you borrow your own money, and pay interest on it, is not attractive. Keep it simple--and keep your insurance coverage separate from your investments.

Term insurance comes in two flavors--annual renewable term or term certain. What's at issue here is whether your cost keeps going up each year or whether the rate stays the same for a set time (usually in five-year multiples). You will find it easiest to budget if your premium is kept level for the length of time that you need coverage. So, if your youngest child will be out of college and independent in 15 years, you probably only need insurance for 15 years. Thus, term life insurance with a 15-year term certain should work well for you.

Once you get insurance, however, do not assume that you can put your policy away and forget about it. Every three years you should check with your insurance agent. If you continue to be in good health, your agency may be able to find a more economical policy for you. Plus, your needs may have changed and you will want to be sure you have adequate coverage. Of course, if you should adopt another child, you will need more coverage. In that case, don't wait three years to contact your agent!

How much insurance do you need? Basically you will need to provide for your child or children until they are self-sufficient (including college), plus you will need to pay off any outstanding debts and get yourself buried. To figure out how much life insurance to buy:

1. Add up the burial costs ($10,000 is a good guess), your debts, college costs as if you had to pay them now, and the amount of money you wish to leave for your child(ren) for immediate needs that they might have upon your death (moving, therapy, etc.).

2. Figure out the monthly income that is necessary to support your children. This amount needs to be enough for the prospective guardian to care for your children either in their current lifestyle or a style comparable to that of the guardian's own children. If you want your children to be able to do something-- say, summer camp--that the guardian is not able to afford for his or her own children, you will want to provide enough funds so that all the children can go to camp.

3. Subtract all of the income to which your children would be entitled (your pension, Social Security to minor children, annuities, trusts etc.) from the total in #2. This gives you the net monthly income needed to support your children.

4. Multiply the net monthly income from #3 by the number of months from now until your youngest child will be independent.

5. Add the total from #1 and #4.

6. Subtract from #5 the total amount of your current investments and any life insurance you may already have, including employer-provided coverage.

Result: The amount of life insurance coverage you need to purchase.

Do your children need life insurance? Remember the logic of why you buy life insurance--because you have dependents to protect. Since your children do not have dependents, they do not need life insurance.

**V. Get more insurance: disability coverage.**

Even worse than dying, from a financial standpoint, , is being disabled. If you die, someone else is dealing with the financial problems. If you are disabled, YOU have all the problems to deal with at a time when you are unable to work and earn a living and when you are probably dealing with emotional issues related to being in such a fix!

Rule #1: DON'T count on whatever coverage you have from your employer. It is rarely enough and often has a limited definition of disability. Contact an insurance broker who is able to get you proposals from several different insurance companies (prices and benefits can vary considerably).

One way of determining how much coverage to buy is to look at what the sources and amounts of income would be in the event of disability. Unfortunately in most situations the income would be either short term (such as sick leave or a leave bank) or extremely difficult to qualify for (i.e. Social Security disability). It is usually best to buy as much basic coverage as you can. The most coverage an insurer will sell to you is usually 65% of your earned income. If you buy this coverage for yourself, the disability income (should you ever be unfortunate enough to need it) would not be taxable to you. Generally this 65% would come close to replacing your current after-tax income. If, on the other hand, you have disability coverage that your employer pays for, that income-- should you ever receive it--WOULD be taxable to you. In that case, the income would be inadequate for your needs.

You can choose waiting periods of 30, 60, 90 days (or even longer) during which you would be disabled before you are entitled to receive a benefit. Since disability insurance is expensive (think 2% of your income!) you will want to keep costs down. If you are able to go 120 days without a paycheck, choose a 90-day waiting period before your benefits would be paid. Yes, that's correct--if you have a waiting period of 90 days before you are entitled to a benefit, you will actually wait 120 days in all--because the insuror won't make a payment to you until the end of the month!

You are thinking, "Wow--2%! What other ways can I keep my costs down?" You can also cut costs by getting what is called a social insurance rider. Basically that prevents you from receiving your full Social Security check on top of a full disability benefit. Rather, it allows you to receive a defined benefit amount (usually 65% or so of your income) whether it comes all from the insurance company or partially from the insurance company and partially from Social Security. Since Social Security is hard to qualify for, and since you are trying to protect yourself from a bad situation (and not to win the lottery!) this is a prudent choice. Other bells and whistles the insuror might offer are luxuries you can probably do without.

If you belong to a professional group that offers disability coverage that is much less expensive, you might consider that as a supplement, but it is always best if you can buy your own individual policy. Group policies can come and go at the whim of the insurer, but if you have an individual policy, it cannot be taken away from you as long as you pay the premium.

## VI. Understand and use your employee benefits.

There are two kinds of mistakes people make with employee benefits:

1)  Thinking they have something they don't have (like assuming that they have disability coverage and finding out when they're disabled that the only employee benefit they have is short term disability that pays a few hundred dollars a week for no more than six months); or

2)  Not knowing that they could have a benefit if they took specific action--like being able to increase life insurance coverage upon the adoption of a child if they merely fill out the necessary form. A common example: Individuals often lose some of the benefits to which they are entitled under their health insurance because they haven't understood the rules and procedure.

You may already have some, if not all, of the life and disability coverage you need through your employer. Hence, it is important to know exactly what is being provided for you and also, if you have to do anything to obtain these benefits (sign something? pay something?). Be aware that benefits offered by an employer require careful scrutiny in order to understand fully what is being provided and what you still need to take care of yourself. A very common situation is one where disability coverage is offered, but the insurance only pays benefits for a limited period of time, or only if you meet a very stringent definition of disability. In such situations, you may well need to buy additional supplemental coverage.

There may also be the reverse situation---you may have benefits at work, say for saving on a tax-deferred basis for retirement, that you are trying to replicate on your own because you aren't fully aware of your employee benefits.

Additionally, check at work to see what else there is that you may want to use--a medical reimbursement plan? a childcare spending account? These things are called "benefits" for a reason, so don't neglect to find out what you do and don't have. Employee benefits can be worth as much as 30% of your salary, so it's worth spending time making sure that you are getting everything you're entitled to.

Lastly, there may be five or more different employee benefits that your heirs would be eligible for upon your death, and each of these benefits probably has a designation of beneficiary form that needs to be completed for the benefits to be distributed as you wish. (You'll read in the estate planning section about how to decide about beneficiaries.) The forms relate to unpaid salary, life insurance benefits, pension benefits, investments in tax-deferred accounts of various kinds, and possible unpaid benefits from disability insurance. Be sure that you have completed these forms and that you know you have the appropriate beneficiary designation on them. The safest thing to do is to file all new copies of the forms. Or, ask your Benefits Director for copies of the most recent beneficiary designations in your file. If you need to change them, do so. If not, date and sign the form once again, so that it will be clear that this is the most recent document in your file.

### What if you don't have employee benefits?

The other Financial Commandments cover the necessary areas, except for health insurance. Make sure you have good health insurance coverage for yourself and your children! A policy that you have to pay for yourself will be more expensive than a group policy, but it is important to fit this expense into your spending plan.

## VII. Invest for the Future.

One of the pieces of advice often given to parents is to enjoy the present time with your child, as the moment is all too fleeting and they grow up all too fast. The implied message here is that the future is just around the corner--then you'll be looking at college educations, cars, weddings, and even your own retirement.

The best time to save for that future is . . . thirty years ago. The next best time is right now! You know what your goals are and you know how much you need to put aside to accomplish those goals. It may seem that the amount you are able to set aside for future goals is so insignificant that it's hardly worth doing. It's important to start saving as soon as possible; that is NOW, even if what you save is small. Consider this: If you could save only $100 a year (less than $2.00 a week) over the 40 years of your average working lifetime, and that money grew at 12%, when you retired you would have over $77,000!

Or consider the "magic of compounding": A $10,000 investment compounding for ten years at 7% would yield $19,671; at 12% you'd have $31,058. The same returns over a 20-year period are truly mind-boggling: With 7% you'd end up with $36,697 but with 12% you'd have $96,462.

But where do you put this money--especially if you want to get a 12% return? Stocks are the only kind of investment that historically has returned rates substantially above inflation and taxes. Thus, for long term money, where inflation is a big bugaboo, stocks are the investment of choice. The stock market has volatility (ups and down) but for time frames of at least three to five years, you can expect stocks to work for you. Time is on your side!

The best way to get together a diversified selection of stocks, without having to become an investment expert, is to use no-load mutual funds. Mutual funds are companies in business to invest money on behalf of their shareholders. So, your investable money gets put together with money from lots of other people and then the managers of the funds do the investing for you. (No-load means you do not pay a commission just for the privilege of putting your money into a mutual fund; hence all the money you are investing goes directly to work for you in your investment instead of as much as 8-1/2% ending up in a broker's pocket.)

Basically, if you are using no-load mutual funds, your job becomes that of picking an investment manager who does a good job and is investing with the same goals that you have in mind. There are thousands of mutual funds to pick from. The key for your long term money (more than five years before you intend to spend it) is to invest for growth. You want growth so that the total return on your investment will keep ahead of both taxes and inflation. If you have $10,000 gathering dust in a fixed-income account paying 5%, in thirty years it will be worth $43,200. Put that same $10,000 into a stock account averaging 10%, and your account in thirty years will be worth $174,500. At 12%, you'll end up with $300,000.

If you have an opportunity to save on a tax-deferred basis (401(k), 403(b), Thrift Plan, Keogh, SEP, IRA, Roth IRA, etc.), do so! Your accounts will grow even faster since you won't have to be paying taxes on the interest and dividends--instead, all that money can go to work for you. Even within these plans, invest for growth. Don't worry about the volatility (the fluctuation in value) of your investment--over time things will even out. You may think that volatility is "risky," but the greatest risk you face otherwise is that your money would buy even less in the future than it will buy you now. Historical records indicate that you MUST accept volatility in order to get the return you need.

You'll find that opening an account with a mutual fund company is as simple as opening a bank account--it's a matter of filling out a simple form with name, address, and a few other facts. Check the library for The Individual Investor's Guide to No-Load Mutual Funds, which the American Association of Individual Investors publishes each year. Pick growth funds that match your objectives and your risk tolerance. Look for funds with long, consistent, good track records--not for last year's high flier (which is more likely than not to take a big dive this year).

Also, don't try to figure out the market and shift your money around from one investment to another--buy and hold is just the kind of low maintenance approach that can fit in your busy schedule and give you the higher return you're looking for.

**Investments for Children:**

You may also be considering putting money in your child's name, in a Uniform Gift to Minors Account (UGMA) since there are some tax benefits. What are they? With such an account, the first $700 of annual income is tax free. The next $700 after that is taxed at the child's tax rate (probably 15%). Greater than $1400 of investment income is taxed at the parent's rate until age 14 when once again the income is taxed at the child's rate.

But, what's the trade-off? The money will be under your child's control, not yours. What if, when your child reaches maturity, s/he decides to spend that money on a sports car--a motorcycle--drugs? Even if you and your child both agree that it's college money--that's exactly how a financial aid officer will look at it also. If you have assets in your name, you will be expected to spend some of them for your child's college. If your child has assets, it will be expected that the total amount is available for college. The establishment of a UGMA account needs to be carefully considered.

There is, however, an interesting alternative. Twentieth Century Giftrust, an aggressive growth mutual fund offered by the Twentieth Century family of funds (1-800-345-2021), allows an individual to make a gift in trust for a child. The trust is irrevocable--which means you can't change your mind about it and take back the money in the future. The individual who makes a gift to the trust gets to say when the shares can be distributed from the trust. Thus, you could give the money to your children but not have them able to receive the money until after they have completed college or reached some particular age. The minimum investment in the Giftrust is $500 and subsequent contributions need to be at least $50.

## VIII.  Teach your children about money

Teach them it's only a tool, a means to an end. Children learn by example, and seeing you follow the ten financial commandments for yourself is going to be the most important way you have of teaching your children about financial responsibility. Money is a major tool that everyone needs to learn how to handle. Start young and you'll have few problems when your children are older.

Involve the children in making choices about money: Should we buy this box of cereal or those cookies?-- we need to make a choice. Let them hear you think through: Should we have a big birthday party or take a day trip?--we need to make a choice. They'll be learning planning. They will also learn about reality, discipline, dealing with frustration. There are many adults who wish their parents had taught them these lessons!

From an early age, it's good for your children to have some of their own spending money. Families differ about whether children should be given an allowance just because they are members of the household, or if they should work to earn their spending money. Both approaches have their merits; for the sake of learning how to handle money, it only matters that children have some money over which they have full control.

If you're afraid actual cash will get lost, consider what some families do--they use poker chips that are exchanged for cash. The parents may also assist in the budgeting process by giving different colored poker chips for different purposes--clothing, school supplies, movies, etc.

In any case, make sure that your child understands what is to be covered from the allowance. Also make sure that the amount you give them is carefully determined--they need to receive enough so that their choices are not severely limited but also not so much that they don't have to set priorities. Allowances should not be used as punishments--so don't withhold their allowances.

This is also a good opportunity to teach your child about charitable giving. You can help them understand that you give a part of your money to others less fortunate, and that can be one of the uses for part of their money also.

Once your child has learned the importance of accumulating assets for significant purchases, you'll even be able to teach them about saving. You can also teach your children about investing. It used to be that parents would buy their children a few shares of a stock their children could identify with-- MacDonald's or Disney, for instance. Now some mutual funds are even designing funds especially for young investors so that they can have the same kind of diversified investments their parents have.

## IX.  Get your estate in order.

The worst thing that could happen to your family is for you to die and leave them with a mess because you had not made adequate plans for how the children were going to be cared for and supported after your death. You'll want to make it a top priority to have all the necessary documents in order so that your child will be cared for as you wish, even if you are not around. Perhaps for the first time in your life you will need a current will. You will also need a general durable power of attorney, a health care power of attorney, a living will (also known as a health care directive).

A will tells how your assets are to be distributed but also who and how you wish your children to be cared for. If you have minor children, you will want to indicate whom you wish to be appointed as guardian. A durable power of attorney allows your designated agent (a family member or trusted friend) to handle your finances in the event that you are unable to do so. A health care power of attorney is similar, except that it allows someone to make decisions about your health care in the event that you are not competent to do so. The living will or health care directive will provide your doctors and your agent with specific information about what care you wish and what care you wish to decline in the event that you are not able to provide that direction at the time.

You will want a competent estate planning attorney to draft your documents for you. You may well want to create a trust in your will (called a testamentary trust) that allows for your assets to be handled by a competent adult until your child/children reach what you consider to be a mature age. Or, depending on your level of assets, you may even want to set up a trust now, while you are around and competent so that you can test out the management skills and decision-making of your trustee. These are issues that you can work through with a financial planner or an attorney.

Remember also, as discussed above, that you need to have the beneficiary designations on all of your employee benefits accurate, up to date, and coordinated with the plans reflected by your will. Your attorney will ask to see copies of your completed beneficiary designation forms and will advise you of any necessary changes.

While you are at it, look into estate planning that your parents or other relatives may have done. If they intend for your adopted child to be treated equally with all natural born children, they will need to have an attorney check the language in their document.

## X. Lastly, seek help if you need it.

Being a single parent, and in addition dealing with the unique concerns of adopted children, is a demanding job. Organizing your finances is one task that falls to you. Just like other tasks that you choose to delegate (changing the oil in the car, painting the house), financial planning is one for which you may well wish to hire assistance.

Your major job is to get competent, objective advice. You can, of course, ask friends, relatives, and trusted advisors for referrals. Or you can contact one of the following:

National Association of Personal Financial Advisors
1-888 FEE-ONLY, or info@napfa.org

The Financial Planning Association
1-800-282-PLAN, or www.FPAnet.org

American Society of Chartered Life Underwriters and Chartered Financial Consultants
1-800-392-6900, or custserv@financialpro.org

It is important to know how planners are compensated. Many individuals who call themselves financial planners are selling something--investments or insurance. They do not get paid unless they sell you something. These people earn commissions on what they sell.

Other planners operate on a "fee only" basis. This means they are paid by you (and only by you!) just the way an accountant or an attorney is. They are only selling their advice.

They can, of course, make very specific recommendations about everything, including insurance and investments, and will help you shop for and buy those products. But they do not have a vested interest in your buying any particular products; they are working solely for you, the client. Fee-only planners are free to recommend a course of action based only on strategic financial considerations.

Still other planners do what they call "fee offset." They charge you a fee, but then any commissions they get if they sell you investments or insurance are applied to the fee, so that you only have to pay the difference between the fee and the commissions. But what happens in the very frequent case where the commissions are higher than the fee? Don't count on getting a refund!

Don't be your own expert. Find an advisor who sells no products, and receives no remuneration of any kind except for fees from the client. Have a "team builder" who will look only to your interests while working with the attorney, the CPA, the insurance agent, the stockbroker, the banker, etc.

---

Peg Downey, CFP, founding partner of Money Plans, a financial planning firm in Silver Spring, Maryland, has been chosen by Worth Magazine in its 1996, 1997, and 1998 lists of the "Top Financial Advisors in America." She has over 18 years' experience in providing financial advice to individuals and small businesses. She has been active in professional and other associations related to her field, and is past Chairperson of the National Association of Personal Financial Advisors.

---

* U. S. Department of Agriculture Center for Nutrition Policy and Promotion, "Expenditures on Children by Families," 1999 Annual Report. Miscellaneous Publication No. 1528-1999, March 2000.

These expenditure figures are for single-parent families. Estimates for single-parent families are noticeably lower than for couples, but a majority of this category is made up of divorced parents who, as a whole, tend to have a more difficult time financially than single adoptive parents.

(c) Peg Downey 2000

# Income Statement

(for an average month)

## INCOME

Salary, Wages _____
Bonuses _____
Interest _____
Dividends _____
Rents (net) _____
Royalties _____
Self-Employment (Net) _____
Alimony/Child Support _____
Pensions and Annuities _____
Social Security _____
Trusts _____
Other _____
____ Total Income _____

## EXPENSES - FIXED

Savings/Investments _____
Federal Taxes _____
State/Local Taxes _____
Social Security/Medicare _____
Retirement Funds _____
IRA _____
Mortgage (P.I.) _____
Rents _____
Real Estate Taxes _____
Interest _____
Utilities _____
Home Insurance _____
Auto Insurance _____
Life Insurance _____
Disability Income Insurance _____
Loan Payments _____
Auto Loans _____
Credit Card Payments _____
____ Subtotal Fixed Expense _____

## EXPENSES - VARIABLE

Alimony _____
Allowance(s) _____
Animal Care _____
Auto Operation _____
Books, Papers, Tapes _____
Child Care _____
Child/Parent Support _____
Clothing _____
Contributions _____
Education _____
Entertainment _____
Fees/Dues _____
Gifts _____
Groceries _____
Health (including Insurance) _____
Home Furnishings _____
Home Maint./Improvement _____
Job-Related Expenses _____
Meals outside Home _____
Personal Care _____
Professional Fees _____
Telephone _____
Vacations _____
Miscellaneous _____
Other (Explain) _____
_____
_____
_____
_____

Subtotal Variable Expenses _____

Total Expenses, Fixed and Variable: _____

NET INCOME:

Total Income less _____

Total Expenses _____

# Solo Parenting, Socially Speaking
by Andrea Troy, MSW

*Socially, my life actually improved after I adopted my son. By that I mean going, doing, and being with others.*

Choosing single parenthood as a way of life is probably the hardest-won yet most gratifying decision you'll ever make. But neither the decision to do it, nor the road to get there, is short, simple, or sweet.

Most of the single women I know have come to adoption nearing 40 or on the far side of it, although there are exceptions and a substantial number of earlier achievers. (In the world of adoption, a "young" parent connotes something very different from being young in ordinary society--it's all relative.) From what I see, men tend to become single fathers sooner, due to a different set of social circumstances and options.

I know, from first-hand experience as an adoption social worker and single-over-forty-adoptive mom, that my "story" and those of other women are very similar, except in specific details. They go something like this:

*I've always had relationships and figured I'd get married and have a child within a traditional family. Frankly, I'm surprised it has turned out this way.*

*I expected to have a family by now---husband, kid, dog. Here I am at 42 without that. I can do without the husband, or the kid, but not both..*

*I've wanted a child since who knows when. I'm 40 and my window of opportunity will evaporate unless I act now.*

*What do you do when you wake up 45 and decide you want a child? You act quickly, very quickly.*

These women, who hadn't *planned* all of their lives on becoming single moms or single adoptive moms, find themselves influenced by the clock. Even adoption clocks tick, particularly if an infant is the goal. And there are many singles for whom adoption, rather than birth, is a first choice.

So, at a point in real time, becoming a mother becomes *the* goal.

This may sound like a desperate grab to find love by forgoing a loving adult relationship in which one raises a child as a couple. For some, it may be. But for the majority of others, like myself, it is a conscious decision to raise a child alone, feeling that it can be done without harm to oneself or the child and, for that matter, be a fulfilling and complete experience. I caution women and men who are undertaking adoption as a substitute for marriage and/or a mate to rethink their plan. One must assume that raising a child solo is a positive, worthwhile endeavor, an end in itself, regardless of how their life plays out. Otherwise, how will you convince family and friends who view raising a child alone as a nightmare fraught with unbearable consequences, that your decision is a wise and realistic one? That it can work? How will you counter their assertions that "You'll never find a man now!" or, "It's unfair for a child not to have a father." Single men, and gay and lesbian singles and couples, contend with the same "How could you!" attitudes.

Before adopting a child as a single man or woman, you should feel very sure that you want to do it, can do it, and look forward to doing it. In other words, it's for the "right reasons" as you understand them in relation to your life.

Friendships are often overlooked when we speak of a social life, as in "How is your social life?" The question implies "going out," "dating," "having an affair," "a love relationship." But that is a conventional, narrow definition. Socially, my life actually improved after I adopted my son. By that I mean going, doing, and being with others. No longer could I luxuriate (or hibernate) in bed on a Saturday or Sunday morning. And since I was averse to the prospect of spending the day indoors with a ball of non-verbal atoms, and later a ball of exploding toddler atoms, I developed getting-out-of-the-house syndrome. I gravitated toward other parents, other single and adoptive and older parents. We had a lot in common, we *understood* each other. Finally! I discovered the true salvation of adult relationships. Many of those adults came from New York Singles Adopting Children, a support group for single adoptors and the gateway to my new life.

The general lack of adult conversation and, in particular, trying to discuss real ideas with a two-year old, or teenager for that matter, just doesn't cut it for many single parents. One mother, trying to find some adult company, attended Parents Without Partners and church singles groups without much success, but found that invaluable friendships came through child-related activities--soccer, afterschool programs, scouting etc. Single dads can do the same. Adoptive parent support groups are invaluable.

Another great source of adult connectedness is the single friends you had B.C. (Before Children). Those who don't disappear because they are envious, threatened, or annoyed by your new lifestyle can be your biggest supporters. Often they have the time to help---and listen---that other harried parents don't.

And what about those people who said you'd never meet anyone with a kid around your neck? In my case, romance wasn't a big part of my life before I adopted---in part because I wasn't really looking---and it isn't now. So, not meeting men had nothing to do with being a single mother. Some women and men in the group did, and still do, date and enjoy it. Some have subsequently developed committed relationships or married. Others who didn't care about a relationship before, feel it would make their life easier now and want one, while still others have found that having both a relationship and a child is difficult and don't covet it. There are also men and women who do not like coupledom but enjoy parenthood. The best part is, it all works.

If you want a child, the experience is unbeatable. The "social you" might/could/can/does/will change after you adopt, making you a more complete person . . . with or without a partner to accompany you.

---

*Andrea Troy is an adoption consultant, social worker, and personal crisis coach practicing in New York City. She is past-president of NY Singles Adopting Children, and the adoptive mother of an 11-year old son. Her e-mail address is ATROYNY@Aol.com.*

## *Ohio Researchers Find*
# Better Language Skills in Preschoolers from Single Parent Homes

Two researchers from Baldwin-Wallace College in Berea, Ohio conducted a study in 1989, following up in 1992, in day care centers and nurseries throughout Cleveland, on whether family structure affected a preschooler's speech and language abilities. Dierdre Madden, Ph.D., and Deanna Laurence, M.A., found that the one factor predicting language skills was the marital status of the parent(s).

"Children from single parent homes appeared to have an advantage over two-parent families," said Dr. Madden. "While speech sounds and hearing acuity in the two groups were similar, the children from single parent homes had better receptive and expressive language on average and were less likely to have communication problems."

Only 25% of the children needing to be referred for communication problems were from single-parent families, while 44 percent came from households with married, working parents. The total number of children referred in the follow-up 1992 study fell, but the ratio between children of single parent versus two-parent families remained about the same.

Dr. Madden suggested that "Children in single parent homes may get more intensive, one-on-one communication time with their parent than those who have two working parents. Women who have children know how much a little person has to tell you about their day when they get home." Single parents, she continued, may be more likely to develop close relationships with their child, in which not only are there more chances to communicate, but the conversations are likely to be more complex.

Day care workers supported this finding, she added. "One of the [teachers at the day care centers with children enrolled in the study] said they can always tell by the maturity level of the kids when they come into the day care whether or not they come from a single parent family. She said that the kids from single parent homes are usually a lot more mature than the others."

*Reprinted from ADVANCE for Speech-Language Pathologists & Audiologists, March 11, 1996.*

# Medical Primer for the Adoptive Parent

## by Jerri Ann Jenista, M.D.

### Adopting from North America

If you are adopting domestically, don't fool yourself. Just because your child was born and/or raised in this country does not mean that:

1) he got good medical care,
2) that you will be able to get some or all of her medical records, or
3) that records were kept at all.

Many medical centers and offices destroy or microfiche charts that are inactive for periods even as brief as three years. So, today is the best time to start collecting your child's records.

If the child is a newborn, you have the best possible chance to obtain complete medical records. Every baby should arrive with at least:

1) a basic description of the health and ethnic origin of the parents and any genetic conditions known in either family; for example, diabetes, heart disease, mental illness, immune defects, etc.

2) a description of the pregnancy and delivery including the results of any maternal screening such as hepatitis B, HIV, syphilis, gonorrhea or drug testing.

3) the newborn discharge physical examination with commentary on any unusual aspects of the nursery course.

4) results of the "newborn metabolic screening tests" (usually PKU and thyroid but others are included in some states) or a plan for getting those results when they are available.

Most newborn domestic adoptions are without major medical issues. Problems, when they occur, generally fall into two categories: parental or infant. Typical concerns about the birth parents include drug or alcohol use; mental illness, particularly schizophrenia; sexually transmitted diseases, such as HIV, syphilis, hepatitis B or C and genetic conditions such as diabetes or some forms of mental retardation. Particular to the infant are prematurity, low birth weight, growth retardation, congenital anomalies, genetic syndromes, intrauterine infection and drug or toxin exposures.

Before you proceed with any newborn adoption, you should select a pediatrician or family physician. Even if this is to be a placement "in the delivery room," you can review what is known about the birth family's health with your doctor. Any questionable items should be addressed before there is any baby to consider. For example, if the mother was treated for syphilis in the first trimester, your doctor will be able to advise you on what tests should have been done to determine success of the maternal treatment and also what other sexually transmitted diseases should have been considered at the same time.

Similarly, if there is a family history of schizophrenia, the physician can help you outline questions to ask: What is the relationship of the newborn to the affected person (cousin, grandchild, niece)? Was the diagnosis made by a psychiatrist in accordance with recognized standards (DSM-IV)? Counseling on the implications of such conditions for your potential child is available from most university genetics clinics.

No matter how open the adoption or how accessible the medical history seems now, it is essential to have at least the above records in written form. You do not know what may happen later and the opportunity to collect accurate information will never be as timely again.

### Adopting the Foster Child

If the child is older, especially if he has been in multiple placements or hospitalized, you may have great difficulty in getting complete and accurate records. Even if you have been the foster parent of this particular child before making the decision to adopt, it is likely that your child received other medical care before she lived with you. The health care of foster children is notoriously fragmented, often with many different providers. You should insist on at least:

1) a record of all immunizations and their dates, often found in school records.

2) As complete a birth family medical history as is possible, including that of siblings.

3) a list of any major past illnesses, allergies, medication reactions, injuries.

4) a copy of the discharge summary for each hospitalization.

5) a copy of any specialist consultations (as these usually result in a typed summary).

6) copies of any special education evaluations and the resulting IEP (Individual Education Plan) summaries.

7) a summary or the discharge diagnosis of any psychiatric treatment or hospitalization.

8) records of any dental care or procedures.

9) an assessment of the child's risk for past physical, emotional, or sexual abuse and/or drug or alcohol exposure.

10) HIV screening may be important for some children.

11) A straight-on, expressionless, close-up photograph of the child's face (i.e., similar to the photos obtained when a person is booked into jail).

Again, before placement (or finalization of the adoption) is your best, and possibly only, opportunity to collect these records. You will do yourself and your child a disservice if you allow an agency or social worker to ignore these items. If the materials are not available, ask for a written explanation of why they are missing and what efforts have been made to obtain them. In some states, the child's entire agency file must be made available to the adoptive parent at the time of finalization. Be sure to check the laws in the state where the child resides.

Children in foster care who become available for adoption frequently have medical problems. Conditions may not have been diagnosed (for example, mild hearing loss from recurrent eaveinfections) or

may have been erratically and poorly managed (for example, asthma). In one survey in Oakland County, CA, 82% of children in foster care had at least one chronic medical problem and 29% of children had three or more such issues. Most common were retarded growth, recurrent or congenital infections, and neurological or respiratory abnormalities.

In addition, children who have lived in foster care have a high risk of emotional, behavioral, and developmental conditions. Studies in California and Washington note that 60-80% of children in foster care have problems in one or more of these areas: developmental delays, especially in language; poor social relationships and coping skills; adjustment reactions; depression, educational deficits and others.

Photographs may be useful in detecting evidence of dysmorphic (abnormal) facial features leading to suspicion of genetic or other syndromes such as fetal alcohol syndrome (FAS).

Regardless of the age of the child you adopt and/or his apparent health, it is always wise to schedule a full physical examination with a pediatrician or family doctor within two weeks of arrival. Such a visit establishes the beginning of a long-term and hopefully supportive relationship. It allows the physician the chance to review past records and rectify any deficiencies in immunizations or screening tests. A comprehensive "well child check-up" will also document abnormalities, no matter how minor or as yet undiagnosed, as "pre-existing" the adoptive placement. In some states, such pre-existing emotional, behavioral, or medical conditions make the child eligible for adoption subsidy or other health care benefits. It never hurts to have a complete record of the child's condition at arrival.

**Adopting from Abroad**

If you are adopting a child from another country, be realistic. You are never going to get every piece of information that you want. Ideally, any child should be accompanied by the same records as listed above for a US-born child. However, abandonment, overstrained medical facilities, translation problems and cultural differences will always intervene.

The minimum acceptable information should include:

1) the date of the examination (should be within one or two months for the child under one year old, within six months for the child under five

years old, and within one year for older children). Children with an undiagnosed or changing medical condition, regardless of age, should have had an examination within two months.

2) the birth date or the estimated birth date and how it was chosen.

3) the actual height, weight, and head circumference with units of measurement (kilograms or pounds, etc.). All measurements should be labeled with the date they were obtained.

4) a list of the parts of the physical examination performed and a description of any abnormalities.

5) an assessment of the child's growth and development; how does it compare to other children of this age? to other children in this same environment (orphanage, foster care, etc.)?

6) any details, no matter how insignificant, known about the birth family, the pregnancy, delivery or siblings.

7) a list of any hospitalizations, illnesses, treatments, medications, injuries.

8) dates of any immunizations including BCG.

9) results of any laboratory tests.

10) A description of any current medical treatment.

11) A straight-on, expressionless, close-up, full-face photograph of the child.

A simple form including all the above is available in Spanish/English or Portuguese/English from International Concern for Children, 911 Cypress Drive, Boulder, CO 80303. The same form can be adapted easily for other languages or countries. There are some pitfalls, however, in using a form. The physician or social worker may feel that the only information required is that outlined on the form, omitting vital data about a child's personality or development which might otherwise have been included in a narrative description.

If the above basic information cannot be provided, ask why not. The child may be in a remote rural area with no medical facilities or in a very restricted access environment such as a government orphanage. The best you may be able to ask is, "How

does this child compare to others of the same age living in the same place? Are her health, growth, mental and physical development and behavior the same, better, worse or, in some way, different? If so, how?"

Sometimes you can request an examination by someone outside the institution at your own expense. However, when the problem with the medical record is one of terminology or interpretation, you may be paying for another version of the same confusion. For example, in the former Soviet Union and Eastern Europe, phrases such as "spastic tetraparesis" and "perinatal encephalopathy" are frequently used to describe an infant with risk factors for health problems or delayed development due to institutional living. In North America, these terms would only be used to describe a severely neurologically impaired child. A "new" evaluation using these same words is not going to add to your understanding of the child's potential.

Be careful, too, that you are not insulting the judgment of the adoption workers in the other country. Continued insistence on additional details, especially if the agency considers them trivial, may produce reports with "what you want to hear," which may not be at all related to the truth. Under **no** circumstances should you ever complete a final adoption without either the medical evaluation outlined above or having seen and cared for the child yourself.

For children with special needs, especially with handicapping conditions that affect daily living, or for children from areas under former Soviet control, photographs and/or a videotape are often invaluable in assessing the degree of handicap or in confirming or refuting the medical records. Good quality, close-up facial photographs are essential in evaluating for Fetal Alcohol Syndrome. Even a brief videotape can be extremely important in the decision to proceed with or halt an adoption, despite contradictory medical reports. For example, a two-year-old with cerebral palsy who is shown running, jumping, feeding himself and stacking blocks probably only has a mild impairment. A four-year-old who is said to be "cheerful and pleasant with only mild neuropsychic delay" who has an unsteady gait, is unable to play a game of catch and has unintelligible or garbled speech is likely to have one or more significant neurological or developmental issues.

In most cases, you will have the chance to review any medical records you receive with your pediatrician or family doctor. No matter how normal the child, such a "pre-adoption" visit is very important. Use this opportunity to:

1) make sure the physician is sympathetic to adoption, especially of this age child, from this country, with these special needs, to a single parent family. If he is not, start looking now for a new doctor.

2) discuss the medical information provided, what it means and if there are questions that should be resolved with further testing or another examination.

3) arrange when the child should be seen after arrival and how those appointments will be made.

4) review what screening tests should be done on the child after arrival and when.

Occasionally, you will identify and adopt a child in another country without returning to the United States before the process is finalized. If there is any question about the medical information you receive or about the condition of the child, immediately seek a second opinion, at your own expense. Get a recommendation for a reliable English-speaking physician from the U.S. Embassy or consulate; Western medical training is a plus but not always essential. Alternatively (a poor second choice but sometimes the only one), call, fax, or e-mail your physician at home with what you have and the questions you have raised.

Such desperation measures are rarely needed. If you still have serious doubts, then consider stopping the adoption. Remember, however, that becoming a parent overnight and in a strange country can be extremely stressful. Is this over-anxiety and culture shock, or a genuine concern about this specific child? Often, it is helpful to talk things over with another adopting family or somebody at home. Yes, it will cost a fortune but you will have this child for life.

**When Your Child Comes Home**

After the arrival, both you and the child will be in shock and tired, no matter how happy the occasion. If the child seems sick with fever, extreme crabbiness, extensive sores, vomiting or diarrhea, a new rash or pus coming from anywhere (eyes, ears, etc.), take the child to your doctor within a day. About one-half of children will have some acute infectious disease such as an ear infection within the first month after arrival.

Even if the child appears well, many parents like to take the child in to the doctor's office in the first day or two for a brief examination. Usually, even just height and weight will do, so you'll have something to write on the arrival announcement. All children with an identified special medical need, such as a cleft palate, should be seen within the first few days after arrival.

However, it is best to schedule the comprehensive evaluation for about two weeks after arrival. This gives everyone the opportunity to recover from the travel and to adjust to new climate, new food, etc. By two weeks, you will have a much better assessment of what the child's behavior is truly like, what he can do, how he eats or sleeps, is that head-banging a habit or just being overtired?

**After the Adoption**

At the comprehensive visit, every child, regardless of past medical history, age, or country of origin, should have:

1) a complete clothes-off physical examination, including height, weight, and head circumference measurements. Note any evidence of past abuse, neglect, or medical procedures.

2) a developmental assessment. School-aged children or children with known disabilities may have such evaluations done in a specialty clinic or by the school district for special education placement.

3) assessment of vision and hearing, especially if the parent has concerns. These can be done quite accurately even if the child does not speak English or cannot cooperate with the examination.

4) assessment of immunization status.

5) any screening tests that normally would be done at this age: For example, PKU for a newborn or blood pressure measurement for a teenager. Just because a child is from an adverse background does not mean that you can ignore standards for ordinary health care.

6) a preliminary estimate of age for children without a confirmed birthdate. Final determination should be left as long as possible, preferably a year, as many children will have dramatic gains in physical size and sexual and dental development over the first one or two years after placement. It is quite awkward to change an eight-

year-old boy's age to six years because of his size and maturity and find out two years later, as his voice changes and he grows a beard, that he was really 11 or 12 when you got him.

7) special screening tests for all immigrants, including:
   a. VDRL or some other syphilis test.
   b. Mantoux (PPD) tuberculosis test; NOT the four-prong skin prick (tine) TB test. This is important even if your child has received BCG vaccine.
   c. complete blood count.
   d. urine analysis.
   e. hepatitis B serology, including surface antigen, surface antibody and core anti body. This is essential even if you are sure your child received hepatitis B vaccine or was screened before arrival.
   f. stool specimens for ova and parasites, collected into preservative containers; at least three specimens with at least one week between specimens.
   g. HIV screening, regardless of whether it was done in the country of origin. The only exception might be children from countries of extremely low risk, such as Korea.
   h. referrals for any condition that will need specialist care. About 20% of childrne will have some need for expert care, usually for dental, surgical, ophthalmo logic, special education or infectious disease questions.

(These "international adoption screening tests" are discussed in more detail along with other infectious disease concerns in the American Academy of Pediatrics' "Red Book," also known as "The Report of the Committee on Infectious Diseases." This book is found in every pediatrician's office and is considered the standard of care.)

Beside poor growth and deficient immunizations, other problems that are common and/or annoying include: skin rashes and scars, lice, scabies, food intolerance, poor appetite or overeating, poor muscle tone, sleeping problems and lactose (milk) intolerance. These are manageable but can surely make those early months miserable. It's always helpful to talk to others who have "gone before" in your parent group. It can be quite reassuring to learn that "this, too, shall pass."

More serious concerns include very small size, past sexual or physical abuse, mental retardation and emotional or behavioral problems. Most small stature is the result of genetics and past malnutrition. Extensive evaluation is usually fruitless early. If the child does not begin to show some catch-up within a few months, or is progressively smaller than his age-group over one or two years, then a bone-age (wrist x-ray) should be done and you should discuss an endocrinology referral with your doctor.

## Over the Long Term

This article is not meant to cover other more serious life-long problems such as attachment disorder or past sexual abuse. These do exist, especially the older the child at the time of adoption. The best advice is always to seek help *early*. Your agency, parent group members, school teachers, therapists or your doctor can give you suggestions for adoption-sensitive counselors. There are also many e-mail discussion groups on the internet for every kind of adoption and every kind of adoption issue. However, the information and advice is not always monitored and may be of variable quality. Remember, you are not alone in any problem you may have. Many other parents have been through the same and are willing to help.

Finally, a prepared parent is the one best able to deal with the medical issues of adoption. Ask your homestudy agency for any materials they may have. The references on the following list are highly recommended, even for the non-medical audience.

## Selected References

Ames, E.W. et al: The development of Romanian orphanage children adopted to Canada: Final Report. Summary is $4.00 and the full report (highly recommended) is $15.00 from Adoptive Parents Assn. of British Columbia. Box 890 #101-1001 West Broadway, Vancouver, B.C. Canada V6H 4E4 604-588-7300.

Benoit, T.C., L.J. Jocelyn, D.M. Moddemann, J.E. Embree, Romanian adoption: the Manitoba experience. *Archives of Pediatric and Adolescent Medicine, 1509, 1278-1282.*

Conjeevaram, H.S., A.M. DiBisceglie (1995). Management of chronic viral hepatitis in children. *Journal of Pediatric Gastroenterology and Nutrition, 20,* 365-375.

Edelstein, S.B. (1995). Children with prenatal alcohol and/or other drug exposure: Weighing the risks of adoption. Washington, D.C.: Child Welfare League of America Press, 105 pp. (Order from CWLA at 440 First Street, NW, Suite 310, Washington, DC 20001-2085).

Fisher, L., E.W. Ames, K. Chisholm, L. Savoie (in press) Problems reported by parents of Romanian orphans adopted to British Columbia. *International Journal of Behavioural Development.*

Frank, D.A., P.E. Klass, F. Earls, L. Eisenberg (1996). Infants and young children in orphanages: One view from pediatrics and child psychiatry. *Pediatrics, 97,*

Hershow, R.C., S.C. Hadler, M.A. Kane (1987). Adoption of children from countries with endemic hepatitis B: Transmission risks and medical issues. *Pediatric Infectious Diseases Journal,* 6, 431-437.

Jenista, J.A.: Adoption. (1999) in Dershewitz, R.A. ed. Ambulatory Pediatric Care, 3rd ed. Lippincott-Raven, Philadelphia.

Jenista, J.A. (1995). The immigrant, refugee, or internationally adopted child. In Jensen, H.B. R.S. Baltimore, R.I. Markowitz, A.B. West (Eds.) *Pediatric infectious diseases: principles and practice.* Norwalk, CT: Appleton and Lange.

Kaser, J.S. (1983). Parenting the ageless child. Albuquerque, NM: Joyce S. Kaser, 18pp. (Order from Dr. Kaser at 3301 Don Quixote Place NW, Albuquerque NM 87104).

Lien, N.M. K.K. Meyer, M. Winick (1977). Early malnutrition and "late" adoption: a study of their effects on the development of Korean orphans into American families. *American Journal of Clinical Nutrition,* 30, 1734-1739.

Miller, L.C., N.W. Hendrie, (2000) Health of children adopted from China. *Pediatrics 105, e76*

Szilagyi, M. (1996). Medical issues in children adopted from foster care: Guide for physicians. *Adoption/Medical News,* II (5), 1-5. (Order from A/MN at 1921 Ohio Street, NE, Palm Bay, FL 32907).

Winick, M. K.K. Meyer, R.S. Harris (1975) Malnutrition and environmental enrichment by early adoption. *Science,* 190, 1173-1175.

Many topics of interest in back issues of *Adoption Medical News* can be accessed at www.adoptionmedicalnews.org.

## *In addition:*

Dr. Jenista recommends:

### Hepatitis B. Foundation
101 Greenwood Ave. Suite 570, Jenkintown PA 19046 (215) 884-8786. Dr. Jenista says it publishes an inexpensive newsletter and provides many printed free materials on Hepatitis B prevention and treatment. Their newsletter is "B Informed."

"Needle Tips & the Hepatitis B Coalition News" published by the Immunization Action Coalition, 1573 Selby Ave. Suite 229, St. Paul MN 55104, (612) 647-9009, or editor@immunize.org, www.immunize.org.

Jerri Ann Jenista is the single adoptive parent of four girls and a toddler boy, all from India, and two U.S.- born cats. She has specialized in infectious diseases and other medical problems of adopted children for many years, and now has a night job in the Emergency Room of St. Joseph Mercy Hospital.

# SINGLE ADOPTIVE PARENT SUPPORT GROUPS

**CAUTION:** This information is valid as of June 2000. Inevitably, contact people will change and addresses and phone numbers will change, before this Handbook is revised again.

**ALABAMA**
Single Adopt. Parents Subgrp, Ala.Friends Adopt.
Sherry Atkinson, contact (205) 733-0976 CST
2407 Titonka Road, Birmingham, AL 35244
Semi-active.

**ARIZONA**
Advocates for Single Adoptive Parenting
Torin Scott, (480) 951-8310 MST/MDT
8702 E. Malcomb Dr.,Scottsdale, AZ 85250
Annual dues $25, newsletter

**CALIFORNIA**
Single Adoptive Parents, South Bay Chapter
Jan Johnson (408) 292-1638 PST/PDT
385 S. 14th St., San Jose, CA 95112
50 families, most already parents; monthly social, educational, recreational meetings

Single Adoptive Parents, North Bay Chapter
Peggy Scott, (510) 524-5050 PST
1839 Catalina, Berkeley, CA 94707
60 members, bimonthly mtgs, dues

Single Adoptive Parents of Los Angeles
Jane Reben, (818) 769-3376 PST
12720 Burbank Blvd. No. 218
N. Hollywood CA 91607
Monthly informal social/family meetings,dues

**CONNECTICUT**
Contact: Connie Royster, (203) 431-6652 EST
228 Barlow Mountain Rd., Ridgefield, CT 06877
73074.2212@compuserve.com

**D.C., VIRGINIA, AND MARYLAND**
Association for Single Adoptive Parents
P.O.Box 3618, Merrifield, VA 22116-9998
(703) 521-0632 EST/EDT
70 members, some in Maryland and D.C. half parents,$20/year, newsletter, bimonthly meetings

**GEORGIA**
Alliance of Adoptive Parents
Sharon Hilley , (404) 755-3280 EST/EDT
687 Kennolia Drive S.W., Atlanta, GA 30310-2363
most are parents, quarterly meetings, dues

**Georgia, cont.**
Single Women Adopting Children
Johannah Smith, (770) 640-0495 EST
865 Whitehall Way, Roswell GA 30076
20 members,monthly meetings varying kinds

**ILLINOIS**
Single Adoptive Parent Support Group
(847) 604-1974 CST [Chicago area; address and contact unavailable]
50 members, most parents; $25/year; periodic meetings and other activities

**MASSACHUSETTS and NEW ENGLAND**
Single Parents Adopting Children Everywhere
Claire Ryan, Director, (781) 641-9816 EST
40 Smith Street, Arlington, MA 02476
Betsy Burch, Executive Director, (508) 655-5426
6 Sunshine Ave., Natick, MA , 01760
Dues, 200 members, monthly mtgs, **biennial national single adoptive parent conference.**

**MICHIGAN**
Michigan Association of Single Adoptive Parents
Barbara Knight, (734) 729-6989 EST
946 Forest St., Westland MI 48186
70 members, 90% parents, varied activities. quarterly newsletter, dues

Singles Adopting from Everywhere
Lori Streeter, (616) 285-9979 EST/EDT
2645 Knightsbridge St., Grand Rapids, MI 49546
30 members, most parents, monthly meetings for support, playgroups, newsletter

Singles for Adoption
Carol Powell, (616) 381-2581 EST
619 Norton Drive, Kalamazoo MI, 49001
Small group, all parents, monthly meetings

**MISSOURI**
Single Adoptive Parents Support Group
Buffy Atkins, (573) 445-1262 CST
1800 Fairview Rd., Columbia MO 65203
semi-active

## NEW JERSEY
Adoptive Single Parents of New Jersey
Marie Corwin, (908) 322-0813 EST/EDT
marie.corwin@ey.com
163 Hunter Ave., Fanwood NJ 07023
75 members, 90% already adoptive parents;
social and family activities, $15/year

## NEW YORK
New York City and Surrounding Area
New York Singles Adopting Children
P.O.Box 472, Glen Oaks, NY 11004
(212) 259-9402 EST/EDT
100 members, mostly parents, monthly social,
informational, education meetings; dues, very
good quarterly newsletter. To reach Long Island
chapter,call above number.

Long Island
Contact: Maureen Reichardt, (516) 938-7252
EST/EDT
11 Lynn Place, Bethpage, NY 11714
mreichar@optonline.net

Capitol District--Albany, Troy, Schenectady, Saratoga
Upstate New York Single Adoptive Parents,
affiliated with Adoption Coalition
Florence Abrams, (518) 489-4322 EST
38 Shaker Drive, Loudonville, NY 12211
also: Kathy McGee, (518) 581-0981
21 Concord Dr., Saratoga Springs NY, 12866
25 members, informal meetings

## OHIO
Single Parents by Adoption
Marilou Priestle, (513) 661-5170 EST
mpriestle@aol.com
2547 Talbott Ave., Cincinnati OH, 45211
15 members, monthly social, family meetings

## PENNSYLVANIA
Single Adoptive Parents of Delaware Valley
(Philadelphia and suburbs)
Kathy Rupert, Pres.(610) 272-7956 EST/ EDT
710 Noble St., Norristown PA 19401.
Susannah Starkweather, Membership secretary,
40 Aberdale Rd. Bala-Cynwyd PA 19004,
(610) 617-1197
Monthly social and informational meetings;
35 members,75% parents, $15/year, newsletter

## SOUTH CAROLINA
Single Adoptive Parents of South Carolina
J. Kirk Mixson , (803) 263-4502 EST/EDT
jaykirk@earthlink.net
P.O.Box 417, Norway, SC 29113-0417

## TEXAS
Adopting Children Together
Contact Donna Chatman, S.A.P. subgroup
(817) 465-1825 CST, or ACT,
P.O.Box 120966, Arlington, TX 76012
Periodic meetings, about 30 members, news-
letter, $15 dues.

Contact: Avelia Funderburk, Esq.
3321 Creek Bend Dr., Garland TX 75044
(972) 675-6336; office (972) 866-9800 CST
Information, advice, encouragement

## WASHINGTON
Advocates for Single Adoptive Parents-NW
Joyce Hamack, (425) 485-6770 PST/PDT
5706 N.E. 204th St ,Kenmore, WA 98028
25 members, most parents, monthly meetings

## WISCONSIN
Wisconsin Association of Single Adoptive Parents
Laurie Glass, (414) 962-9342 CST/CDT
4520 N. Bartlett Ave.,Shorewood WI 53211-1509
30 members, five meetings a year, $15 dues,
frequent events,newsletter.

Wisconsin Single Parents of Adopted Children
Diane Karrow (920) 262-2540 CST/CDT
810 Richards St., Watertown, WI 53094
Small group; quarterly meetings

Wisconsin Single Parents of Adopted Children
Anne Handschke, (715) 886-5572 CST
annehand@wctc.net
403 Vilas Ave. Nekoosa WI, 54457
12 members, all parents. Bimonthly meetings,
social, educ., recreational, family

---

## CANADA
Single Adoptive Parent Support Group
Heather Keillor, 905) 939-8441 EST/EDT
5400 17th St. Rd. R.R. 3
Schomberg, Ont. L0G 1T0, Canada
also, Donna McKie, (905) 771-8441
168 Bayview Fairways Dr.
Tjprmjo;; Pmt/ :3T 2Y8
50 members, most parents; newsletter. Bimonthly meetings, $20 yearly dues. Maintains
contact with governmental or child-concerned
local, provincial, and federal level agencies.

## Single Parent Groups, continued

### NATIONAL SINGLE PARENT GROUPS

**Adoption Resource Exchange for Single Parents(ARESP)** 8605 Cameron St. Silver Spring MD. 20910. (301) 585-5836; e-mail: aresp@aol.com ARESP advocates for and promotes the adoption of older and special needs children by single men and women, including non-traditional families. It offers orientation classes, assistance, and information; and can link prospective parents with individuals who have faced the same situations. ARESP appears to be reorganizing at present.

Single Mothers by Choice
Jane Mattes, Founder and Director
(212) 988-0993 EST/EDT
P.O.Box 1642, Gracie Square Station
New York, NY 10028
Contact Jane Mattes for chapters or contact people actoss the U.s. and Canada. Members network and share information and resources on the national and local level. Annual membership dues being a member ship directory for the member's area, a resource packet, and literature on single parenthood, as well as a subscription to the newsletter.

# Country-of-Origin Support Groups

## LATIN AMERICA

**Latin America Parents Association**
   New York headquarters, P.O.Box 339, Brooklyn N.Y. 11234, (718) 236-8689 EST  This chapter can provide links to LAPA chapters across the country, many of which publish newsletters and offer regular meetings and informational and social programs supporting Latin American adoptions and culture.

## CHINA

**Families with Children From China:** This is a very active and growing network of chapters in the U.S., Canada, and the United Kingdom.  Their goals are: to support families who have adopted children of Chinese origin, to encourage adoption from China and support waiting families, and to advocate for and support children remaining in Chinese orphanages. Chapters offer family picnics, celebrations of Chinese festivals, pre-adoption information meetings, playgroups, Chinese language and culture classes for children, and parent speakers. To locate the chapter nearest you, contact the web-site: www.fwcc.org. The webmaster, Jim L. Weaver, can be reached by e-mail at jimlweaver@aol.com.

## EASTERN EUROPE

**Families for Russian and Ukrainian Adoption**
   7616 Trail Run Road
   Falls Church, VA     **(703) 560-6184 EST**

**Romanian Children's Connection**
   Mary Thomas, Editor    (703) 548-9352 EST
   1206 Hillside Terrace, Alexandria, VA 22302
   300 members; annual dues, newsletter

## INDIA

**Supportive Parents of Indian Children Every -
   where** SPICE, a national organization, runs an Indian culture camp for families and their children at a different place in the U.S. each year. Half a day is spent on Indian culture and the rest on social activities.  Curriculum director is Dr. Jerri Jenista, single adoptive mother of five children from India, and noted adoptive child medical specialist.  (734) 668-0419 EST

Iowa Parents of [East] Indian Children
   Jackie Sparks, President   (515) 792-7843 CST
   420 First Ave. W. Newton IA 50208 This group operates a culture camp in Iowa.

Parents of [East] Indian Children
   Lynn Malfeld        (612) 645-9068 CST
   1395 Simpson Street, St. Paul MN 55108
   100-150 members, many single; newsletter, culture camp

NAMASTE, Foreign and Indian Adoption
   Nancy Reinbold        (262) 968-4564 CST
   546 Black Earth Court, Wales, WI 53183

Families Interested in Adoption
   Emily Eisenbaum      (716) 837-6657 EST
   P.O.Box 56, Williamsville, NY 14231-56

Gail Walton edits **Connections**, an international quarterly publication for families adopting or hoping to adopt children from India and its subcontinent. it contains a mix of cultural material on India, book reviews, medical advice, and personal stories.  One of its aims is to put people in touch with each other. Address: 1417 East Minor St. Arlington Hts. IL 60004, (847) 255-8309 CST

# Adoption Resources and Registries--Nation-wide

## Adopt America (formerly Adopt a Special Kid--AASK America)

Edieann Didham, Exec. Dir.(419) 534-3350 EST
1025 N. Reynolds Rd., Toledo, OH 43615,
adoptamer@aol.com; adoptamericanetwork.org.

Promotes the adoption of special needs children; networks with agencies across the country registering their waiting children with Adopt America; families also register to adopt special children.

## Children Awaiting Parents (CAP)

700 Exchange Street, Rochester, NY 14608
(716) 232-5110 EST; cap@adopt.org;
www.capbook.org.

CAP publishes The CAP Book, a national photo-listing of children waiting for adoptive families that is one of the most effective such registries in the country. CAP has joined with the NAC (below) in its computerized photolisting. Those interested in adopting a special-needs child **who have a home study** may ask their agency to contact CAP about a particular child. See NAC for the URL. Publishes Adoption Link newsletter.

## The National Adoption Center

1500 Walnut St., Suite 701; Philadelphia, PA 19102
1-800-862-3678 or (215) 735-9988 EST

The Center and CAP have joined in a national computerized photo-listing of waiting U.S. children and information about adoption of waiting children. People interested in special-needs adoption, who do not yet have a home study, should use this website or contact NAC by mail or telephone: www.adopt.org

## Adoption Medical News

Publisher and Editor, William L. Pierce, Ph.D., P.O. Box 1253, State College PA. 16804, (814) 364-2449.

This has been one of the most valuable newsletters in the adoption field. In only 4-8 pages each issue, the former editor, Jerri A. Jenista, M.D. took up a range of medical and related topics with clarity and nerve: the pros and cons of circumcising, the value of videotapes, the con cern over tuberculosis, a parents guide to attachment problems. Under the new publisher, who has assembled an impressive advisory board, we can expect that the same high quality will continue.

## Jewish Children's Adoption Network

P.O.Box 16544          Steve and Vicki Krause
Denver, CO 80216-0544;   (303) 573-8113 MST

M matches children with families, including single women and men. Does not do legal work or home studies. Has located US Jewish (and some non-Jewish, black, or biracial) children from birth to age 17, usually special needs. Has helped to place hundreds of children 80% special-needs, not all Jewish, with families, not all Jewish. "The most important thing is to respect the child, and the child's culture."

## STARS OF DAVID INTERNATIONAL-- Jewish Adoptive Families

c/o Susan Katz          1-800-STAR-349 CST
3175 Commercial Ave. Suite 100
Northbrook IL 60062-1915
Information to prospective families coast to coast, in 35 Chapters.  e-mail Starsdavid@AOL.Com

## NATIVE AMERICAN RESOURCES
### Fost-Adopt Program

American Indian Child Resource Center
522 Grand Ave., Oakland, CA 94610
(510) 208-1870 PST, aic@aicsc.org

**Rainbow Adoption Services and Family Tree Foster Care:** Program s of the Council of Three Rivers American Indian Center.Margaret G. Gold. Director, 120 Charles St., Pittsburgh, PA 15238 (412) 782-4457 EST
Resource and technical aid for lawyers and case workers involved with native American adoptable children under the Indian Child Welfare Act. Native enrolled children may be adopted only by enrolled members of tribes.

# Disabled or Deaf *Parents*

National Resource Center for Parents with Disabilities 2198 Sixth St. Suite 100, Berkeley CA 94710-2204 1 (510) 848-1112 PST

"Through the Looking Glass" program is devoted to prospective adoptive parents with disabilities, including deafness. It published the book You May Be Able to Adopt: A guide to the adoption option for parents with disabilities, and their partners. TTLG, 112 pages, 1997.

# Adoption Registries and Resources--Regional and State

Family Builders by Adoption (Bay Area)
528 Grand Ave.            Jill Jacobs
Oakland, CA 94610         (510) 272-0204 PST/PDT

The Adoption Exchange
14232 E. Evans Ave., Denver, CO 80014
(303) 755-4756 MST/MDT, www.adoptex.org.
Works in CO, MO, NV, NM, SD, UT, and WY.  Publishes
newsletter, Heartlines. Photolisting. Can work nationally.

Lutheran Child & Family Services
333 W. Lake St.           Lanell Hill
Addison, IL 60101         (630) 628-6448 x222 CST

Adoption Information Center of Illinois
188 West Randolph, Ste.600
Chicago, IL 60601(312) 346-1516 CST/CDT

Indiana Special Needs Adoption
402 W.Washington St. W-364   Jody Pearce. Audrey Dabney
Indianapolis IN 46204     (317) 233-1743 EST/EDT

Lutheran Social Services
1855 North Hillside
Wichita, KS 67214(316) 686-6645 CST/CDT

Protection and Permanency Planning--DSS
275 E. Main St. 3rd Floor, Frankfurt, KY 40621
(502) 564-2147 CST/CDT

Maryland Adoption Resource Exchange
311 W. Saratoga St.       Eloise Mooney
Baltimore MD 21201        (410) 767-7359 EST/EDT

Massachusetts Adoption Resource Exchange, SSA
45 Franklin St. 5th Floor
Boston, MA 02110-1301  (617) 542-3678 EST/EDT
Serves Mass., Rhode Island, Connecticut.

Spaulding for Children Foster Care and Adoption,
National Resource Center for Special-Needs Adoption
16250 Northland Dr. No. 120, Addie Williams, Pres. & CEO
Southfield, MI 48075      (248) 443-0300 EST/EDT

N.Y. State Dept. Social Services, Adoption Svcs.
40 N. Pearl St., Riverview Center, 6th Floor, Albany NY
12243. Bruce Bushart   1-800-345-KIDS EST/EDT
www.dfa.state.ny.us/adopt
Publishes The Blue Book, "New York's Waiting Children."

Women's Christian Alliance--Family Builders
1610-16 N. Broad St.      Theresa King
Philadelphia, PA 19121    (215) 236-9911 EST/EDT

Children's Institute--Project STAR
6301 Northumberland St. Pittsburgh, PA 15217
(412) 244-3066 EST/EDT, Tim Bittner
Serves Western Penna. residents only.

Tressler-Lutheran Adoption Services Inc.
836 So. George St.        Barb Holtan
York, PA 17403            (717) 845-9113 EST
Serves Central Penna. residents only.

Pennsylvania Adoption Exchange, Dept. Pub.Welfare
P.O.Box 2675              Jewel McCliment
Harrisburg, PA  17105-2675  (717) 772-7015 EST

Three Rivers Adoption Council (TRAC)
307 Fourth Ave. Ste.710  Pittsburgh, PA 15222
(412) 471-8722 EST/EDT, Sherry Anderson
Serves Penna., West Virginia, Ohio.

Children Unlimited
P.O.Box 11463             Linda J. Eisele
Columbia, SC 29211        (803) 799-8311 EST/EDT

Southeastern Exchange of the US--SEEUS
P.O.Box 1453              (864) 242-0460 EST
Greenville, SC 29602-1453
Serves AL, FL, GA, KY, MS, NC, SC.

Spaulding for Children--Southwest
710 N. Post Oak Rd. Ste.500,Houston, TX 77024
(713) 681-6991 CST/CDT

Texas Adoption Resource Exchange, MC-E559
State Dept. of  Protective & Regulatory Services
Austin, TX. (512) 834-3279    1-800-233-3405 CST
www.adoptchildre.org

Adoption Resource Exchange of Virginia
730 E. Broad St. 2nd Fl., Richmond, VA 23219
(804) 692-1280 EST/EDT, Tonya Martin

Medina Children's Services
123  16th Ave., Seattle, WA 98122
(206) 461-4520 PST/PDT, Rebecca Heartz, Exec. Dir.

West Virginia Adoption Resource Network
350 Capitol St. #691,  Charleston, WV 25301
(304) 558-7980 EST/EDT

Northwest Adoption Exchange
600 Stewart St. Ste. 1313, Seattle, WA 98101
(206) 441-6822 PST/PDT, Barbara Pearson
Serves WA, OR, UT, ID, AK, NV.

# Major National Adoption Organizations

**Joint Council on International Children's Services**   Sharon A. Kaufman, Director
1320 19th St. N.W. Suite 200, Washington DC 20036. www.jcics.org Nonprofit association of large and small licensed international adoption agencies and advocacy groups, dedicated to professionalism and ethics in international adoption. Tracks developments affecting international adoption, including laws and regulations. Annual conference, quarterly newsletter.

**National Council for Adoption**
1930 Seventeenth St. N.W.
Washington, DC 20009, (202) 328-1200 EST
A nonprofit adoption information and education organization representing well over 100 adoption agencies and individual members across the U.S. Works for federal and state legislation promoting and encouraging adoption. Several publications for its members and subscribers.
Annual meeting.

**International Concerns for Children**
911 Cypress Drive, Boulder, CO 80303
(303) 494-8333 MST, ICC@ Boulder.net, www.iccadopt.org. Publishes **Report on Foreign Adoption** listing, first, licensed adoption agencies placing children for adoption, with countries each agency works in; second, countries from which applicants may adopt (and the agencies working there). Also, on the internet, publishes photo-listing of children available for adoption, as well as much other invaluable information and counsel. Quarterly newsletter

**The Adoption Education Institute** New non-profit serving adoptive and prospective adoptive families: providing personal, printed, and on-line assistance to families who need information, advice and referral to resources for pre-adoption questions and post-adoption issues. Website to be on line by Jan. 2001, with network of peer counselors,personal consultations, list-ings, printed materials. Until then, limited e-mail service at sfreivalds@adoptioneducation.org.

**American Academy of Adoption Attorneys** P.O. Box 33053, Washington, DC 20033-0053 (202) 832-2222, www.adoptionattorneys.org Most attorneys who conduct or assist with adoptions are members of this organization. Many are very able and experienced.

**North American Council on Adoptable Children (NACAC)** 970 Raymond Ave. Ste 106 St. Paul, MN 55114-1149, (612) 644-3036 CST
A nonprofit organization founded in 1975 to support and facilitate the right of every child to a permanent family. Publishes the quarterly newsletter Adoptalk, and conducts an annual four-day conference, rotating among the eastern, midwestern, and western United States and Canada. It also issues publications to assist groups and individuals working for the goals they share with NACAC.

**National Adoption Information Clearinghouse** 330 C Street S.W., Washington DC 20447
1-888-251-0075 EST, http://www.calib.com/naic e-mail: naic@calib.com. Mary Sullivan, Director. NAIC is federally mandated to collect and disseminate information on adoption. Also prepares information reports on important issues. An extremely valuable source of information on all areas of adoption.

**Child Welfare League of America (CWLA)**
440 First Street N.W. Suite 310, Washington, DC 20001-2085, (202) 638-2952
Advocates for all aspects of children's interests, including adoption, at national and state levels. Publishes newsletter and prepares reports on problems in child welfare. Annual meeting.

**American Public Human Services Association**
810 First St. N.E., (202) 682-0100. APHSA develops, provides, and implements policies that improve health and wellbeing of families, children, and adults. The APHSA serves as the secretariat for the Interstate Compact on the Placement of Children [across state lines] and the Interstate Compact on Adoption and Medical Assistance.

**Voice for Adoption** P.O. Box 77496, Washington DC 20013. (202) 543-7372; FAX: 202-543-7371. A national coalition of organizations devoted to insuring permanent families for waiting children. VFA advocates action to overcome legal, policy, and funding barriers to the adoption of waiting children. E-mail: cholden1 <cholden1@netzero.net>

# DOCTORS WHO WORK WITH ADOPTED CHILDREN

NOTE: This information has been checked through August 2000. We expect that many more doctors will be added to this list. A good place to check would be theAmerican Academy of Pediatrics' Section on Adoption: call 1-800-433-9016 (ask for the Section Administrator) or the AAP website at www.aap.org. Another is the website of the National Adoption Information Clearinghouse, http://www.calib.com/naic.

## CALIFORNIA

Tina Gabby, M.D., (415) 381-3255 PST
21 Fifer Ave. Suite 200, Corte Madera, CA 94925
Foreign-born children only. Behavioral and Developmental Pediatrician. Director, Early Childhood Clinic; Asst.Clinical professor U. Cal. San Francisco. Assessments including pre- and post-adoption consultation and treatment.

Rowena Korobkin, M.D. (415) 923-3822 PST
fax 415-923-3506
California Pacific Medical Center, 2340 Clay St. No. 303,San Francisco CA 94115
Pediatric neurology consultation

Deborah Lehman, M.D., (310) 423-4471 PST,
fax 310-423-8284
Cedars-Sinai Medical Center, 8700 Beverly Blvd. Los Angeles CA 90048
US- and foreign-born children. Pre- and post-adoption medical evaluation. Infectious disease practice.

## COLORADO

Sarah Carpenter, M.D., Matthew F. Daley, M.D. The International Adoption Clinic, 1056 E. 19th Ave. B032, Denver, CO 80218. (303) 837-2830, MST, fax 303-764-8072
Pre- and post-adoption consultation, post-adoption developmental evaluation. General pediatrics, multidisciplinary team evaluation.

## CONNECTICUT

Margaret Hostetter, M.D. (203) 737-5970 EST
Yale Child Health Research Center,
464 Congress Ave., New Haven CT 06520
Foreign-born children only. Pre-placement evaluation & consultation only.

Margaret K. Ikeda, MD , (203) 458-7410 EST,
fax 203-458-6960, Moose Hill Pediatrics
705 Boston Rd. Guilford CT 06437
U.S. and foreign-born children. Post-Adoption pediatric care. General pediatrics, infectious disease

## DISTRICT OF COLUMBIA

Nina Scribanu, M.D. (202) 687-8635 EST/EDT
Fax 202- 687-8899;
scribanu@gunet.georgetown.edu
Department of Pediatrics
3307 M St. N.W. Washington DC 20007
Foreign- and US-born children. Clinical geneticist, developmental problems: FAS, parental substance abuse etc. Fluent in Russian & Romanian.

Phillip Pearl, M.D. (202) 884-2120,
fax 202- 884-5226
Dept. of Neurology, 111 Michigan Ave. N.W. Washington DC 20010
Foreign- and US-born children. Neurological evaluation.

Marie Tartaglia, M.D. (202) 537-1180
fax 202-244-7410.
3301 New Mexico Ave., N.W. Suite 238
Washington DC 20016
US and foreign born children. Pediatric care.

## GEORGIA

Patrick Mason, M.D., Ph.D., Amy Pakula, M.D.
(404) 727-9566 EST, fax 404-727-9519
e-mail adopt@marcus.org
1605 Chantilly Dr, Suite 100, Atlanta GA 30024
Foreign-born children only. Pre-and post-adoption evaluations, special interest in child hood growth and development, early life stress; related services

## ILLINOIS

Todd J. Ochs M.D., Adoption Pediatrics S.C.
(773) 769-4600 EST; fax 773-975-5989,
e-mail t-ochs@northwestern.edu
1945 W. Wilson St. Chicago IL 60640
> Foreign- and US-born children. Adoptive parent (China)

Ira Chasnoff, M.D. (312) 362-9607 CST
fax 312-362-9609. Child Study Center, 200 So.
Michigan Ave. Sts. 1430, Chicago, IL 60604
> US- and foreign-born children. Pre- and post-adoption review & evaluation and post-adoption medical evaluation. Developmental pediatrics, parenting classes and attachment therapy.

Tina Tan, M.D., (773) 880-4187 CST, fax 773-880-8226. Children's Memorial Hospital, 2300 Children's Plaza, Chicago, IL 60614
> U.S. &foreign-born children. Post-adoption medical evaluation. Infectious disease practice.

## INDIANA

James Conway, M.D. (317) 274-7260 EST
fax 317-278-3031. Riley Hospital for Children
702 Barnhill Dr.Rm.5845, Indianapolis IN 46202
> Newly arrived foreign-born children only. Post-adoption medical evaluation.

## MAINE

Nancy W. Hendrie, MD, (207) 442-7612 EST
fax 207--386-0307. The Sharing Foundation
P.O.Box 399, Woolwich MD 04579
> Pre-adoption review for China, Cambodia, Vietnam, Korea, India. General pediatrics

## MARYLAND

Johns Hopkins-Kennedy-Krieger (410) 955-8032
International Children's Clinic, N. Wolfe St.,
Baltimore MD 21287.
> Pre and post-adoption evaluations.

## MASSACHUSETTS

Lisa Albers, M.D. (617) 355-5209 EST
fax 617-730-5529
Children's Hospital
300 Longwood Ave. Boston MA 02116
> Foreign- and US-born children. Pre-placement evaluations, developmental & behavioral pediatrics

Laurie Miller, M.D. (617) 636-8121 EST
fax 617-636-8388; www.nemc.org/adoption
International Adoption Clinic,
The Floating Hospital for Children,
New England Medical Center, Box 286
750 Washington St. Boston MA 02111
> Foreign-born children only. Pre-adoptioncounseling, evaluation; adoption medicine and pediatric rheumatology. Monthly pre-adoption seminars, monthly adoptive parents group with speaker, strong post-adoptive program for school-age US- or foreign-born children with school, learning, behavioral or emotional problems. Contact Carol Curtin, (617) 636-7242

Linda Sagor, (508) 856-4198, fax 508-856-7745
lindasagor@banyan.ummhc.edu
Univ. Massachusetts Medical Center
55 Lake Avenue No., Worcester MA 01655
> U.S. and foreign-born children; pre-place ment and post-adoption evaluations; pediatric primary care

Claire D. Wilson MD, (781) 744-8083, EST
fax 781-744-5244. Lahey Clinic, 41 Mall Rd.
Burlington MA 01805
> U.S. and foreign-born children. Pre- and post-adoption review and evaluation. Post-adoption pediatric care.

## MICHIGAN

Jerri A. Jenista, M.D. (734) 668-0419 EST
fax 734-668-9492, St. Joseph Mercy Hospital
551 Second St. Ann Arbor MI 48103
> Foreign- and US-born children. Pediatrician; specializing in infectious diseases, developmental and behavioral issues, medical impairments. Adoptive parent of five(India).

Dennis Murray, M.D. (517) 353-7806 EST
fax: 517-355-1679; murrayd@pilot.msu.edu
C 204 East Fee Hall, Michigan State University
East Lansing MI 48824-1316
> Foreign and US-born children,pediatric infectious diseases, Hep.B & C etc. by referral from child's physician.

## MINNESOTA

Dana E. Johnson, M.D. Ph.D.
(612) 626-2928 CST, fax 612-624-7176;
johns008@maroon.tc.umn.edu
International Adoption Clinic
D-136 Mayo Building, Box 211,
420 Delaware St. S.E. Minneapolis MN 55455
Foreign-born children only. Pediatric and
teen consultation. Parents call first; may go
to clinic or request consultation by mail.

Leah Willson, M.D., (320) 587-2020 CST,fax 320-
234-3317. Hutchinson Medical Center/Pediatrics,
3-Century Ave. SE, Hutchinson MN 55350
U.S. & foreign-born children. Pre- and post-
adoption evaluations, post-adoption developmental evaluations, regular pediatric care.
General pediatrics.

## MISSOURI

Mary K. Bowen, M.D. (314) 845-1780 CST, fax
314-845-1781, bowenmd99@yahoo.com, Unity
Medical Group, 4305 Butler Hill Rd. Ste. 2,
St. Louis MO 63128-3717
U.S. & foreign-born children, pre- and post-
adoption review & evaluations, developmental evaluations. General pediatrics plus
neurology.

Jennifer S. Ladage, M.D. (314) 577-5643CST
fax 314-268-4028, Foreign Adoption Clinic and
Educational Services, Cardinal Glennon
Children's Hospital, 1465 Grand Ave. St. Louis
MO 63104
Foreign-born children only. Pre-and post-
adoption reviews, consultation.

## MONTANA

Marie Mitchell, R.N. Pediatric Nurse Practitioner
(406)585-924,MST, 475 Concord Dr. Bozeman
MT 59715, mariem@msu.oscs.montana.edu
Foreign and US-born children, any age.
Consultations, referrals, pre-adoption
evaluations, post-adoption physicals.

## NEBRASKA

Sandra Iverson, Pediatric Nurse-Practitioner
(402) 561-6854, iverson@novia.net
c/o Dr. Dana Johnson, as of Sept. 2000
Foreign-born children only; evaluations, pre-
placement and post-adoption counseling and
referrals. Moving to Minn. in September.

Edward Kolb, M.D. (402) 354-7252 CST
fax 402-354-3032
International Adopted Children's Clinic
Children's Hospital
8301 Dodge St., Omaka, NE 68114-4114
Foreign-born children only. Clinic open two
days a month for pre- and post-placement
evaluation, counseling & referrals

## NEW JERSEY

Lisa Nalven, M.D. (201) 447-8151 EST
fax 201-447-8526
Center for Child Development
505 Goffle Rd. Ridgewood NJ 07450
U.S. and foreign-born infants & children.
Developmental and behavioral pediatrician.
Pre-placement consultation & post-adoption
evaluation.

## NEW YORK

Andrew Adesman M.D. (718) 470-4000 EST
fax 718-343-3578
Evaluation Center for Adoption, Suite 139
Schneider Children's Hospital
269-01 76th Ave. New Hyde Park NY 11040
Foreign and US-born children. Developmental and behavioral pediatrician. Pre-adoptive
screening.

Jane Ellen Aronson, M.D.
(212) 727-0627 EST, jaronmink@aol.com
Director, International Adoption Medical
Consulting Services.
151 E. 62nd St. Suite 1-A, New York NY 10021
Foreign-born children only. Pre- and post-
adoption reviews, consultations, post-
adoption general pediatric care. Pediatric
infections diseases, complicated cases.

Steven Blatt, M.D. (315) 464-5831,
fax 315-464-2030
University Health Care Center, 90 Presidential
Plaza, 3rd Floor, Syracuse NY 13202
US. and foreign-born children. Directs a
foster care clinic. Pre-placement reviews and
evaluation of videotapes, pediatric care

Boris Gindis, Ph.D. Licensed Psychologist, (914)
357-2512, fax 914-369-6830 International
Adoption Psychological Consultation & Services.
13 South Van Dyke Ave. Suffern NY 10901
U.S. and foreign children. Post-adoption
comprehensive Russian-English educational
and psycho-developmental evaluations &
consultations.

Mary Anne Kiernan, M.D. (716) 225-0950, EST
fax 716-225-9093. Long Pond Pediatrics
2350 Ridgeway Ave. Rochester NY 14626
    U.S. & foreign-born children. Pre- and Post-
    adoption review & evaluations, post-
    adoption developmental evaluations,
    regular pediatric care.

Susan Levitzky, M.D. (212) 213-1960, fax 212-
213-5809, 161 Madison Ave. New York NY 10016
    U.S. & foreign-born children. Pre- and post-
    adoption reviews and evalutions, regular
    pediatric care.

Daniel R. Neuspiel, M.D. MPH, (212) 844-8309
fax 212-844-8401, Beth Israel Medical Center
10 Union Squ. East Ste. 2J, New York NY 10003
    U.S. & foreign-born children. Pre- and post-
    adoption review & evaluation, developmen
    tal evaluations,pediatric care.

Moira Szilagyi M.D., Ph.D., (716) 274-6927
fax 716-292-3942, Foster Care Pediatrics,
Monroe County Health Dept. 111 Westfall Rd.,
Rochester NY 14692
    U.S. children only. Pre-adoption review for
    children being adopted out of foster care &
    adolescents in and adopted from foster care.

Michael Traistor, M.D. (212) 787-1444 EST, or
(Scarsdale) (914) 725-7555; fax 212-799-8620
390 West End Ave. Suite 1E, New York NY 10024
    Foreign- and US-born children.

Elaine Schulte, M.D. (518) 262-7745 EST, or
(518) 262-6086; fax 518-262-5589
Dept. of Pediatric Medicine, Albany Medical
College A-88, Albany NY 22314
    Foreign and US-born children.
    Pre-placement evaluation.

David Soule M.D. (716) 271-2937
fax 716-271-3575
15 N. Goodman, Rochester NY 14607
    Foreign- and US-born children. Specialist in
    FAS, ADHD, ADD. Retiring soon.

Lawrence Sugarman, M.D., (716) 271-0860
fax 716-271-1383
2233 Clinton Ave., Rochester NY 14618
    Foreign- and US-born children. Pediatric, bio-
    feedback and hypnotherapy. Pre-placement
    evaluation.

NORTH CAROLINA
    Elizabeth Blair, M.D. Ph.D. (252) 355-3773 EST,
    fax 252-355-1958 111 Berkshire Drive, .
    Winterville  NC 28590
        U.S. & foreign-born children. Pre- and post-
        adoption review and consultations and
        developmental evaluation.

OHIO
    Deborah Borchers M.D. , (513) 753-2820 EST
    fax 513-753-2824;  debbiborch@juno.com
    Eastgate Pediatric Center, 4357 Ferguson Dr.,
    Suite 150, Cincinnati,  OH 45245
        Foreign- and US-born children; pre-place
        ment review, post-adoptive treatment,
        adoptive parent (China).

    Karen Olness, M.D., Ann Madalakas M.D.
    Marisa Herran, M.D.  (216) 844-3224
    fax 216-844-7601  e-mail RCIC@po.cwru.edu
    Rainbow Center for International Child Health
    11100 Euclid Ave. MS 6038, Cleveland OH 44106
        Foreign-born children only.

    Mary Staat, M.D., M.Ph. (513) 636-2877
    fax 513-636-6936
    Director, International Adoption Center
    Children's Hospital Medical Center
    3333 Burnet Ave. Cincinnati, OH 45229-3039
        Foreign-born children only. Pre-placement
        and post-adoption evaluation. Specializes in
        infectious disease, preventive medicine.

    Wendy Schmidt, OTR/L, MA-Occupational
    Therapist (216) 231-1981, fax 216-368-0116
    2219 Devonshire Dr. Cleveland OH 44106
        Chiefly foreign-born children. Pre-adoption
        review re growth and development;
        recommendations & on-site treatment
        techniques; post adoption development
        evaluation. Occupational Therapy treatment
        related to issues in the post-institutionalized
        infant.

PENNSYLVANIA
    Stephen Aranoff, M.D. (215) 707-6605 EST
    Fax 215-707-6629, Temple University Children's
    Medical Center, 3509 N. Broad St. Philadelphia
    PA 19140.
        Foreign and US-born childen. Advice to
        adoptive parents on infectious diseases.

**Pennsylvania, cont.**

Sarah Springer M.D., Scott Faber, M.D.
(412) 575-5805, fax 412-232-7389
Mercy Center for International Adoption
Dept. of Pediatrics. 1709 Blvd. of the Allies,
Pittsburgh PA 15219
Foreign- and US-born children.
Pre-placement evaluation; initial
consultations at early stages of adoption.

Gail Farber, M.D. (215) 590-7525, EST
Adoption Program of the Philadelphia Children's
Hospital, 34th and Civic Center Blvd. Philadelphia PA 19104
US/ & foreign-born children. Pre- and post-
adoption reviews, evaluations,post-adoption
pediatric care. Evaluation and management
of adoption-related issues,through childhood
and adolescence.

Carl Meyer, D.O., (724) 588-1400,103 Woodfield
Drive, Greenville, PA 16125
U.S. and foreign-born children. Pre- and
post-adoption review & evaluations,
post-adoption developmental evaluations,
pediatric care.

Leslie E. Sude, M.D. (215) 752-8700, fax 215-
741-1147. DMVA/Oxford Valley Pediatrics,
825 Town Center Drive Langhorne PA 19147
U.S. & foreign-born children. Pre-and Post-
adoption review and evaluations, pediatric
care.

**RHODE ISLAND**

Boris Skurkovich, M.D. International Adoption
Clinic, Hasbro Children's Hospital, 593 Eddy St.
Providence, R.I. 02903 (401) 444-0400.
Pre- & post-adoption review and evaluation,
post-adoption developmental evaluations.
General pediatrics, infectious diseases.

**TEXAS**

Gale L. Haradon Ph.D., OTR, (210) 567-8889 CST
Fax, 210-567-8893. University of Texas Health
Science Center at San Antonio, 7703 Floyd Curl
Dr. , San Antonio TX 78229-3900
Foreign-born children only. Pre-adoption
review, consultation; post-adoption
developmental evaluations.

**VIRGINIA**

James R. Baugh, M.D. (703) 573-2432, fax 703-
280-9350, Fairfax Inova Hospital, 3020 Hamaker
Court, #220, Fairfax, VA 22031
U.S.& foreign-born children. Pre- and post-
adoption review and evaluation. Pediatric
care. Russian & French spoken.

Ronald S. Federici, Psy.D., (703) 548-0721 EST
fax 703-836-8995, 620 Wolfe St., Alexandria VA
22314.
U.S. and foreign-born children. Develop
mental neuropsychologist. Foreign-
and US-born children. Pre-placement review
and counseling, neuropsychological testing,
referral. Adoptive Parent (Romania)

**WASHINGTON**

Julie Bledsoe, M.D. (206) 598-3006 PST
fax 206-598-3040; jbledsoe@u.washington.edu
Pediatric Care Center, Center for Adoption
Medicine, University of Washington
4245 Roosevelt Way N.E., Seattle WA , 98205
Foreign- and US-born children.
FAS expertise. Adoptive parent.

Jacqueline Farwell, M.D. (206) 505-1101
www.pacmed.org
International Adoption Medicine Clinic
1101 Madison St. Suite 301, Seattle WA 98104
Foreign-born children only. Pre-placement
evaluation, diagnostic information and
referral. Adoptive parent (Romania)

---

**Good Doctors in Foreign Countries:** IAMAT, the International Association for Medical Assistance to Travellers, is a little-known worldwide network of doctors and medical institutions in other countries. Its world directory lists 125 countries with the location of "English-speaking doctors who make house calls for no more than US$55." All have been trained in either North America or Europe. This is a membership organization---membership is free, donations of $25 entitle members to health safety information on 1,440 cities and risk charts for several diseases. Head office is 40 Regal Road, Guelph, Ont. N1K 1B5, Canada (519) 836-0102 EST. Also located at 1287 St. Clair Avenue West, Toronto, Ont. B6E 1B8, Canada. (416) 652-0137 EST; iamat@sentex.net, website: www.sentex.net/~iamat

# Books, etc. about Adoption in General

Following is a selection of the many excellent **books** available for those thinking about adoption. The best mail-order sources are: Tapestry Books, at 800-765-2367 EST (e-mail: http://tapestrybooks.com/), whose catalog lists over 240 books for adults and children; and Perspectives Press, the infertility and adoption publisher, at (317) 872- 3055, EST (e-mail: ppress@iquest. net). Adoption books are also sold at adoption support conferences.

## General Interest

**Real Parents, Real Children: Parenting the Adopted Child** by Holly van Gulden and Lisa M. Bartels-Rabb, 1993. For international, interracial and same-race adoptions, infancy through adulthood. Dr. Jerri Jenista calles this book the "Dr. Spock of raising adoptive children."

**Raising Adopted Children: A Manual for Adoptive Parents,1986**, by Lois Ruskai Melina. Looks at the child's physical, emotional and psychological development at every age. "This book should be on the reference shelf of every adoptive family," says Tapestry Books.

**Adopting on Your Own: the Complete Guide to Adopting as a Single Parent**, by Lee Varon. Farrar, Straus & Giroux, New York, 392 pages, 2000. A thorough and helpful manual dealing with all types of adoption. The author teaches workshops for single people considering adoption. Each chapter ends with exercises and activities to help the prospective adopter think through reasons and choices.

**Perspectives on a Grafted Tree; Thoughts for those touched by adoption**. Perspectives Press, Indiana, 144 pages, 1983. This is a lovely book, and every adoptive parent should have it. There are 84 poems, written by birthmothers giving up a child, adoptive parents receiving a child, grown adoptive children. Some are lyrical, a few are bitter, and some make you cry.

**National Council for Adoption FACTBOOK III.** NCFA, Washington DC, 2000, 637 pages. This encyclopedic book provides statistics and short articles on almost every topic conceivably related to adoption, by experts in their respective fields.

# Periodicals:

**Roots and Wings,** Chester, NJ quarterly adoption magazine with candid articles on all facets of adoption, special-needs and other; happy or problematic. (908) 637-8828 EST

**Adoptive Families**, New Hope Communications, New York, NY. Under new management, this popular bimonthly aims to keep readers informed about current adoption news and to address important adoption issues at all stages of the adoption process. 1-800-372-330; info@adoptivefam.com.

**Adoption Today**, (formerly Chosen Child) Loveland, CO. Bimonthly written by adoptive parents, adoptees, and professionals in medicine, international and domestic adoption law, social work, and education. 1-888-924-6736; www.adoptinfo.net.

**Adoption Access**, Evan B. Donaldson Adoption Institute, 120 Wall Street, New York, NY. Provides, on a quarterly basis, an up-to-date annotated list of published research and policy and practice literature relevant to adoption, and a brief overview of the most significant studies and analyses both published and unpublished.

**The Future of Children**, Vol. 3, No. 1, Spring 1993, Adoption; Center for the Future of Children--the David and Lucile Packard Foundation, Los Altos, CA 94022. Each issue deals with a different aspect; some touch adoption.

**Adopted Child**, Moscow, ID 83843, (208) 882-1794 MST. In each 4-page monthly issue, Editor Lois Melina researches one adoption-related issue, presenting all major aspects lucidly and fairly.

**Adoption Helper**, Toronto, M4C 1Z6; Monthly publication "Devoted to helping people adopt" with articles, news of national and provincial legislation and international developments.

**Guide to Adoption** New Hope Communications, New York, 2000. Step-by-step overview of the adoption process plus detailed listings for hundreds of licensed adoption agencies, support groups, and attorneys nationwide. Also an overview of adoption options and details on the most common ways to adopt a child today. 1-800-372-3300

# Developmental Delays, Effects of Substance Abuse

## Fetal Alcohol Syndrome, Fetal Alcohol Effect

## Books

**The Broken Cord**, by Michael Dorris, Harper & Row, 1989. Account by single adoptive father of his oldest son, born with severe FAS. Tapestry says: Anyone who adopts a child with a family history of alcohol or substance abuse must read this book.

**Reaching Out to Children with FAS/FAE**, a Handbook for teachers, counselors, and parents who work with children affected by Fetal Alcohol Syndrome and Fetal Alcohol Effects, by Diane Davis. Center for Applied Research in Education, West Nyack, NY. 10995

**Fantastic Antone Succeeds!:** Experiences in Educating Children with Fetal Alcohol Syndrome, edited by Judith Kleinfeld and Siobhan Wescott, University of Alaska Press, 1993.

## Articles, Periodicals, Support Groups

*FAS/FAE: A Practical Guide for Parents* by Jim Slinn, 1994: helpful hints for parents of children with FAS/FAE, from Parents Resource Network, 540 W. International Airport Rd., Anchorage, AK 99518-1110. (907) 474-6389

**"Fetal Alcohol Syndrome: The Impact on Children's Ability to Learn,"** National Health/Education Consortium, 1001 Connecticut Ave. N.W. Suite 310, Washington, DC 20036, (202) 822-8405, fax 872-4050.

**F.A.S. Times**: Fetal Alcohol Syndrome. Family Resource Institute Newsletter, P.O.Box 2525, Lynnwood, WA 98036. E-mail, vicfas@hotmail.com; www.fetalalcoholsyndrome.org. Excellent newsletter listing suppot networks in 28 states and Canada, New Zealand and Sweden. Editor, Jocie DeVries; 1-800-999-3429 or 1-253-531-2878.

**FAS/FAE Information Service**, Canadian Centre on Substance Abuse. Information, bibliographies of recent publications. www.ccsa.ca/fasgen.htm

**National Organization for Fetal Alcohol Syndrome**, 216 G St. N.E., Washington, DC 20002, 1-800-666-6327. www.nofas.org. Information and referrals to support groups and specialists, training and materials in the U.S. and abroad.

**Council on Alcoholism & Drug Abuse of Bergen, Inc.** Support Network for Adoptive, Foster and Biological Parents of FAS/FAE and Other Drug-Affected Children. Ms. Ronnie Jacobs, (201) 488-8680 EST. Information on US support groups, services, and specialists.

**Growing with FAS**, 7802 S.E. Taylor, Portland, OR 97215. National parent-founded and operated information network on FAS; Pamela Groves, editor of quarterly newsletter: (503) 254-8129.

## Other Developmental Delays

Guidelines for Adopting Drug-Exposed Infants and Children. Dr. Ira J. Chasnoff, the Child Study Center, Chicago IL (312) 362-9607; e-mail nti@cr-triangle.org Dr. Chasnoff, the leading expert on the effects of prenatal drug or alcohol exposure, presents a complete review of what is known about the effects of prenatal alcohol and other drug exposure on the infant and child. An easy to use guide for parenting interventions for children through school age.

New Developments: New angles on Developmental delays. Developmental Delay Resources, Patricia S. Lemer, M.S. Bus. NCC, Executive Director. Quarterly newsletter. (301) 652-2263; www.devdelay.org. referrals for doctors and therapists throughout U.S.

Exceptional Parent Magazine: Parenting Your Child with a Disability. P.O.Box 1807, Englewood Cliff NJ 07632, 1-800-535-1910. Information, guidance, and emotional support for parents of children with physical disabilities, developmental delays and special health care needs; also rights and laws.

The ARC of the US, 500 E. Border St. arlington TX 76010, 1-800-433-5255 or (9817) 261-6003. Non-profit organization for mentally retarded citizens, with 1500 chapters across the U.S., Newsletter.

**Learning Disabilities Association of America,** 4156 Library Road, Pittsburgh, PA 15234, or call 412-341-1515. Many chapters across the U.S.; support, advocacy and information on all aspects of LD.

**Parents and Educators Resource Center.** Information on ADHD, dyslexia, speech and language delays etc. related to learning disabilities. www.perc-schwabfdn.org/

# Attachment Disorder and Other Special Needs

## Books

**Adopting the Hurt Child,** by Gregory C. Keck, Ph.D and Regina M. Kupecky, LSW, Pinon Press, Colorado Springs, CO 1995, 239 pages. An excellent and readable handbook for parents of emotionally damaged children, by two professionals at the Attachment and Bonding Center of Ohio.

**ADHD Parenting Handbook:** Practical Advice for Parents from Parents. Proven techniques for living with your hyperactive child. Taylor Publishing Co. Dallas TX, 1-800-275-8188 CST.

**Adopting and Advocating for the Special Needs Child**, by Rita Laws and Anne Babb, Bergin & Garvey, 1997. This will be the bible for prospective parents planning a special-needs adoption, and the agencies seeking to place these children. The authors cover every aspect of adopting hard-to-place children readably, clearly, and with good humor.

**Attachment, Trauma, and Healing: Therapy for Children and Families,** by Terry M. Levy and Michael Orlans, 328 pages, 1998. Examines causes of attachment disorder and provides in-depth discussion of effective treatments.

**Hope for High Risk and Rage-Filled Children,** by Foster W. Cline, Ph.D. The concept of intrusive therapy as practiced at the Evergreen Center om Colorado, toward the goal of bonding and attachment. 287 pages, 1992.

**Residential Treatment: A tapestry of many therapies**, edited by Vera Fahlberg, M.D., Perspectives Press, Indianapolis IN 1990, 320 pages. Identifies the forces behind emotional and behavioral problems, and the ways that the child can lock the family into relstionships that prevent healing; and helps the family to find and use different methods that permit healthy development.

**Adoption and the Sexually-Abused Child**, ed. by Joan and Bernard McNamara, U. of Southern Maine, 1990. Funding contributrd by the U.S. Dept. of HHS, Children's Bureau. The editors have authored several books on understanding and helping sexually abused children. This is most helpful for parents who are considering adopting a sexually-abused child.

**Adoption and Disruption; Rates, Risks, and Responses,** by Richard P. Barth and Marianne Berry, Aldyne de Gruyter, Hawthorne N.Y., 1988. Classic study concluding that factors tending to prevent disruption include good pre-placement preparation, preferably with a group-process home study; accurate information about the child; and intensive and long-lasting post-placement services to the child and the parent.

**Can This Child be Saved?** by Foster W. Cline, M.D. and Cathy Helding. City Desktop Publications, Inc., 1999. Examines the causes of hurt children's actions and why conventional approaches often fail to reach them. Explores and validates parents' feelings and offers struggling families detailed parenting techniques that succeed with disturbed children.

## Periodicals

**News from FAIR**, quarterly newsletter of Families Adopting In Response, Palo Alto CA., a support group for adoptive or fost-adoptive parents whose children have special emotional, developmental, or physical needs; or with transracial or transcultural issues; or parents experiencing crises. An excellent publication. (650)494-3057 PST.

**the Roundtable,** Journal of the National Resource Center for Special Needs Adoption. Spaulding for Children, Southfield MI 48075. For professionals in the field, but it also lists books and videotapes, many of which could be of interest to people adopting or thinking of adopting special-needs children. 1-810-443-7080 ESTwww.Spaulding.org

**Handbook for Treatment of Attachment-Trauma Problems in Children,** by Beverly James, Lexington Books, 290 pages, 1994. Clinical suggestions for instilling trust and security in children to help them develop lasting normal relationships.

**The Post**, published by the Parent Network for the Post-Institutionalized Child, Box 613, Meadow Lands, PA 15347. (412) 222-1766, EST. Information on the serious neurological and behavioral problems that can be exhibited by many children coming from orphanages, and ways parents can identify and treat these problems.

## Support Groups

**National Information Center for Children and Youth with Disabilities** P.O. Box 1492, Washington DC 20013, (202) 884-8200, www.nichcy.org. Clearinghouse for routing parents of children with disabilities to support groups in their states; especially helpful advice on accessing educational services under the Individuals with Disabilities Education Act

**Parent Network for the Post-Institutionalized Child,** Box 613, Meadow Lands, PA 15347. A national parent-founded and operated support group for parents of children from orphanages. Bimonthly publication, The Post; many references to sources of support and information. E-mail address: NPIC@aol.com, or (412) 222-1766.

**Attachment Disorder Support Group Home Page** www.syix.com/adsg/ Articles, message forum, and answers to frequently asked questions.

**ATTACh** Association for Treatment and Training in the Attachment of Children, Joanne Fix, Director. (949) 76 0-9109 PST. www.attach.org. A nonprofit organization committed to education, training, and advocacy for all parties interested in the attachment and bonding process. Publishes Connections, a quarterly newsletter.

**Attachment Disorder Network**, Leawood KS. (913) 381-9026; publishes Hoofbeats, a newsletter serving children and families affected by attachment disorder.

## Deafness:

National Deaf Education Network and Clearinghouse is associated with Gallaudet University, 800 Florida Ave. N.E. Washington DC 20002-3695. A centralized source of information, it collects, develops, and disseminates up-to-date information on deafness, hearing loss,services to and national organizations for the deaf and hard of hearing. The cearinghouse helps to design, produce, and disseminate books, videotapes, periodicals, and other publications related to deaf and hard of hearing chileren, their families, and the professionals who serve them. It published the the 1996 pamphlet, "Adoption and Deaf People."

Voice and TTY: (202) 651-5051. (202) 651-5054 (fax). E-mail: clearinghouse.infotogo@gallaudet.edu. Web site: clerccenter.gallaudet.edu.

## Fostering or Fostadopting

**Fostering or Adopting the Troubled Child:** A Guide for Parents and Professionals, by Janet Clayton Glatz, 1998. Audenreed Press, Biddle Publishing, Brunswick ME. 152 pages. Comprehensive and realistic handbook on fostering or adopting the minority of foster children who are seriously troubled. How to reach out for skilled help and respite, and what financial aid is available.

**A Guidebook for Raising Foster Children**, by Susan McNair Blatt, M.D. Greenwood Publishing Group Inc., Westport CT 2000, 146 pages. Very new book said to be a comprehensive guide to the care of foster children; includes health, behavior, school and many other aspects of a foster child's life.

**Helping Children Cope with Separation and Loss**, by Claudia L. Jewett. The Harvard Common Press, Harvatd MA. 1982, 146 pages. A child and family therapist talks about telling a child about separation and loss, the stages of grief, and its effects---sometimes long term--on the child.

## Support Organizations

**You Gotta Believe!** The Older Child Adoption and Permancy Movement, Inc. Coney Island NY 11224. Pat O'Brien, Director. An agency promoting and locating permanent families for older foster children. 1-800-601, 1779 EST

**Orphan Foundation of America,** Vienna, VA. Eileen McCaffrey, Director. Assistance to emancipated foster children, with training and scholarships. 1-800-950-4673, or (703) 281-4226. e-mail eileen@orphans.org www.orphan.org

**Voice for ADOPTION**, Washington DC 20013, (202) 244-0926 EST. Courteney A Holden, Director. A national coalition to advocate for the adoption of waiting children and to educate the public, media, and decision-makers to their needs.

# Adopting Black, Biracial or Other-Ethnic Children

## Books

**Adoption Bibliography and Multi-Ethnic Sourcebook**, compiled and annotated by Elizabeth Wharton Van Why. Open Door Society of Connecticut, 1977, Hartford, CT 06101. Part I is a list of books, articles, periodicals, films, and some laws, and Part II lists all kinds of multi-ethnic books, toys, gifts, records, periodicals. Many of the sources given will have gone out of business by now.

**Parenting Resource Manual,** Transracial Parenting Project, North American Council on Adoptable Children. Compiled by Susan Cunningham, B.A. and Jeanette Wiedemeier Bower, M..A. July 1998, 300 p. A useful reference book for a parent planning to adopt a child of a different ethnic group, and wondering how to help the child's adjustment to American culture, and to help the child adjust to the pain that sometimes goes along. There are chapters on parenting skills, youth perspective, medical and hair care, and racism. Ethnic groups included are African-American, Hispanic, and Asian. Included are parent support groups, ethnic culture camps, publications, and organizations in existence as of 1998.

**Inside Transracial Adoption**, by transracial adoptive parents Beth Hall and Gail Steinberg, co-Directors of PACT Adoption Alliance. Perspectives Press, Indianapolis IN. 46290. 2000, 416 pages. Practical advice, recommended resources and more, for parents who are couples or single, heterosexual or gblt, and parenting children who don't match them racially. The authors deal candidly with issues of race, adoption, and children's developmental issues. (317) 872-3055; ppress@iquest.net, www.perspectivespress.com.

## Periodicals

**Black Child** by Candy Mills, 1955. (404) 364-9195, on health, education, and parenting black children, including adoption, single parenting, and black family life.

**The Red Thread** 5900 SOM Center Road #194, Willoughby, OH 44094. Edd Schultz, Publisher. A quarterly connecting the adoptive families of Chinese children, staffed by parents of Chinese children.

## Related Organizations

**Our Chinese Daughters Foundation**, supports single women and their adopted daughters from China. Quarterly OCDF Newsletter with resources, ListServ, annual Chinese Culture Camp. P.O.Box 1243, Bloomington IL 61702, (309) 862-1326, ocdfnewsletter @ yahoo.com.

**The African American Project**. apublic-private collaboration, a specialized adoption program designed to place African American children in African American homes, and reduce the number of African American children waiting for adoption. St. Paul, MN 55101,

**PACT, An Adoption Alliance.** A non-profit adoption agency solely devoted to placing newborn children of color with parents of the same or different ethnic background. PACT works with birthparents who have already decided to place their children for adoption, helping them to choose the adoptive parent)s) and working to ensure that connections to birthfamilies are maintained, if possible. San Francisco CA 94111. (415) 221-6957 PST (San Francisco) (323) 464-4005 (Los Angeles); info@pactadop.org, www.pactadopt.org. outside CA? Photolisting?

**One Church, One Child** is a national organization with chapters across the U.S. working to place black children into black adoptive homes instead of foster care, following the example of its (single!) founder, Father George Clements. Enlists churches to undertake programs to place children and assists them with brochures and follow-up information. OCOC also walks the adopting family through the process before and afterwards with hook-ups to support groups and needed assistance. Address: 1000 16th St. N.W., Suite 702, Washington DC 20036. Phone, (202) 789-4333 EST, e-mail ocoaocoi@aol.com.

**Afro-American Adoption Permanency Planning Agency,** 1821 University Ave., St. Paul; MN 55104. Marquita Stephens, Director. AAAPPA runs a nationwide photolisting program of children who are wards of the various states. The children range from newborns to fifteen years old, about evenly divided by gender. Address: 821 University Ave. St. Paul MN 55104. (651) 659-0460 CST; www.aaappa.org, and aaappa@aaappa.org.

**Institute for Black Parenting** 9920 LaCienega Blvd., Inglewood, CA 90301, (310) 348-1400.

# Adoption by Gays and Lesbians

## Periodicals

**Gay Parent Magazine: Gay Parent resources for creating and nurturing your family.** Forest Hills NY 11375. Bimonthly magazsine. (718) 793-6641, gayparentmag@banet.net. gayparentingmag.com.

**Alternative Family Magazine**, River Forest, IL 60305. Includes a long list of resources, national and state-by-state. (708)386-4770 info@altfammag.com, www.altfammag.com

**In the Family** Magazine, Takoma Park, MD 20913. Sponsors annual conference in San Francisco for mental health professionals helping glbt families with concerns. (301) 270-4771 lmarkowitz@apo.com www.inthefamily.com

**Alternative Family Matters** newsletter,Mission: to help LGBT people realize their ambitions for family, to help the mainstream community become more familiar & receptive to L?GBT families, and to promote a thriving LGBT community with new models of family and community life.Cambridge MA 02139, (617) 576-6788, altfammat@msn.com

"Two Steps Forward, One Step Back: Single and Gay Adoption in North America," in **Adoptalk,** the newsletter of the North American Council on Adoptable Children, Summer 1999. (651) 644-3056 CST. The article covers several victories and some ongoing challenges, ending on the importance of non-traditional families and hopeful signs for the future.

"Serving Gay & Lesbian Youths---the Role of Child Welfare Agencies" Recommendations from a Colloquium convened by the Child Welfare League of America on Jan. 25-26, 1991. Although addressed to the federal or private agencies that serve these youths, it is worth examining the issues faced by "this high-risk group," in the words of the pamphlet.

## Support Organizations

**Center Kids**, Lesbian and Gay Community Service Center, 1 Little West 12th St,(moving soon), New York, NY 10014, (212) 620-7310. Terry Boggis, Director. Supports glbt parents (biological or adoptive) in the tri-state area of NY, NJ, and CT. Newsletter, dues. E-mail: terry@gaycenter.org;

**Children of Lesbians and Gays Everywhere--**COLAGE. Support network organization for children of all ages, San Francisco CA 94110, (415) 861-5437 PST. kidsofgays@aol.com www.colage.com

**Family Pride Coalition** (formerly Gay and Lesbian Parents Coalition International) P.O.Box 34337, San Diego CA. 92163, (619) 296-0199 PST Family Pride is a gold mine of information for glbt parents: guides, books, newsletters, and bulletins for gay parents, children of gay parents, and spouses of gay parents. While it is chiefly aimed at biological parents, adoptive parents will find FPI a generous support source. E-mail: pride@familypride.org; www.familypride.org.

**Gay AParent**, a list-serve for lesbians/gay men interested in adoption. Good place to explore/ discuss adoption options. listserv@maelstrom.stjohns.edu

**National Center for Lesbian Rights**, 870 Market St. Ste. 570, San Francisco CA 94102. Provides legal materials, information, and referrals. (415) 392-6257 PST, www.nclrights.org., info@nclrights.org

**Gay and Lesbian Advocates & Defenders**, 294 Washington St. Ste 740, Boston MA 02108, Legal referrals and information throughout New England. (617)426-1350 (this number is a hotline from 1:30-4:30 M-F), gladlaw@glad.org, www.glad.org

**Lambda Legal Defense and Education Fund**, 121 Wall St. Ste 1500, New York, NY 10005, National legal organization, with offices in other regions of the U.S. as well. Takes on legal cases likely to be precedent-setting. (212) 809-8585. e-mail lldefny@aol.com. www.lambdalegal.com.

More websites:

website for prospective lesbian/gay parents: www.geocities.com/WestHollywood 3373.

# Adopting Internationally

## Books and Booklets

**How to Adopt Internationally---A Guide for Agency-Directed and Independent Adoptions**, by Jean Nelson-Erichsen and Heino R. Erichsen. Mesa House Publishing Div. of Two Coyotes, Inc. Fort Worth TX, 2000, 288 pages. The Erichsens founded and still direct Los Ninos International Adoption Center, one of the oldest placement agencies in the U.S., and have observed the best and some of the worst practices in intercountry adoption. Experts in ethical international work themselves, they have included a blue-ribbon group of experts. This book gives the entire process down to the forms that applicants need, from choosing an agency to post-placement and naturalization.

**With Eyes Wide Open; a workbook for parents adopting international children over age 2,** by Margi Miller, M.A. and Nancy Ward, LICSW, Childrens Home Society of Ninnesota, St. Paul MN 55108. Strongly recommended by Dr. Jenista. (651) 646-6393, www.chsm.com.

**Across the Seas---guidelines for adoptive parents**, by Ira J. Chasnoff, M.D., Margo Mahan, Psy..D, and Linda Schwrtz, Ph.D., published by the Child Study Center, Chicago, IL. Booklet, 2000. Dr. Chasnoff, one of the leading experts on international adoption medical issues, and his colleagues have listed specific and important medical and social questions parents should ask their placement agency and the orphanage, before adopting a particular child. Doctors would need the answers in order to recommend treatment and, in fact, whether or not to recommend adoption. (312) 362-9607; www.cr-triangle.org.

Health Issues in International Adoption. **Adoption Helper,** Robin Hilborn, Director. Helper Publishing, Southampton, Ont. N0H 2L0, Canada. Discusses risks, health of intercountry adoptees, pre- and post-adoption asessments, resources. (519) 797-1441 EST

## Articles

"Medical Supervision of Internationally Adopted Children," by Dr. Dana Johnson, M.D. Ph.D. and Margaret Hostetter, M.D. in **Pediatric Basics,** No. 77, Summer 96, p. 10-17. Published by Gerber Products Co. Fremont MI 49413.

"The Value of Videotapes," Adoption Medical News, Vol., VI, No. 2, January 2000, available from Adoption/Medical News, State College PA. (814) 364-2449. Authors: Marie Mitchell, RN, PNP, and Jerri A. Jenista, M.D. The vital role of videotapes: for the prospective parent(s), in presenting the child; and for the health professional, in assessing the child's growth and development. Concerns about videotape quality are included as well as recommendations for the length and content of a good tape.

## Web Sites

International Adoption, Department of State, at http://travel.state.gov/adopt.html. Short but important compilation of applicable INS regulations on immigration and naturalization, plus comments on prevention of adoption fraud and the validity of foreign adoptions in the U.S. This is one of many useful topics on the State Department site; among others are status reports on current situations with respect to adoption from particualr countries.

U.S. Centers for Disease Control and Prevention, at www.cdc.gov, offer information on diseases, travel health, prevention and more.

---

## Some characteristics of children adopted from other countries

The U.S. Immigration and Naturalization Service tracks the number of "orphan visas" issued to children adopted from abroad. In FY 1999 the total was 16,389; the highest number so fa.r. In 1996 foreign adoptions formed a little over 17% of all unrelated U.S. adoptions (NCFA Factbook); the percentage may have risen slightly since them. The five countries from which the largest number of children came in FY 1999 were Russia (4,348), China (4,101), Korea (2,008), Guatemala (1,002), and Romania (895).

# Chapter IV

## Handling Challenges

*The Jenista Guide*
## to Single Parenting

**by Jerri Ann Jenista**

(who does not cook, clean, or mow the lawn except as necessary for public health)

Being a single parent has taught me a lot of stuff. Things you don't learn by growing up in a family of nine children or even practicing as a pediatrician. Stuff you never wanted to know or thought you would ever need. Things that seem so obvious you can't understand why it took you so long to figure them out. Courtesy of four teenage girls, two cats and one extremely spoiled toddler boy, here are a few clues to simplify your life (and justify your bad habits to your mother).

Reliable day care is the key to survival. Approval for additional children should be sought from your day care provider, not your adoption agency or your family.

Good friends, usually other single parents, are a must. These are the people who will bail you out when you need to go Christmas shopping without children or you are in the hospital with pneumonia.

Never do anything when your children are asleep that you could have done when they were awake. Sleeping time should ALWAYS be reserved for more essential activities such as balancing your checkbook, taking a bath or helping the tooth fairy.

Toilet training, learning to tie shoes and other similar tortures should be put off as long as possible. Most kids will learn all by themselves, thereby saving you the trouble. And it keeps the manufacturers of Pull-ups and Velcro tennis shoes in business.

You will never have enough time, money, patience, or sex.

Your kids won't care if you have a spotless house, brand new clothes or gourmet meals. But they will remember the 105 times you played Chutes and Ladders, all the books you read together, and the Ninja Turtle costume you made out of a cardboard box.

The telephone is the link to the sane world and allows you time to fold the laundry while commiserating with your other single parent friends.

Talking to the cats is worth hours of therapy. They are never critical and (almost) never talk back.

The four food groups are diet Coke, chocolate, Taco Bell and take-out Chinese.

Making beds is a waste of time you could use more productively doing something else, like talking to the cats. Besides, a made bed inhibits you from taking a nap at 10 a.m.

Any fire drill at home should include a plan to save the cats, the Christmas ornaments and the photo albums.

Books are more important than food.

Handicapped children grow up into handicapped adults, not just larger versions of their younger selves.

Use your nice towels and linens, the good dishes and glasses and all those scented soaps right now. You won't care about them later.

Sleeping in their clothes, eating pizza for breakfast, putting away their own laundry and not having a TV does not harm children.

You can adjust to almost any degree of physical, mental, or emotional abnormality in your household and still think your life is "normal."

The plumbing, electrical and heating systems in your house are always in a merely temporary state of good repair.

Everything you hate most about yourself, your children will copy. But they make up for it by doing something great you never would have thought of.

When you are gone, the only people who will miss you longer than a few days are your family. So, start making good memories for them right now.

The Jenista Family, 1996: Anni, 11; Ro, 13; Subhendu, 2; Louisa, 13; Julia, 11

## A Note on Two Specific Problems:

# 1. Fetal Alcohol Syndrome

**Fetal Alcohol Syndrome** — FAS — and the less severe **Fetal Alcohol Effect** are the miserable results when a pregnant woman drinks alcohol. The baby is irreversibly damaged, to a greater or lesser degree. The degree of injury depends on the mother's age, the amount she drinks, and the periods during her pregnancy when she drinks most, and most steadily. The damage appears to be permanent, even if the children are adopted by loving parents determined to provide as much stimulation and education as they possibly can. The long-term studies that produced this conclusion were made at a time when FAS and FAE were not widely recognized, however, and new programs designed to circumvent some of the specific symptoms may offer hope of a better outcome.

**The Effects:** FAS children often show central nervous system abnormalities, including seizures; they usually display moderate to severe mental retardation, learning disabilities, and memory problems. They may have malformations of the skeleton, heart, kidneys and other organs, especially if the mother also took drugs (less likely in Eastern Europe). They can show psychosocial problems such as poor judgment, difficult behavior, short attention span, inability to "connect" with other children and adults, sometimes hyperactivity. Children who only have Fetal Alcohol Effect may have normal or almost normal IQs, but are likely to display moderate to serious behavior problems as they grow older.

**Detecting Fetal Alcohol Syndrome** or Fetal Alcohol Effect is not easy. In severe FAS there are identifiable facial deformities: a small head (less than 33 cm at birth), small, almond-shaped eyes with "oriental" folds at the inner corners, a broad nose with a low bridge, no vertical groove between the nose and upper lip, thin upper lip, small and low-set ears. By adolescence, however, these characteristics may decrease, and many children whose mothers drank during pregnancy do not appear to have FAS. The most reliable indicator is prenatal alcohol use. Many women who use alcohol also take other drugs, or smoke, and the small head size or behavioral abnormalities of a newborn can be induced by these other maternal behaviors as well.

What the adoption agency, or hospital or custodial body in the United States, must do is to collect as much information as possible, especially on the birthmother--was she an alcoholic? Why was the child surrendered? If the child is a toddler or older, are there photographs at different stages of the child's life? If the child is developmentally delayed, are there other reasonable explanations, such as institutional living, chronic illness, past neglect or abuse? How well is the child's daily behavior recorded? Does the agency seem to try to downplay problems and stress only favorable aspects? **Videotapes of the child may be helpful here.** If there is a question in the prospective parent's mind, she/he should borrow the tape and show it to her pediatrician and/or a pediatric neurologist.

**Varying Impact of FAS:** If the mother was quite young, she is less likely to have ingested enough alcohol to injure her fetus severely; if this is the mother's fourth or fifth child, however, the likelihood increases. If she drank only part of the time she was pregnant, certain effects may not have occurred. It is said that body structure and the neural system develops in the first trimester, growth in size and the beginning of intelligence in the second, and further intellectual development in the third.

Judith Kleinfeld, co-editor of *Fantastic Antone Succeeds!* (See Resources, Chapter III) points out that the level of damage and characteristics of FAS/FAE varies with the individual. She takes a much more optimistic outlook than other professional observers, writing: "It is not true that all children prenatally affected by alcohol are severely damaged . . . prenatal alcohol abuse has very different effects on different children. Some children have indeed suffered severe damage to the brain and central nervous system, are mentally retarded, or have severe learning problems, despite average IQ scores. But other children . . . have only subtle learning problems. Moreover, some children appear to escape entirely, even though their mothers abused alcohol during pregnancy."

The leading expert on the effects of prenatal drug or alcohol exposure is Dr. Ira J. Chasnoff, medical director of the Child Study Center in Chicago, IL. Dr. Chasnoff agrees that some children show little long-term effect, and says the degree is not only related to the amount of fetal drug and/or alcohol ingested, but to the environment the child is raised in. Each child needs to be evaluated separately. The most frequent and noticeable effect was in the child's behavior, a significant problem with about 20% of the children he has seen. Difficulties in learning were sometimes diagnosed under Attention Deficit Disorder, with or without Hyperactivity; Difficulties in peer relationships often included aggression and impulsivity.

Among children with similar behavior problems in both groups, he found the severity less among adopted children, and feels that many of the issues with prenatal drug exposure can be addressed through early recognition and intervention.

Dr. Chasnoff advises parents considering the adoption of a drug-exposed child first to find out the resources available in the community. He suggests contacting the pediatrics department at a university-based hospital for a child-development program, or finding a pediatric psychologist or a Fetal Alcohol Syndrome program. Look for a program with a strong clinical component, that does not minimize the problem of drug exposure. His program sometimes uses medication, but the treatment in most cases involves a variety of behavioral management techniques individually designed for the child.

## 2.  Are Children Endangered by Orphanage Life?

Orphanages are widely used throughout China, in some Latin American countries, and throughout Eastern Europe in Russia and the countries formerly part of or under the influence of the USSR, for children from infancy to the teen-age years. Struggling with the economic calamity of communism and its aftereffects, the Eastern European countries have not been able to afford good pay for training of caregivers in these orphanages, or equipment and supplies to the degree necessary. Often, though, good medical personnel are available, if not on staff, and medical care is provided to correct such disabilities as club foot, cleft palate, hare lip, etc. On the other hand, other diagnoses or information on the child or the child's background and history before coming to the orphanage are sketchy or puzzling.

Information on Latin American orphanages is not widely available. Despite scare stories in international media, conditions in Chinese orphanages appear to be adequate and responsible, despite staff limitations.

The most important aspect of child development is the way the infant brain develops: From day one, an infant needs to have the stimulation that comes with touch, eye contact, and comforting; with response to hunger, wet diapers, and tummyaches; and, if possible, with love. This sensory input helps the neurons and the synapses connecting them in the entire brain to develop and subsequently to process sights, sounds, smells, taste, and touch to create an understandable environment for the child. Comforting and response teaches the child to trust, and to respond to others, particularly caregivers. In much of the time, in far too many institutions, caregivers are too overburdened or too ignorant of good practice to provide this attention, and the result is

developmental delay to a minor or extremely serious degree.

What is the result of inattention? Thais Tepper, founder of the Parent Network for the Post-Institutionalized Child, cites study after study showing that the lack of stimulation of the senses can produce symptoms including over-sensitivity to touch, motion, sights, or sounds. Conversely, there may be such under-sensitivity that the child seeks out self-abusive or even painful activities such as autism-like rocking or head-banging; coordination problems; delays in speech, language, motor skills or academic achievement. The term for this pattern is Sensory Integration Dysfunction. The other serious problem that some children from some orphanages display is Attachment Disorder, which arises when an infant learns that when he is hungry or in pain, no one comes; and that the adults around her constantly change, and that no one of them is devoted to her personally. A child with Attachment Disorder, all studies agree, can exhibit some or more of these symptoms: indiscriminate affection with strangers, lack of ability to give or receive affection appropriately, extreme efforts to control self or others, chronic lying, learning delays and disorders, lack of conscience, and poor peer relationships. Such a pattern can drain a parent of energy and hope.

What is the degree of risk? Opinions vary on the degree and extensiveness of "orphanage developmental delay." Several studies have been made of the early, horrifying days of Romanian adoptions after the fall of Ceausescu; Lois Melina (editor of *Adopted Child*) cites one by Victor Groze, Ph.D., from Case Western University, who looked at 475 children adopted between 1990-1993, two-thirds of whom had been in orphanages or other institutions. Only thirty percent or less had marked developmental problems, but a high proportion of the latter came from the institutionalized group. Of those who rocked themselves, for instance, 93% were from institutions. Of the oversensitive children, 87% had come from institutions.

Admittedly, Romanian orphanages under the Ceausescu regime were uniquely awful; no other country had anything like them. Dr. Groze found, however, that parents of the children in his study reported remarkable progress in their children's physical, language, and other developmental milestones. There seems to be a feeling on the part of trained observers that Russian orphanages provide generally better care than the earlier Romanian institutions, and that Romanian orphanages today are able to provide better care since the outpouring of attention and assistance in reaction to the revelations of the early 1990's.

What should parents look for? Parents should ask their agency to find out how old the child was when he/she came to the orphanage, and how long the child has been there. Dr. Liz Randolph at the Attachment Center at Evergreen, Colorado seems to feel that ideally a child should be removed from an orphanage to a permanent family before age one; before age two at the latest. Pediatrician Myron Winick, in a 1975 study of undernourished children, found that those who had been adopted by age three were normal in growth and intellectual development, in contrast to children adopted at a later age. Even older orphanage children, however, may well have come into care as toddlers or later after a reasonably normal family life, and may have achieved normal developmental milestones, including ability to attach to parental figures, before they were orphaned.

Dr. Mary K. Alvord is a psychologist in Silver Spring, Maryland, who specializes in children and families in her clinical work. She speaks Russian and has traveled to Russia, where she visited at least one orphanage and spoke with groups of doctors, psychiatrists, and orphanage and government officials. She takes a calm and organized approach to adoption from abroad and to working with any problems observed after adoption. Look at the child in the context of his or her environment, she advises: look at the cultural attitude toward adoption in that country, the location (urban or rural) and size of the orphanage. Try to determine the child-adult ratio, the medical and nutritional care. Ask whether the care-givers attempt to stimulate the children and respond to their needs, and the kind of schooling provided. Find out, if you can, the child's preplacement history, and how many changes of place and caretaker the orphan has undergone already. What is the child's medical condition, how well does he/she get along with the other children, how well does the child speak his/her own language?

One excellent tool is a videotape of the child in the playroom, playground, or crib, with sound if possible. Find a good pediatrician who knows something about institutionalized children and is willing to look at the videotape and the medical and social information provided. Sometimes this information is pretty sketchy, and the translation of the medical diagnoses can be scary because of different understandings of medical terms. Ask the pediatrician if you can call him or her from Eastern Europe, if you feel it necessary. [See Doctors, p. 64]

Much of this information will be hard to obtain from the source agency in this country, but press for it. Most agencies will do their best to provide information, but if you get the feeling that the agency is primarily interested in the fee, look elsewhere.

When the child comes home to a completely strange environment, populated with talkative and demonstrative people whom he cannot understand and who do not understand anything he says, take him for a medical examination but otherwise, let the adoption settle down for a few weeks or even months, advises Dr. Alvord. Hasty psychological examination of a non-English-speaking child can miss and misinterpret: for example, a child intensely frustrated at not being able to communicate verbally can be seen as full of rage, a child with chronic ear infections can appear to have difficulty with auditory processing. If, after a reasonable time for observation, and a comprehensive evaluation (bilingual if possible), you still feel that your child has problems in one or more areas, Thais Tepper recommends that you not ignore these problems. "Do not believe that your child's problems will disappear with time. Early evaluation and therapy is imperative." There are steps you can take, and steps for which you need the advice and help of specialists.

Think of the future: You may consider your child to be healthy and normal, or you may discover problems you can handle, or you may feel that you want to adopt **this child** no matter what the risk. Many children are survivors; in most cases the damage, if any, from institutional life can be ameliorated or counteracted. Look down the road, and try to imagine your child as a teenager, and a young adult, and what will be involved in helping this child adjust and grow for the rest of his or her life.

# Common Medical Problems Seen in Newly Arrived Adopted Children

**by Jerri Ann Jenista, M.D.**

*The parent who is prepared in advance of the placement to face a broad range of medical problems is likely to cope well. The worst scenario is having to deal with an unexpected and possibly life-threatening condition at the same time you are trying to adjust to new parenthood.*

I could write several books on all the medical issues that you might have to face with your newly adopted child. The following is neither comprehensive nor all-inclusive. I have attempted only to give you an outline of the most common or worrisome problems. Resources for detailed evaluations and advice are listed at the end of the article.

There are several kinds of problems one has to consider in any adoption:

o   short term infectious diseases (i.e., lice, chicken pox, hepatitis A)
o   chronic infectious diseases (i.e., tuberculosis, hepatitis B, HIV)
o   chronic medical conditions (i.e., cerebral palsy, fetal alcohol syndrome)
o   issues related to growth (i.e., malnutrition, pubertal timing, dental problems)
o   issues related to neglect or institutional care (i.e., delayed development, sexual abuse).

Although some of these are clearly more important in international adoption and others are bigger concerns for domestic placements, in the past decade the problems of adopted children have become more universal. "Exotic" diseases such as tuberculosis can be seen in a child born in the United States. Previously "unheard of" issues in international adoption, such as fetal alcohol syndrome or recognized sexual abuse, are almost as common in foreign as in domestic waiting child listings.

The parent who is prepared in advance of the placement to face a broad range of medical problems is likely to cope well. The worst scenario is having to deal with an unexpected and possibly life-threatening condition at the same time you are trying to adjust to new parenthood. If you thought a new baby and a trip to China or Russia was hard, throw in unexpected chronic hepatitis B. Or how about an acting-out pre-teen who has her first menstrual period in second grade?

I advise prospective parents to study the following list carefully. You will feel enormously relieved when you can cross off anything your child **doesn't** have. You'll feel so much better than if you count up all the diagnoses your child **did** bring along.

## Short-Term Infectious Diseases

You may worry lots about these conditions but, for the most part, they should be the least of your concerns. In general, the short-term infectious diseases are easily managed if you are prepared to deal with them.

**Diarrheal Diseases:** Viral infections are the most common cause of diarrheal illness in children; however *Salmonella, Shigella, Campylobacter* and the like are sometimes encountered in children coming from orphanages or homeless shelters. Pediatricians are all well-versed in the management of diarrhea as it is one of the most common complaints seen in offices and urgent care centers. For the most part, all you have to do is pour in enough fluid at the top to match the amount of fluid coming out the bottom. It is the unusual child who will need intravenous fluids or antibiotics. However, be sure to wash--scrub--your hands with soap **and water**, including under the fingernails, as adults don't do well with these kinds of illnesses.

**"Exotic" conditions:** Included here are infections such as typhoid fever, cholera, and yaws. When you have to look on a map to find the country where your prospective child lives, you begin to worry about every weird disease ever known to man. Fortunately, these very strange diseases are extremely uncommon in immigrant or adopted children. If your child has something this unusual, neither you nor your pediatrician is likely to figure it out. This is what infectious disease specialists are for. However, remember that even if the condition has life-threatening symptoms (such as the severe diarrhea of cholera), the treatment to prevent death is usually not something special; it is standard pediatric intensive care. Pediatricians and children's hospitals know how to provide that kind of care, even while they are trying to figure out what disease is going on.

**Hepatitis A:** Hepatitis A is a viral infection of the liver. It is endemic in most developing countries and epidemic in child care centers in the U.S. Spread by contaminated food and water, it usually causes no symptoms in the infected child. Adults, however, can be very sick for several weeks. If you are traveling, protect yourself by getting immunized with either of the new hepatitis A vaccines (Vaqta or Havrix). Skip immunoglobulin shots. They hurt, don't protect as well, and cost the same.

Since hepatitis A is shed in the stool for only a few days or weeks and does not cause chronic disease, it is not necessary to screen your newly arrived child for this condition. Just be sure to wash your hands.

**Helicobacter pylori:** Found in people living in crowded or poor circumstances, *Helicobacter* is common in institutionalized children and in Americans from lower socio-economic conditions. it is probably transmitted mostly by poor hygiene but possibly also from person-to-person. Most people with *Helicobacter* infection of the stomach are completely asymptomatic. However, this peculiar spiral shaped bacterium is the major cause of peptic ulcer disease. It also may be related to some cases of stomach cancer after many years of infection.

Although this is not really an acute infectious disease and screening is not routinely recommended for adopted or immigrant children, *Helicobacter* isa disease to keep in the back of your mind. If your child has gastro-intestinal symptoms such as chronic pain, bloating, poor weight gain and so on that are not explained by more common problems such as giardiasis or lactose intolerance, then think *Helicobacter*.

Although the best diagnostic technique is biopsy of the stomach wall, there are blood tests available also. Treatment is by a combination of antibiotics and anti-ulcer drugs over a period of several weeks. Occasionally, a second course is necessary to get rid of the organism.

**Intestinal worms and parasites:** The creepy crawly worms that most parents are worried about are unusual except in the older child or the child who has lived on the streets. Don't panic if you see these in the stool even many months after arrival. They've been there a long time. Most are not contagious to the family. Just be careful about handwashing and see your doctor soon. There are excellent safe drugs for virtually all parasites, although they may have to be specially ordered.

Small infants and older children who have been exposed to poor quality water are more likely to have protozoal (one-celled) parasites such a *Giardia* or *Entamoeba histolytica*. These are diagnosed by microscopic examination of the stool. Often, in the child who has been infected for many weeks or months, there are no symptoms. Thus, all children should be screened at least once after arrival for these parasites. Because these are spread by poor hygiene, you can acquire them from your child. Be sure to wash your hands carefully after diaper-changing and toileting activities.

**Lice:** Lice are common in poor crowded institutional settings but, as any parent can tell you, they are also the bane of many U.S. elementary school classrooms. Except for Korean or Guatemalan foster care, you should anticipate that your child may have lice.

Lice are little hopping grey bugs about 1/8 inch long. Usually what you see are the nits or egg cases. These are dandruff-sized white dots stuck to the hair shaft. You have to pull them off one at a time. **They do not brush or comb out.** Nits on the hair shaft more than one-half inch out from the scalp are not live. The best places to look for nits are behind the ears and at the nape of the neck. If in doubt, treat.

Treatment is easy. The best drug is Nix (permethrin) bought without prescription. It is safe at all ages. Wash the hair, put on Nix like creme rinse for ten minutes and then rinse. It is 99% effective. To be safe, re-treat ten days later. If you have been living with the child longer than a day before you recognize the lice, you may want to treat yourself also. Don't believe the instructions on the Nix box. The fine-tooth comb does not remove the nits. Pick them out, ignore them, or cut the hair.

While you are putting on the Nix, wash all clothes and bedding. Alternatively, run them thorugh a hot dryer or leave them in bright sunlight for a day. There is no need to treat rugs, furniture, etc. You may want to wash a cloth car seat cover.

**Malaria:** Malaria, a parasite of red blood cells, is spread by the bite of certain mosquitoes. In North America, transmission is highly unusual except in certain special circumstances. Thus, you are not going to acquire the disease from your child. Malaria is actually quite rare in adopted children but can be life-threatening if not diagnosed and treated properly. Suspect this condition in a child with an unexplained high fever who comes from near the U.S.-Mexican border, Africa, any Asian country, the southern states of the former Soviet Union, and low-lying areas of Latin America.

**Measles:** This viral infection is rarely encountered in the U.S. and so your doctor may not recognize it. Within the first two weeks of arrival, if your child develops a high fever with cough, conjunctivitis and runny nose with an all-over red rash, think measles. This is an important diagnosis to make as your doctor may want to take special infection-control precautions before seeing your child. The infection is extremely contagious to unimmunized children; the pediatrician will probably want to see your child after hours when there are no small babies in the office.

There is no specific anti-measles treatment; however, children should receive an injection of vitamin A to try to prevent a more serious course.

**Scabies:** Like lice, scabies is a very common skin condition in children from poor or crowded settings. This skin parasite may be very difficult to recognize, especially if the sores are infected or partially treated. If in doubt, ask your dermatologist to scrape a lesion to look for the mite under the microscope. If in doubt, treat anyway.

Skip the old treatment, Kwell (lindane). The new, safe drug is Elimite (permethrin), available by prescription only. Apply from head to toe on kids, below the neck on adults, at bedtime. Wash off the next morning. Repeat **once** in 10-14 days.

The itchy lesions will NOT go away with anti-scabies treatment. This is not recurrent scabies; it is the allergic reaction to scabies. Treat with hyrdocortisone cream. The day you wash off the Elimite, wash all bedding and clothing. Bleaching is not necessary; it is the heat that kills the mites. Coats, stuffed toys, pillows, etc. should be run through a hot dryer or left in a closed plastic bag for two weeks. Vacuum rugs and furniture but anti-mite sprays are not necessary.

**Chronic Infectious Diseases:**

Knowledge about treatment and the long-term prognosis for many chronic infectious diseases is changing dramatically. Because of AIDS and the complications it induces, the pace of research seems to be advancing almost monthly. What your doctor knows and what you read in medical textbooks about many of these infections is outdated every few months.

Although none of the conditions listed below is to be ignored, most are quite manageable. Often the social questions are worse than the disease itself.

**CMV:** Cytomegalovirus is in the class of herpes viruses along with chicken pox and the cold sore virus. It causes diseases like the common cold and infectious mononucleosis. Once you have the virus, it is in your body for life although it will not cause you harm unless your immune system is destroyed (as in AIDS or cancer treatment). CMV is spread by contact with body fluids such as saliva and urine and is endemic in child care centers in North America and in any situation where there is crowding or poor hygiene.

In most people, CMV is an inconsequential infection. However, if a mother acquires infection during the pregnancy, the unborn baby can suffer severe effects such as mental retardation, seizures, deafness and blindness. The condition may be progressive so that the child will actually get worse for months to years. The only treatment is experimental and has not yet proven to be of any benefit to such children.

CMV is acquired by virtually all people in developing countries before the age of ten years; thus, congenital CMV is highly unusual. In North America, about 50% of adults have not had infection and so congenital disease is occasionally seen in newborns. Infection acquired before pregnancy can be passed on to the baby but with much less severe effects. The infants are born normal and have a small risk of mild progressive hearing loss in the pre-school years. For this reason, routine screening at birth for CMV is practiced in Canada. In the U.S., we rely on normal well-child check-ups to detect any children with suspected hearing problems.

CMV occasionally comes up in domestic adoption when it is one of several sexually transmitted diseases a mother may have had, or when the newborn has suspicious symptoms. Evaluation of the child is not difficult and you should be able to get appropri ate counseling about this disease from any neonatologist or pediatric infectious disease specialist.

In older children and children from other countries, screening for CMV is not recommended unless the child has symptoms specific to CMV. Since the infection is so common in institutional settings, routine screening will identify many positive children. Without symptoms, there is no treatment and knowing this result will only unfairly label the child.

**Hepatitis B:** Chronic infection (that is hepatitis B surface antigen persisting for longer than six months), occurs in about 5% of all international adoptees and in less than .5% of U.S. children. There are many excellent resources for information about this infection, its prognosis and treatment, and the social and emotional implications.

The knowledge of a child's chronic infection belongs to you and the child. You do not need to tell everyone you know while you learn about the disease. You can make that decision later. Day care centers, schools, churches and others usually do **not** need to be informed of your child's status.

Do not be alarmed by what is written in old textbooks or what your doctor tells you unless he keeps up on hepatitis. Hepatitis B research is moving very rapidly. Treatments for adults and for selected children, especially Eastern European and Russian adoptees, are available. Research is active in childhood protocols.

Hepatitis B is not a death sentence. It is a manageable disease. Most people lead full normal lives. It is only spread by blood, sexual contact, or from mother to baby, just like HIV. Household members can be protected with a three-dose vaccine series.

**Hepatitis C:** Like hepatitis B, hepatitis C causes chronic infection of the liver. Most children have no symptoms. Routine screening is not recommended for children from the U.S. or from other countries because the long-term prognosis and treatment options are unknown. (In other words, the disease may be serious but we don't have anything to offer children right now, so why bother to test?) The disease is not spread by household or casual contact, so you are not likely to acquire it from your child.

Except for a few sporadic infections in Russian children, isolated epidemics in occasional Chinese baby nurseries, and perinatally transmitted infections from intravenous drug-using mothers in the United

State, hepatitis C does not seem to be a common condition in the adopted child.

**Hepatitis D:** This viral infection of the liver is only of concern if your child also has chronic hepatitis B. Any child who is hepatitis B surface antigen positive for six months should also have a one-time screen for hepatitis D. Most children with hepatitis D have originated from Albania, Romania, and other countries around the Mediterranean.

Although the textbooks say that the combination of the two infections is extremely serious, our recent experience in the U.S. has shown that most of these children do very well. Treatment options (interferon and the like) are limited and anyone with this combination of infections should be followed by a pediatric infectious disease specialist or a gastroenterologist to take advantage of new treatments as they become available.

**HIV (Human Immunodeficiency Virus or AIDS virus):** Current U.S. immigration law does not allow a person who is HIV-positive to obtain a permanent residency or orphan visa. However, the law does not **require** testing of children under age 16 years. In countries with high rates of HIV infection, such as Haiti, Uganda, Romania and Thailand, the agency or lawyers will almost invariably test in advance of adoption proceedings. The U.S. Embassy in those countries will likely request testing if it has not been done. As of August 2000, the only known HIV-infected internationally adopted children have come from Romania, Panama, Vietnam, Cambodia, and Russia.

In low-risk areas such as Korea or the Pacific-rim countries, testing may be refused by the local authorities or may be completely unavailable. Unless the child has a high-risk history (born of a U.S. serviceman, blood transfusion from a Western donor, etc.), you are not likely to get a test and probably should not insist on it.

Most other areas of the world, South and Central America and Asia, especially India, China, and Vietnam, are epidemics waiting to explode. The risk is lower than in the U.S. but will become rapidly worse in the next decade. You must weigh carefully the true risk of HIV based on the child's history versus the risk of becoming infected during testing, i.e., by use of poorly sterilized blood-drawing equipment. In some situations, the best policy is to provide your own disposable needles and syringes, especially if you will be with the child during the blood-drawing.

HIV is not a serious risk for most adoptive families but you need to consider all local circumstances. Some judges will require HIV testing of the potential adoptive parent. Regardless of result, **any** HIV test must be repeated after arrival. HIV tests are fairly accurate but many other factors may intervene before the test result reaches a piece of paper.

In domestic adoption, HIV risk is somewhat different for newborns versus older children. Theoretically, the birth mother will have been counselled and will have received appropriate screening during pregnancy for many diseases, including HIV. However, many states have laws in place that prevent you from requiring a person to be HIV tested or even to ask if the person has ever even had a test. Unless the mother is voluntarily tested, you will have to wait until the birth parents' rights are terminated or until a court or agency has custody of the child before requesting testing. However, for most newborns, some assessment of risk can be made ahead of time by a well-trained social worker.

Although a baby under 18 months of age who tests positive may not have HIV infection (but only antibody from his infected mother), it is not necessary to wait until after this age to make a determination of true infection. For the child already residing in the U.S., university and research hospitals are now capable of making an accurate diagnosis of HIV infection within days or weeks in virtually all children. Such tests should routinely be undertaken in any child who tests positive, whether or not the child is to be adopted, as early treatment will vastly improve the quality and length of the child's life.

Older children, especially those from multiple foster care placements, have often been tested as part of their own medical assessment. Again, you must know the laws of the child's state before you can request a test; however, an assessment of risk should have been done long before you ever get to that point in an adoption proceedings.

**Parasites:** Long-term parasitic infections such as paragonimiasis, schistosomiasis, neurocysticercosis and others are quite unusual in internationally adopted children. Domestically born children have little risk unless they have traveled or have had contact with immigrant communities. Older children may have acquired these parasites in the toddler or preschool years, remaining without symptoms for many years. Do not screen for any of these conditions. Just keep in mind that, if your child develops an unexplained chronic illness, especially of liver, lung, or nervous system, that you should remind the physicians where he was born and lived his first few years of life.

An excellent resource for thinking about and diagnosing strange conditions from around the world is found in:

Jenista, J.A. (2001). The immigrant, refugee, or internationally adopted child. In Jensen, H.B., R.S. Baltimore, R.I. Markowitz, and A.B. West (Eds.). *Pediatric infectious diseases: principles and practice,* 2nd edition. Norwalk, CT: Appleton and Lange. *or*

Wilson, M.E. (1991). *A world guide to infections: Disease, distribution, diagnosis.* New York: Oxford University Press.

**Syphilis:** Syphilis is encountered in the medical records of many children referred for adoption from the republics of the former Soviet Union. Although some of these diagnoses are in doubt, the infants do seem to get appropriate antibiotic treatment. In the United States, there is a dramatic increase in congenital syphilis; many states have reinstated their old policies of screening all babies at birth, regardless of the mother's history.

In older children, a new diagnosis of syphilis is highly unusual. When the child comes from a tropical country, a positive syphilis test may actually be an indicator of another disease such as yaws or pinta.

Although untreated congenital syphilis may have severe and irreversible effects on the child, especially on the brain, early treatment may prevent all complications. The best scenario is when the mother's infection is found and treated early in pregnancy. The worst case is when the baby is born with signs of infection and is not treated for the first months or years of life.

Any record with syphilis indicated should be scrutinized carefully. The majority of children will have complete resolution of all laboratory signs of infection without any physical signs of disease at all. Don't reject a referral because of syphilis alone. Look at the whole baby and consider all the evidence before making a decision.

Long-term follow-up with the child who has had anti-syphilis treatment is basically following laboratory tests to normal, making sure there are no associated infections such as HIV or hepatitis B and monitoring the child's developmental status.

**Tuberculosis (TB):** TB is a relatively common diagnosis in adopted children, both in the U.S. and from other countries. The same social conditions that allow a child to become available for adoption (homelessness, prison, poverty, poor medical care, drug or alcohol use and so on) are the same conditions that allow for the spread of TB. Tuberculosis is easily treated if diagnosed early (preferably when the only sign is a positive skin test). The greatest problem in diagnosing the disease is failing to test for it.

The majority of children from other countries will have received the anti-tuberculosis vaccine, BCG. Many doctors have a difficult time deciding what to do about skin testing if the child has had BCG. If the child is well and the BCG site is still oozing or crusted, wait one year past the BCG date to place a PPD. If the child develops a tuberculosis-like illness in that year, place a PPD anyway.

If the BCG is healed or more than one year old, the PPD is accurate. Read it like any other PPD. A positive PPD must be treated with at least one drug. More drugs may be needed if there is chest x-ray or other evidence of active TB. Children with TB are not contagious to family members because they usually do not have cavitations (holes) in their lungs. Neither the child nor the family needs to be isolated.

# Chronic Medical Conditions:

The clue to dealing with chronic medical conditions is understanding your level of comfort with uncertainty. For certain well-defined conditions such as thalassemia (a blood disorder), ventricular septal defect (hole between the lower two chambers of the heart) or a missing limb, you can pretty much guess what treatment will be needed, what complications are to be anticipated, and what the best and worst outcomes might be.

More vaguely defined conditions such as moderate cerebral palsy, neurofibromatosis (a disease of skin, nerve, and other tissues) or extreme prematurity with multiple complications carry a far higher degree of uncertainty. You can be sure some deficit is present but only time will tell you whether the course will be benign, expensive or life-threatening.

**Neurological Conditions:** Chronic neurologic conditions such as cerebral palsy, learning disabilities, attention deficit and hyperactivity are common in waiting children in all countries around the world. Although some of these problems are clearly traced to prematurity, low birth weight, neonatal infection, maternal illness, prenatal drug or toxin exposures or severe malnutrition, many children have no suspicious antecedent history. Because of this, and because of the difficulty in accurately diagnosing these conditions in infancy, there can never be any guarantees in infant adoption.

The best neurological evaluation can only tell you how the child is doing on the day of the examination. There are no tests of development or intelligence that have perfect "predictive value," that is, that can tell who is going to succeed in school or need lifetime support. Of course, some good estimates can be made about a child's potential based on our past experience with similar children.

This is relatively simple when we are talking about a straightforward case such as a baby born at appropriate weight, eight weeks early with no complications. Such a scenario is common in the nurseries of North America; we have good statistics and long experience to use in advising families. However, when you throw in neglect, institutional living, unknown drug or other exposures, malnutrition and inadequate developmental evaluation, it is much harder to make predictions for prospective families. Often, the best you can hope for is a judgment about how this child looks and acts compared to children who have come from the same circumstances.

Remember, that although the prospect of trying to predict outcome for any one child is incredibly daunting, the majority of children are normal: that is, with appropriate support in the family and educational setting, they can do well.

**Cocaine or drug exposure:** Our knowledge about prenatal cocaine exposure is changing continually. Some babies, but not all, have severe neurologic problems such as stroke or drug withdrawal symptoms. Many of the long-term effects of cocaine exposure may be due to social environment rather than the drug itself. Such children may do very well in a new environment, that is, in an adoptive home.

Most of these babies have been exposed to more than just cocaine; usually also to nicotine, marijuana, alcohol and other substances. These babies are smaller at birth and tend to stay in the hospital longer. Their long-term developmental outcome in adoptive families is unknown. A potential parent must recognize that **no one** can predict the outcome for any specific child.

The best resource pulling together the known information on perinatal drug exposure is found in:

Edelstein, S.B. (1995). *Children with prenatal alcohol and/or other drug exposure: Weighing the risks of adoption.* Washington, D.C. Child Welfare League of America Press, 105pp. (Order from CWLA at 440 First Street, N.W., Suite 310, Washington, DC 20001-2085).

**Congenital defects:** Children with various handicapping conditions such as scars, amputations, cleft lip/palate, heart disease, post-poliomyelitis, etc. are frequently available for adoption. When the child is in another country, it may be almost impossible to predict the true diagnosis, the extent of involvement and the prognosis for repair or rehabilitation. In general, physical defects that are devastating in developing nations (such as cleft lip), are easily managed in the U.S. However, there are some things that cannot be fixed no matter how excellent the medical care provided.

When thinking about a child with a chronic medical condition, be sure to consult with an expert in the condition, usually at a university or children's hospital. Ask for the "differential diagnosis," that is, the list of conditions that might possibly be present if the one the child carries is incorrect. Ask what is the range of outcomes for children with that defect. Talk to other parents who have adopted similar children. Make sure your insurance company will cover the full range of services possibly required. Visit a classroom in your school district that this child might be expected to attend.

If the child is in the U.S., full information should be available. If not, ask why. There is almost no circumstance where a child should be placed without having had at least preliminary investigations into the implications of a congenital defect or disease. Virtually all such children, when placed by a public agency, should be eligible for adoption maintenance and/or medical subsidy. You should make sure you have investigated the possibilities for subsidy thoroughly, just in case you lose your health insurance or the child exceeds lifetime insurance benefit maximum.

The National Organization for Rare Disorders provides extensive listings of medical experts, parent support groups, basic information and research centers for almost every condition you could ever think of. Contact the office at 1-800-999-NORD.

**Fetal Alcohol Syndrome:** FAS is the most common preventable cause of mental retardation in North America. Statistics vary on how commonly this diagnosis is made in children in special education programs; however, it is clear from waiting children photo listings that many affected children are available for adoption. This has become an issue in adoptions from Eastern Europe and the former Soviet Union also.

In a domestic adoption, an expert examiner should be able to evaluate an older child for possible FAS without great difficulty. In the newborn, the child with inadequate history or the child who is not available for examination (i.e. overseas), the task is much more difficult. One must often use a combination of guesses about the social circumstance, records of the child's growth and development and frontal facial photographs. Even so, some affected children are surely unknowingly adopted and some unaffected children are probably inappropriately labelled. Each child's case should be evaluated individually as the range of abnormality in both cognition and behavior is great.

For more information and real-life experience on single parenting an adopted child with fetal alcohol syndrome, read *The Broken Cord* by Michael Dorris (Harper & Row, 1989).

Also, an excellent readable reference work is Anne Streissguth's book *Fetal Alcohol Syndrome: A Guide for Parents and Communities.*

## Issues Related to Growth

Growth retardation, early puberty, poor dentition, age determination questions and the long-term effects of severe and moderate malnutrition are common issues as adopted children grow. Although we think about these as problems in children adopted from another country, they may be just as important for an older child adopted from foster care.

True precocious puberty, growth hormone deficiency and other rare conditions are just as rare in adopted children. However, physicians and consultants not familiar with "psychosocial dwarfism" and its associated problems may embark on lengthy, expensive and fruitless investigations of the child who does not meet middle-class American norms. The adoptive parent and the physician have to look carefully for situations that can be ameliorated or "cured" by appropriate treatment without labelling the child as "abnormal" for irreparable "defects," such as small stature.

# Issues Related to Neglect or Institutional Care

Previous sexual abuse, educational problems, abnormal social behavior, "attachment" and "bonding" difficulties are more common the older the child and the longer he or she has lived in institutional care. Little is known about how to treat these problems or even how to sort out the diagnosis in children with multiple adverse risk factors in their histories.

For an adoptive parent, it is often hard to know when a diagnosis or treatment is the current "fad" in adoption, education, psychiatry or behavior management. The best you can do for your child is:

o   Recognize that there is a problem
o   Get help early
o   Get outsiders such as the school, physician, counselor, child care providers to agree that there are issues
o   Investigate treatment options suggested by professionals, adoption publications, parent information groups, etc.

o   Don't try to cure everything; pick out the issues or behaviors that are most important for sanity, safety and the child's future independent functioning
o   Engage the professionals involved in your children's life in a dialog to develop a plan that is appropriate for your family's circumstances
o   Don't be hesitant to change the plan if things are going worse than expected after an agreed-upon period of time.

Remember that you didn't cause the child's problems. Anything you do to improve his life is an opportunity he might never have had otherwise.

A guide to many of the issues found in institutionalized children is found in:

Miller, M., and N. Ward (1996). With eyes wide open: A workbook for parents adopting international children over age one. Children's Home Society of Minnesota, 155pp. (Order from CHSM for $20.48 [including postage] at 2230 Como Ave. St. Paul, MN 55108)

---

## Some Basic Figures about Adoption:

One of the major reasons that couples and even individuals seek to adopt is inability to bear a child. The percentage of women who were infertile was 7.1% in 1995, a rate that has been pretty stable for decades. To that must be added, however, a rising number and percentage of women with "impaired fecundity"---difficulty in conceiving or carrying a child to term. In 1988 they numbered 4.9 million; 8.4% of women in childbearing years. By 1995 that number had increased to 6.1 million, and 10.2%. The pattern holds across all races and socio-economic groups. Some of the increase is probably due to the aging of the baby boom generation. (Fertility, Family Planning, and Women's Health: New Data from the 1995 National Survey of Family Growth. National Center for Health Statistics, Centers for Disease Control, 1997.)

There are five routes to adoption: **public** governmental agencies place children from the public child welfare system; **private** placement (of U.S.- or foreign-born children) by a non-profit or for-profit agency licensed by the state(s) in which it operates; **independent** placement (of U.S.- or foreign-born children) through a licensed or unlicensed facilitator; or doctor, member of the clergy, or attorney; **kinship** placement in a relative's home, with or without the services of a public agency, and

**stepparent** adoption by the spouse of the child's parent. Placement with a single parent can take place through any of the first four methods (NAIC).

The cost of adoption varies with the process: adoption of a US-born child through a public agency ranges from nothing to $2,500---and there may be subsidies if the child has special needs. Private non-profit or for-profit agency fees range from $20,000 to $45,000 (the higher fees for newborns); some agencies use a sliding fee scale based on family income. Independent adoption costs can vary from $12,000 to well over $35,000. Intercountry adoption, through agencies or independently, ranges from $15,000 to $28,000, counting travel and local agency services, depending on the agency and the country of origin (NAIC).

"Disruption" is the term used when a placement falls through before the adoption is legalized (after legalization, if an adoption fails it is said that the legal tie has "dissolved"). It seems to vary directly with the age of the child. Less than 1 percent of infant adoptions disrupt. The disruption rate for children aged 6-12 is 9.7%, and for ages 12-18 it is 13.5% (Barth and Berry, Adoption and Disruption: Rates, Risks, and Responses. Adeline deGruyter, 1988). The rate of disruption for placement of special-needs children of any age is 14.3% (Groze," Special Needs Adoption, Child & Youth Services Review, 1986).

# You Want to Adopt A
# *Special-Needs Child?*

"The flaming drapes did not burn the house down."

*"We only used 18 inpatient psychiatric days in February so we have 12 more to use later in the year if we need to."*

"Protective Services believed our version of the story."

*"I learned to spell psychotic."*

"We got there in time to pump her stomach."

*"He limped when his brother's leg was hurt."*

"I had a week without a crisis call from school."

*"We found a bodybuilder babysitter who is willing to come back a second time."*

"He has kept a job for 6 weeks now."

*"My child said I was the best mother (and he has had 12 to compare.)"*

These upbeat announcements are Selections from Christmas Letters That Were Never Sent, compiled by the participants in an adoptive support group for parents of special-needs children. Not everyone can make a good parent for a child who has been, as he sees it, rejected by his or her birth family, and then suspended in limbo for years during the processes of unsuccessful family reunification/foster care/different foster care/adoption followed by disruption. But in most cases this child can be detoured from where he or she was headed and become a healthy, loving son or daughter.

Tressler-Lutheran Adoption Services in central Pennsylvania, which specializes in placement of waiting children, says that the kind of person who makes a good adoptive parent for a special-needs child (1) has experience working with children-example; a teacher, or a health worker; and (2) has a history of overcoming personal problems herself or himself. These characteristics are more important than the age, the race, the income, the marital status, or the education of the applicant.

**Description**: Almost every waiting child over the age of infancy has hadat least s degree of emotional damage, and the longer the wait, the more intense the rage and the lower the self-esteem. Only a small proportion is retarded, and a small number has physical disabilities--cerebral palsy, spina bifida, visual impairment, deafness, Fetal Alcohol Syndrome/ Effect. Many have a learning disability and Attention-Deficit Disorder, sometimes with Hyperactivity; many have Attachment Disorder.

According to the major adoption exchanges, the great majority of waiting children are boys, and most of them are between the ages of 5 and 12. Ethnicity varies across the country: In southern states, and in large urban areas everywhere, black or biracial children form about 65% of waiting children. In the northwest United States, by contrast, 70% are caucasian. There are lots of sibling groups.

The Children's Bureau of the U.S. Department of Health and Human Services collects data in the Adoption and Foster Care Analysis and Reporting System. In July the analysts estimated that in fiscal 1999 the total number of children in out-of-home care was 550,000. About 117,000 children were in foster care awaiting placement,or in adoptive homes awaiting adoption, or had adoption in their plan, although the rights of their parents had not yet been terminated. An additional 40,000 children had alaready been adopted. This would seem to leave about 393,000 children who were not living with their birth families in 1999 but were not considered adoptable.

**Who's In Charge of Them?** Almost all the children are wards of their state governments, which have removed them from their homes because they were abused or neglected, or orphaned or abandoned. In an effort to place them, some states photolist the children directly with the national listing services-- The CAP Book, Adopt America, The Adoption Exchange; or with regional or state exchanges. In other states, the social services departments purchase the services of private adoption agencies to locate parents for these children. Occasionally, a birth-mother who is working with a private adoption agency bears a special-needs baby, usually drug- or alcohol-affected; sometimes with physical anomalies, and surrenders the baby to the agency to place.

**What are the rewards?** One was expressed by the authors of <u>Adopting the Hurt Child</u> (see Resources, Chapter III): "For all the tears and trials of parenting a hurt child, the payoffs can far exceed the heartache . . . While [the] children may not be perfect (none are), they have been given the tools to become competent, responsible, loving adults who will be contributing members of society. That is a tremendous gift to the child . . . and to all of us."

**How Do You Go About Adopting a Hurt Child?**
First, you need a home study from an agency in your area. Talk to a couple of local agencies and choose one that seems friendly and flexible. Your agency must be willing to send your finished study to other sources, and their postplacement reports as well.

If there is an agency near you that has a purchase-of-service contract with your state or county, you might be interested in a child from their list. If you are not, see if that agency would be willing to work with out-of-state exchanges and sources; otherwise you might get locked in to an agency that has limited sources and kinds of children. Look for an agency that will be actively ready to provide postplacement assistance if you need it; agencies placing waiting children don't generally want to work with applicants who will be out there alone after the child is placed.

Contact the regional or national listing exchanges (listed under Resources) directly and ask them for the nearest location of a listing book. Turn to the several websites photolisting waiting children. When you see a child in whom you are interested, ask the agency to send your home study to the public agency that has custody of the child. This child could be what Tressler-Lutheran Agency calls a "hidden gem."

It seems to be true that the custodial agency (the state or county social services department) usually prefers to place its children in its own or at least neighboring states; the better, perhaps, to keep an eye on the placement in the months following. Nevertheless, placements have occurred from distant states too. It is important to present yourself well in material accompanying the home study: A letter can describe how much you want to adopt, why you want a special needs child, how you plan to care for and locate therapy for him or her, etc. Specific experiences of yours that could illustrate your points should be included.

One good aspect of looking for a special-needs child is that placing agencies relax some of their their usual specifications for the adopting parents---for example, minimum or maximum age, gender, marital status, religious affiliation and, sometimes, sexual orientation.

**What if the Adoption Doesn't Work Out?**

A very few children have been so damaged by the abuse or the neglect of their birthfamilies and subsequent caretakers that they cannot fit into any family. When they express their rage in violent behavior toward the adoptive parents and siblings the parents may conclude that for the sanity, and sometimes the safety, of the family the child has to leave the home. Often, the child goes into residential therapy; sometimes, the adoption is ended. Technically, "disruption" means stopping a planned adoption before it is legally finalized. Ending an adoption after finalization is properly called "dissolution," but in practice the first, stronger term is used for both actions.

Sometimes, public or private agencies placing special needs children do not do an adequate job of describing both the child and the reality of adopting a child with attachment disorder, FAS, post-traumatic stress syndrome or other emotional or behavioral disorders. Sometimes, even if an agency tries to inform them, in their hurry to get a child the prospective parents simply do not listen to what the agency is trying to tell them. They find the books and articles, the actual experiences of parents, "too negative," and block them out. six months later, after the honeymoon period has ended, they may call the agency and demand that the agency take the child back, and claim that "nobody told us."

Disruption is a miserable event for everybody. The child, who may well have come from previous foster or failed adoptions, knows she has failed again, no matter how hard she may have seemed to work to cause it. If there are other adopted children, and no matter what turmoil the child has created, they will wonder if they too could be ejected from the family for bad behavior. The parents know that they have failed, and broken their commitment to the child. Sometimes they face the criticism of unaware friends, relatives, and even the agency.

The key to averting disruption is knowledge. (1) The agency must provide as much information as possible about the particular child, **before** placement, especially in adoptions from abroad. (2) The agency must provide a thorough orientation to the realities the parents may encounter, in group sessions if possible. (3) The agency must commit to providing strong support and services to the family in the months, sometimes the years, after the adoption. If the boy or girl has been adopted from foster care, the parent may have to fight for public funding of therapy, respite care, or placement in a residential institution in the most severe cases.

An article in The Future of Children: Adoption (See Resources, Chapter II) is a roundup of the literature on outcomes of special-needs adoptions. The various studies point in opposite directions a lot, but a few "predictors" and a few placement factors did stand out: Placements in "non-traditional families" (i.e., minority parents, parents with lower socioeconomic status, and **single parents**) tended to work better than those with traditional two-parent white families. Children placed at an older age, especially those in their teens, had a somewhat higher rate of disruption. Foster parents who adopt the children they have had for some time have a high rate of success.

James A. Rosenthal, Ph.D., the author of the article, observed that failure on the part of the agency to provide adequate background information on the child was a strong predictor of disruption. He also noted that financial subsidy may be the most important postadoptive service to adoptive parents and has been "integral in opening adoption opportunities to minority and low-income families and to foster parents; all groups that have experienced distinctly positive outcomes."

Counselling, of individuals and families, was not always successful, and he mentioned **parents' opinions that parent groups and contact with other adoptive parents were perhaps more helpful than therapy services.** [Emphasis added] Dr. Rosenthal commented that if therapists received education "regarding the particular dynamics and goals of special needs adoption" such services might be more successful.

---

## General Adoption Websites

**www.adopting.org** Adoption assistance information, profiles of waiting parents, resources

**www.adopting.com** The largest listing of adoption-related websites, listseres, photolistings, resources.

**www.adoption.org** Volunteer-operated adoption network.

**www.adoption.com** Members of the adoption triad plus prospective adoptive parents. Photolisting.

**www.adoptionagencies.org** Multi-agency adoption site, photolisting.

**www.adoptivefam.com** Adoptive Families Magazine

**www.celebrateadoption.org**. Improving understanding of adoption by education, public awareness.

**www..starsofdavid.org** Support and information for Jewish adoptive families

**http://directory.hotbot.com** Listings and links to other organizations, directories, publications, adoption-related information and items.

## Medical and Behavioral Topics

**www.syix.com/adsg/** Attachment Disorder Support Group of parents with children with ADSD. Articles, message forum, FAQ answers, links to related sites.

**www.ccsa.ca/** Fetal alcohol syndrome information service by Canadian Centre on Substance Abuse, bibliographies.

**www.nami.org** National Alliance for Medical Illness

**www.psych.org** American Psychiatric Organization

**www.mentalhealth.com** Links to various disorders

**www.chadd.org** Attention Deficit Disorder

**www.npnd.org** National Parent Network on Disabilities

**www.healthguide.com/** Information on ADHD, Post Traumatic Stress Disorder, Bipolar Disorder, Depression, Obsessive-Compulsive Disorder

**www.orphandoctor.com** Dr. Jane Aronson

**www.healthfinder.gov** US Dept. of Health and Human Services maintains a gateway with governmental information & links to other sites.

**www.cdc.gov** U.S. Centers for Disease Control and Prevention--information on diseases, travel health, prevention.

## Special-needs Children

**www.adoptamerica.org** Matching families with children who have special needs.

**www.wrightslaw.com** Special education law and advocacy; links to cases

**www.dssc.org/frc** federal resource center for special education

**www.ldonline.org** National Parent Network on [learing] Disabilities

**www.nacac.org** North American Council on Adoptable Children parent support groups and information on subsidies for adopting waiting children.

**www.adoptex.org** The Colorado Adoption Exchange for waiting children

**www.adopt.org** Faces of Adoption--waiting children; co-sponsored by National Adoption Center and Children Awaiting Parents.

**www.clerccenter.gallaudet.edu** information on hearing loss and deafness; also e-mail clearinghouse.infotogo@gallaudet.edu.

# Coping,
# Conscience,
## and the *Difficult* Child

by Barbara Tremitiere

*These children come to us with a history of not being good enough to keep, and with their self-esteem dragging, and their reaction is, "I won't be vulnerable again. I am going to be in control."*

I'm talking about your standard witchy kid who comes to you at the age of one, two, twelve years old; with a background of being moved from one foster home to another, at best, and at worst, a background of abuse. I am talking about the kind of stuff this kid can put you through and how you cope with it--for your sake, and for the kid's.

The agency I worked for, Tressler-Lutheran Services in York, Pennsylvania, is famous for the pre-adoption course they run for people who are thinking of adopting the kind of waiting children they place. They tell you about a lot of the hell that the kids can deliver. They bring in parents who have run this gauntlet and survived--and some that haven't, whose placements have disrupted, and they tell you why. The drop-out rate from this course may be high, but their disruption rate is much lower than normal for adoptions of hard-to-place kids like these. Incidentally, a disruption is not an easy thing for the parent, even if it feels like relief at the time. It's like the death of a child--years later, something triggers a recollection and you cry. I had a parent suicide over a disruption once, and I never take them lightly.

I have fifteen children, most of them adopted. When my former husband and I started out to adopt, my idea was that these little children were all going to gather round my feet in the evening, and raise their little faces, and we were all going to sing . . . in harmony. I was going to be Julie Andrews. I even bought a guitar and started to grow my hair. It didn't work out that way. The children wouldn't cooperate.

But we kept on adding kids anyway and I learned, often the hard way, a number of things which I am now going to pass along to you.

What you have to keep in mind is that these kids lack one important thing when they come to you, and it's called Self-Esteem. They lose it from having been moved from their original families and then from family to family, sometimes ten times. The only thing a kid has to offer is himself and his love, and every time a kid is moved, he is being told "your self and your love are not enough. I don't want it. Take it somewhere else." I remember a little girl once who expressed it like this:

I was staying in this place once, and I really liked it. I liked the parents and I really wanted to stay. The parents had two kids that were born to them who were wild. They even swore at their parents sometimes. I used to tell them "don't do that; they'll give you away," and the kids would just laugh at me. So one time I got brave and sassed the mother. "That's it," she said, "you have to go."

What are we telling these kids when that happens? Whether we love you or not depends on your behavior, not on who you are. Or we do another kind of number on them: Love depends on your looks. All our fairy tales reinforce this: ugly stepsisters, elephants with big ears, reindeer with red noses <u>are not loved.</u> No one has said to these kids, you may have funny ears and you may swear like a truck driver but I still love you. They have not had that kind of unconditional love.

So these kids come to us with a history of not being good enough to keep, and with their self-esteem dragging. A child one year old knows she's been rejected, even if she can't remember it. And what is their reaction? Whether they formulate it or not, it is often: "Nobody is going to get to me again. I won't be vulnerable; I am going to be in control."

They may also come without having developed a conscience. They have been moved around like checkers--where were they going to get a conscience? Where have they picked up a value system? You have got to give them yours, and help them to develop one of their own.

I'm not saying you have to mold these little kids into your image. You can't. Kids come to us genetically programmed by their biological parents. To illustrate, I have a daughter, now twenty-seven, named Chantel. She has been with us since she was two and one-half months old. I have had the chance to mold her little personality, right? Wrong. Ten years ago I met her birthmother for the first time, and we sat down and had a conversation. I asked her to tell me about herself and her family. She said, "my brother played the piano by ear from the time he was four years old. I play the trumpet. Both her birth-father and I were into sports--basketball, volleyball, and track, and we were very good at all three. I was almost going to be a professional basketball player. Oh yes, and I'm an actress, and if I get only one line, I steal the whole show. By the way, one thing that bothered me about her birthfather: when he got mad, he would swear for half an hour and never use the same word twice."

She just described my daughter. Chantel plays the piano by ear, since she was four, and she plays the trumpet. She's good in three sports and guess which ones; she got a college scholarship in basketball. If she has one line in a play she brings down the house, and you **know** what she does when she's angry! We think babies are better because we can "mold" them. Wrong, wrong, wrong! If they are witchy babies, you have them for a lot of witchy years. If you take teenagers, you know not only how they are glued together--weirdly sometimes, but you know how--but you don't have to work with them as long in **active** parenting.

When a child comes to you with a multiple placement history, he has a job to do in order to stay in control, and it's called "Gotcha!" You, the parent, also have a job: not to **be** got. The kid does not know or care what you consider wrong. "You don't kill the neighbor's dog; it's not nice. You don't rip up the neighbor's income tax refund check; that's not nice either." A lot of things in life you wouldn't do, but this kid might. He is always trying to figure out what upsets you--and then he will do just that.

At times, in fact, he may be behaving so obnoxiously that you feel like killing him. I don't spank my kids any more, not because physical abuse is against the law, but because I know how easy it is to get really mad at one of these little darlings, and how easily I could get carried away. Every parent, pushed to the wall, under certain circumstances, could be a child abuser. That's what happens when a little child is stronger than we are. I had to learn different ways of disciplining, and this is what I recommend to the parents I work with.

First of all, a parent who finds that she or he is no longer in control in the family needs to look for help and support. In addition to the pre-adoption course, our agency ran a post-adoption support group. Tressler-Lutheran parents don't hesitate to call me up, or to call on other parents who are going through the same problem areas. These are some of the methods I prescribe:

First, you sit down and figure out what's important to you. Write down all the things or the principles you value in life. Then figure out which of these are enforceable. Honesty may be very important to you, but is it enforceable? No. Take this little scene from daily life:

You are wheeling along the freeway with your family in the family car, and the child in the back seat is observing the speedometer. He says to you, "Ah, dad-dee, um, why does the speedometer say ah-six, ah-five, and the sign by the road says ah-five, ah-five? " and Daddy says, like all fathers say, "If I were going fifty-five on this road, people would run over me on skateboards. You have to go sixty-five to keep up with the flow of traffic." Now let's put a police car just behind you, and let's listen to this wonderful exchange. The policeman comes up to the side of the car and says, "pardon me, sir, did you know you were going sixty-five miles an hour?" Daddy says, "oh, my goodness, was I going sixty-five? I couldn't have been, I had the cruise control set at fifty-five didn't I Mildred?" And the kid is sitting there watching honesty in action.

Out of these (1) important and (2) enforceable values, you pick the five most important to you .

in **your** house, and you enforce them. Your aim is to build a conscience, and to do it without physical abuse. Your two basic rules here are:

1. Your kids are going to take responsibility for everything they do that's wrong. You are not going to excuse them from responsibility on the ground that the poor widdle things have had such a rotten life up to now. Nope nope nope nope. For every single thing they do wrong, they are accountable.

2. You are going to help them make good decisions, and the way you do that is to present them with opportunities to choose. Always be ready to carry out the choices that they make. Put another way, don't offer them a choice you aren't willing to enforce. If you don't like the TV programs they are watching, let them choose between turning them off or losing the TV and then, if you have to, lock the TV up or give it away.

Another example: You are in the supermarket, and the kids are rolling the tunafish cans down the aisle, as kids do. You say to them, "either you stop now, or the next time I come to the store, you do not." If they don't stop, next time you hire a babysitter, and leave them home. You stop at McDonald's on the way home. You don't be finished eating when you come in the door. Oh, ze delicious french fries! Ah, ze chocolate milkshake on ze upper lip! Yum yum yum! The kid says, I think I made the wrong decision.

Kids **want** us to have values, even if they fight against them. Children test because they want to be sure you are in control. When a new older child would come into one of the Tressler-Lutheran families I told the parents to tell him right away: This is not a democracy; this is a dictatorship. Then you can see him relax! What you say is, "I'll be the parent; you may be the child, and enjoy a child's life. In return, I have five rules you have to follow. If you break them, this is what will happen." Then you lay it out.

The five rules in my particular family, based on my values are:

1. You will go to church on Sunday--or at least your body will.

2. You will go to school until you graduate from **something.** If you want to spend five years in the fifth grade, ok.

3. You will do jobs in this house. At 1 a.m. if necessary. (You haven't lived until you have seen a twelve-year-old cleaning up the dog dirt by flashlight.)

4. You will not smoke in the house. (And you will reinforce this by not smoking yourself.)

5. You will not hit your parents.

If a kid breaks any one of these rules, in my house, he goes and lives in the basement until he decides to obey the rules. It's a nice basement, and he is allowed out to go to school, and to eat. But there is no shower down in the basement, and there is no allowance in the basement, and no company and no TV. He needs to **ask** for those privileges until he decides to rejoin the family and live under the family values.

Another punishment which we used ourselves and recommended to our families was for the child to sit on a chair in the living room. He could get up to pee and to sleep and to go to school. But he comes home, he sits in the chair. All weekend he sits in the chair. We all go to grandma's, and we take him <u>and </u>the chair. We are having a ball, and he is sitting in the chair--until he has thought about what he has done, is willing to accept the responsibility, and to discuss what he will do to make up for it. Notice that these sanctions are not physical, and we have not sent the child away from his home. We have simply encouraged him to think. He can get himself off the chair whenever he decides to.

What did you say? He's sixteen, and into competitive weight-lifting? She's fifteen and jumps out her bedroom window? Here are two rules to help cope with that.

Rule No. 1: Set this kind of discipline up in minor situations so that the kids believe you will do what you say you will do. You know that phrase, don't sweat the little stuff? I am telling you the opposite. Sweat out the little things, and when the big crises arrive, no sweat.

Rule No. 2: Enforce your decisions by using peer pressure. You say, "either you will be ready hen when the school bus gets to the end of the drive, you will go as you are." These kids don't want to go to school in their pajamas, and be seen that way. If they do it again, send them to school in their longjohns. I promise you, it will only take one day. But, call the school first, because <u>they</u> tend to freak out.

I remember one time a school called me and the lady said "I am going to report the Smiths for child abuse. Sammy came to school in shorts, in the middle of winter, and that is definitely child abuse." I said, "did uou find out what happed at home?" I had to ask that question ten times, but finally the lady said, "I think I'll call and find out what happened at home." But my dialing finger is faster than her dialing finger, and I got Daphne first.

"That sweet little fellow," she said, "came down to breakfast late. We were all sitting around, eating, and Sammy walks in in pajamas and pees in everyone's greakfast and all over everyone sitting at the table. I thought, kill. It crossed my mind. But I remembered what you said, and I said, 'Sammy, it's time for school. Go upstairs and change your clothes.' Sammy goes upstairs and changes into shorts. The bus is at the end of the lane. I said, 'Bye, Sammy.'" SHE gets reported for abuse? What about peeing in everyone's orange juice?

Take the boy you have just told to go sit in the chair. He is saying, "Hell will freeze over first, lady." So you say to your other child, "Oh, Jennifer, what was the name of that large boy on the football team? Could you look up his number for me? Maybe he would like a little job on the side. He could stand over here behind Johnny and keep him on the chair." Johnny panics. Football players are among the most popular kids in school, and if one of them tells everyone he's got this afterschool job. . . he sits.

The average kid is going to think "I can outlast you any day of the week." OK, your're in the chair, I'm not. Time goes by---the going record, by the way, is three months. Everyone else is having a blast, he's sitting. After a while it occurs to him that he can get off this chair, and so he says, "I'll talk." "Fine," you say. "What did you do?" "I kicked in the plate glass window." "What do you intend to do about it?" "Well, I was thinking while I was sitting there that if I washed the car a lot . . . how much do windows cost anyway?"

Now you are negotiating. You see what has happened? He is now thinking, taking responsibility for his actions. The average kid figures out after the first time that all he has to do is talk about what he did and take the responsibility. You are building in a conscience, and you did it without leaving marks.

Here's another wonderful situation. The School Conference. They are always set up to make you feel guilty. You come into the room, and the whole team is sitting there, down to the janitor, in a horseshoe, and you are the focus. Then they say, "Who would like to start?" "I'LL START," says the first person, and flips open her black book. Twenty-five homework assignments missed. They go around the circle and it's the same story. By the end, you're groveling. I"ll do better next time, honest! You go home, you get out your sharpened lead pencils and your good lighting and you sit beside the kid and help him with his homework every night for five hours and you get to the next marking period and dag, they're requesting your presence again!

You say, wait a minute; something's wrong here. But this time you're a little smarter and you take the kid. This time we get the routine known as "let's all sign papers." They give the kid an assignment, they sign it. He does it, you sign it. He brings it to school and they sign it again. Next marking period comes around, nothing has changed. You finally discover that the sand in the gear is the person transmitting the stuff. He is systematically destroying it between home and school. The kid is saying, "I'm in control, and I am not going to do what you want me to. I am deliberately sabotaging my own education."

Wait a minute. A child's education, unless he is retarded, is his responsibility. So you take the kid to the third school conference and you say, "Obviously my child likes this grade a lot and he plans to spend another year here. So would you please put him back so he can definitely stay in this grade again?" The kid looks at you incredulously and you say, "Your education, my friend, is your responsibility." Somewhere inside of them these kids have to be jolted into the realization that they are responsible for their future, and it's up to you to bring them to that realization.

I don't mean to make this sound easy. It isn't, and if you have more than one kid making your life miserable, or if they have come to you so old or so recently, or so viciously that these rules haven't had time to work, think of this:

They will, eventually, grow up. Think about what you will do after they leave. Myself, I am going to sell my house and buy a mobile home. I am going to visit each of my fifteen kids in turn, plug into their electricity, use up all their water, spoil their kids rotten and move on. Laughing till I cry.

You have given them unconditional love and commitment, not because they were beautiful to see, not because they stood up every time an adult entered the room and cleaned the toilet without being asked, but simply because they were who they were. And in this life you will get your reward. It's called Senior Year.

Take Chantel, the trumpet-playing actress with the basketball scholarship. It took **five minutes** at the end of her senior year for the principal to list all the good things she had done in that school. Take Nikki. Nikki came to us at the age of 18 months, after being severely abused. One of the things that had happened to her was, she was sat in boiling water to help her be toilet-trained. When she came to us she stayed behind the door and just shook. We have had to fight through all kinds of things with her, to build up her self-esteem. Suddenly, in her senior year, she decided that she was Barbie, and a cheer leader, and all the kinds of things that Barbie dolls do. At the end of the year, out of the whole class, Nikki was elected homecoming queen, and crowned, wearing my wedding dress and looking absolutely gorgeous!

All those years of struggle and dag, that kid makes it, and you know you were part of helping her make it, and that makes it all worth while. Our responsibility as parents is to be like the mommy bird who has to prepare for the exact moment when she goes "Ping!" and pushes the babies out of the nest. (Before that, she had another job: Every time she came home, there they were with their mouths open.) She has to time that push exactly right, or the babies fall to the ground and get eaten by the neighbor's cat; if she waits too long, they get too big and push each other out of the nest. So the moment comes, and she knows it and she goes "Ping!" and they fly. What a thrilling moment!

--------

Barbara Tremitiere, Ph.D., ACSW, LSW, was formerly Director of Adoption Services for Tressler-Lutheran Services Associates, Inc., in York, PA. She now works as a consultant and trainer, doing workshops across the U.S. and internationally. This article was based on some of the talks she often gives to parent groups.

All fifteen children are now grown and are productive tax-paying citizens! They range in occupation from cashier at Wal-Mart to career Army to professional basketball player (WNBA--guess who!) Each is very much their own person . . .

# Chapter V
## *Personal Experiences*

## One Man, Eight Children
## ---Adopting as a foster parent

*[The social work system's] goal is still not adoption. It's reunification, and if that's always the goal, foster parents sometimes don't even believe they can adopt . . . Support groups of adoptive parents--these are the people who probably are more successful--they recruit by example. They're not talking about social work, they're talking about kids.*

One of C. Kenneth Johnson's eight adopted children won first prize in a high school contest in 1994 with an essay about his father. He had had a second chance at life, Rodney Johnson wrote, and had given himself completely to children.

Ken Johnson has taken 134 foster children over the years. The eight whom he adopted range in age from 11 to 33. He was a foster parent before he began to adopt, and since 1956, when he graduated from college, he has always held jobs that involved helping children.

Before he became a foster parent, however, his life had gone from pain to partying. His mother died when he was five, and his father sent him and his three siblings to an orphanage, from which he moved to his maternal grandmother and aunt in rural Virginia. His grandmother still lived in a log cabin built by her former-slave parents, without electricity or plumbing. She took in washing for a living, and Ken and his brother and sisters, as well as another boy the two women had informally adopted,

hauled loads of laundry, picked vegetables, and attended a two-room schoolhouse. These were caring and responsible women, but the hard work their life required left them little time or energy for outward affection. They gave the children a rather rigid upbringing. Ken reflected later:

"I really didn't have much of a childhood. I was missing an adult to count on . . . Most kids, to fully develop themselves, need to feed on a close relationship with an adult, need to be loved, hugged, disciplined and taught. Or they become antisocial; or they can turn into what I was, which was very scared, fearful, unsure of myself."

At age 13 he got himself north to New Haven, Connecticut, and reunited with his father. Ken got himself through high school and started college with the help of friends and church brethren, but dropped out, was drafted, and served in Korea. On his return he went back to college and graduated with a degree in elementary and special education.

He taught school in New Haven and loved it, but ten years later, after marriage, two children, and a divorce; followed by another failed relationship and two more children, he moved to Washington D.C. to work on children's programs at the United Planning Organization. He bought a new three-story townhouse in the Anacostia section of Washington, with a huge family room. This he turned into a private night club, with a strobe light, the loudest stereo he could buy, and a very well-stocked bar. Friends and neighbors came and went at all hours of each weekend, and, he remembers, he "stayed half-bombed most of the time." The good times rolled for sixteen years.

Then he opened the front door one evening to two young men he recognized from the neighborhood, and took a bullet in the throat, followed by a beating and a robbery. He was fifty-two. After a long recovery he returned to his roots in the church. While helping out at Shiloh Baptist Church he happened to overhear a presentation by the foster care staff of the D.C. Department of Human Services titled "What Can We Do to Help the Children?" He could not avoid the question: What can *I* do? and decided "to go into the children business again." His second life began.

DHS was looking for black parents to foster black children. It is a myth, says Dr. Sherry David Molock, a clinical psychologist at Howard University, that blacks will not adopt black children. Adoption has gone on for centuries in the black community, most often on an informal basis. In fact, she says, African-Americans have the highest rate of adoption of all ethnic groups in this country. This mis-impression has arisen because of the heavy over-representation of African-American children in the child welfare system, compared to their proportion of the U.S. population. The children also stay longer in the system, partly because their parents' rights are slow to be terminated, and of course, they become less likely to be adopted the longer they stay in the system.

Black applicants also see barriers when they try to adopt children from "the state": For one thing, they have heard it is expensive, and they have the impression that you have to own your own house and have a high income. Moreover, the idea of paying to adopt a child resonates with slavery. What African Americans don't realize is that formal adoption need not cost them much, if anything. The states and large cities, where most of the foster care load is found, take advantage of federal adoption aid

that, matched by state funds, not only makes the adoption process effectively free but provides a continuing subsidy until the child is 18.

DHS gave Ken Johnson a two-month foster training course that disabused him of his vision of "nice, sweet, innocent kids." What you get, he said, are some emotionally abused, very angry children. Now, in talks to other prospective foster parents, he tells them that these are . . .

"children who are not the smiling babies you pictured. They have been through hell before they see you. The children have accepted their life, and often they've accepted that they are at fault: 'If it wasn't for me, Mommy would not hit me. If it wasn't for me, Daddy would not burn me with a cigarette'-- and they nonetheless want to go back home because it's all they know.

"Adopted kids have a fantasy about 'If I could only go back to my parents, everything would be wonderful.' But it isn't based on reality. The reality may be that the parents are in the same situation that caused the removal of the children, or the parents may not want them back." Ken can list examples of each among his own children.

Shortly after the course ended, DHS began sending him children. Some foster placements were brief, some were painful, but others were long, and gradually Ken began to adopt some whose parents' rights had been terminated. First came Danny, a toddler whose mother (who had five other children including one very special-needs) asked Ken to adopt him. Then twins, Rodney and Rakina, aged six; Quinn, aged fourteen; Donna, less than a year old; Harshia, a boy of seven; and lastly, five and a half years ago, another set of twins, Kathleen and Katrina, who were 18 months old when they arrived.

Not that the adoptions were easy, even though each child was already in his home in foster care. The city brought up its "unwritten rule" that an adoptive parent can be no more than 40 years older than the child to be adopted, and Danny was two. Ken might die, the Department said. "I might," said Ken, "and so might a 25-year-old. We do not know how long we will live." When his lawyer threatened to file an age discrimination suit, the Department abrogated its unwritten rule.

Some experts in child development believe that the first eighteen months are the most significant in the formation of a child's intellectual growth and emotional health. They say that the relationships to parents in that year and a half period will mold their relationship to people important to them for the rest of their lives--husbands, wives, lovers, children. At a minimum, a child over a few weeks old must know whether or not the person looking after him/her is the mother whose heartbeat he knew for nine months. Soon afterwards, one child will learn that love and response to crying . . . and another will learn that abuse or at a minimum neglect or abandonment . . . is the way life is supposed to be. Ken Johnson says that every one of his adopted children has suffered a lesser or greater degree of emotional abuse. So, are they going to repeat the same pattern in their own lives? Ken Johnson's opinion is:

"That statement is only partly correct. Children do carry the burden of the damage done, but they do more than survive. I don't like that word, survivor. You can survive an accident and be paralyzed. Children grow, they develop, they continue to develop. I love to see them change. And as for growing, last year Danny grew eight inches in one year! New shoes almost every month. The twins grew six inches in a year--the doctor said, what are you feeding them?

"Yes, they are enjoyable. But I want to be honest; it's work. By the time you finish lunch and clean up, it's time for dinner. By the time you finish dinner and clean up and enforce homework and get them to bed, and you sit down and look at TV, next thing you know the TV's looking at you, because you fell asleep, and you get up and go to bed.

"And you try to figure out, where did my life go? Not just partying--I don't have time to do a lot of the things I like to do. I love to go to the opera. I love to go to symphonies. I can't afford it. Jazz concerts--I haven't been in 27 years. And just timewise. The only time we were down there [The Kennedy Center] I took the kids to see Amahl, which we produced when I was in New Haven. I used to go to the old Metropolitan Opera, standing room only. It was beautiful.

"And children are ruthless, the best in the world at getting to you. They know your buttons and push them, every one. All my kids have severe emotional problems. You can talk about surviving, but you don't outgrow or outlive things that happened to you. The whole thing about being adopted, as kids get older--although Rodney and Rakina asked to be adopted, themselves, but--it's the idea that 'mom and dad didn't want me, they didn't love me, you're not really my father'--it didn't bother me, but it bothers them.

"Harshia has been diagnosed as severely emotionally disturbed--he goes to a special junior high school in the public school system. He is one of 11, 12, no one knows how many children, none of whom live with the mother. All ended up in foster care, or have been adopted. His first seven years, he was living with his mother, his father, his grandfather, his grandfather's girlfriend, other children, and he was just traumatized. He cannot remember or is not willing to remember anything that happened before he came here. He can tell you exactly what happened the day he came, but nothing prior to that. In the five years since he came here he has not even accidentally mentioned his mother. That's amazing to me.

"He can't read and we've been trying all different kinds of ways to teach him. He's not retarded; he has average or above-average intelligence, he's likable--lots of friends. His comprehension is excellent if you read to him. His vocabulary is excellent. He picks up words from TV. He's very good at sports and loves sports. I've got to look for another [special education] school for him after this coming year."

Another of Ken Johnson's children has been diagnosed as clinically depressed; a third, whose mother died of a long illness after she had asked Ken to adopt him, is still sad because he has been unable to locate the rest of his family.

Ken keeps his children busy. Every one, including the little twins, plays tennis, and several have gone in for track as well. The older four have had four years of piano, and the younger ones actually **want** to start learning, at a small institute located at Zion Baptist Church. Choir practice and dance class have also been important--tap dancing for for the boys, modern jazz and ballet for Rakina. Some of the children are tutored as well.

The reactions of friends, acquaintances, and fellow church members has been either admiring or skeptical:

"The question has always been, who does the little girls' hair? And I say, sometimes my neighbors, because I'm not very good at that. And, 'Do you buy their clothes?'-- it's like, men are incapable of selecting clothes that are appropriate for little girls."

The reactions of others, when they were not admiring, were suspicion of a different kind:

" 'You mean your wife agreed to all these adoptions?' When they find out I'm not married, it's 'I know the perfect woman for you!'"

There have been proposals, notably from one woman at his church. When Ken explained that he had eight children, she was amenable: "I have seven."

*　　*　　*　　*　　*

**How could the public social service authorities attract more black adoptive parents?** Ken Johnson feels that for one thing, the social work system is still headed in the wrong direction.

"Their goal is still not adoption. It's reunification, and if that's always the goal, foster parents sometimes don't even believe they can adopt. The judges will always say that the goal is the reunification of the [birth] family. Typically, you have a mother who has been completely dependent on heroin for a number of years. When she's not shooting up, she provides good care, but basically she's unable to care for her child and she will not go into a rehab[ilitation] program. The judge will say that the Department has not spent sufficient time to rehabilitate her. The judges need to be reeducated.

"[Social workers] have always accepted that the child is better off with the mother, or with kinship placements. You know why? The Department doesn't need to pay the relatives for foster care. All it does is help them apply for AFDC. They only monitor the placement for a few months, and then they take no further responsibility. They don't even check to see if Grandma turned the child back to the mother they took the child away from.

"Sometimes the [foster] parents get just a few hours' warning to bring the child in; he's going home. The foster parent knows that the reunification isn't going to work, and the child will be out of there again. One of my children lasted one week back with the parents. And if the foster parent has bonded with the child, they can't bear the separation when the child leaves. After a few such times, either the foster parent learns not to become too attached to foster children, or they get out of the business.

"The social workers and the courts won't change. Their goal is not the best interest of the child, it's the best interest of the parents. Their attitude to the child is: if you're not part of a family, you're nothing. We should be focusing on the psychological needs, or at least the physical needs, of the child. The parents may love the child, but that's not the issue--the issue is to provide proper care for the child. But instead the workers ignore physical abuse until the child is actually injured.

"Social workers should deal with foster parents as partners instead of depositories for children. They don't let foster parents share in decision-making; they tell them what school the children have to go to, they treat the foster parents as outsiders. A good foster care system would be foster parents and social workers working for the best interest of the child, and trying to rehabilitate the mother.

"Evaluate the child--what is happening to her [in foster care]? Has her, or his, emotional well-being stabilized? Has the child grown emotionally? You have to set standards to determine the basis for breaking up the family. But we have some facts--we already know the effect of drugs, the low percent of addicts likely to be rehabbed. If she refuses parent training, job training, drug rehab--she has already forfeited her rights to her child. We are so burdened by the belief that the family unit is sacrosanct, holy.

"You can't set a deadline for TPR, because children vary, not just by age but by personality. Well, you can set a time period to rehabilitate the family, and if a year has been exceeded with no guarantee that she can be rehabbed, terminate her parental rights. A year should be the maximum.

"The government is not the only problem, though. The churches are not doing what they ought to be doing; they are **not**. Even my church. There is no active group sponsoring any adoption fairs, information seminars. Maybe once a year they have something. Some people have gone into foster parenting and adoption because of meeting me at church. [Father Clements] is talking about different ways to bring more people in--less social workers recruiting and more adoptive parents.

"Support groups of adoptive parents--these are the people who probably are more successful--they recruit by example. They're not talking about social work, they're talking about kids. People are still afraid to go through an adoption, because there are a lot of horror stories out there. Some of these foreign adoptions have turned into disasters."

Kenneth Johnson retired in 1994, after working at different jobs since he was eight. His children are beginning to leave home. He is 71, and figures he has a few more years of active parenting. Even if he died then, his oldest, Quinn, who is 33 now, will be able to take responsibility. Quinn is married, with three children, and is a social worker in the D.C. Department of Human Services Child and Family Administration. His wife is a pediatrician in a private clinic.

Rakina is majoring in communications and marketing at Delaware State University and will graduate in 2001. Rodney attends the Univeristy of the District of Columbia, majoring in graphic arts. The rest of the family is still heavily involved with school, church, home chores, tennis, and family fun. That includes playing with the graceful German Shepherd, Princess, who had originally been Quinn's puppy. The children would never let Quinn take her back. Ken says: "Princess has gone through being dressed, bandaged, ridden on, sat on, slept on and kissed. Every night the little girls come downstairs and kiss her good night."

And Ken Johnson is still taking (temporary) foster children--the District of Columbia recently sent him a four-year-old boy.

Photograph by Marc Asnin

Much of the first part of this article is taken from "Autumn of the Patriarch," by Peter Perl, in the <u>Washington Post Magazine</u> September 24, 1995.

# EXPECTATIONS
# and REALITIES --*Adopting the Hurt Child*

# by Lea Wait

Before I had children I was sure I knew what it would be like to be a mother.

To read Dr. Seuss and The tSwiss Family Robinson and Winnie the Pooh over and over. To take little girls in red velvet dresses to see The Nutcracker at Christmas. To get cookie-crumbed hugs. To, once in my life, make a gingerbread house. To teach my girls to knit. To share Katherine Hepburn in Little Women, and to help with school projects on the Egyptians.

My girls--somehow I always had trouble seeing myself as the mother of boys--would be just pretty enough, and very intelligent, and would play Monopoly together and with me. We would eat raw carrots and yogurt and chocolate-chip cookies, and sing songs off-key, and argue, sometimes, and love each other, always. Someday my girls would go off to college or, perhaps, to art or music or carpentry school, and would become independent and self-supporting. They would come home for holidays, though, and we would always be close.

I would be a single parent--at least to begin with. I was in my late twenties and had been married once, so I knew marriage was not a panacea, but I felt that when the right man came along he would love my children, too. I had no doubts. Besides having children and someday finding that right man, the only other thing I really wanted was to write. But I could write after my kids were in bed, couldn't I?

I had a house, several degrees, and a career. I had done volunteer work with abused children, and I loved the idea of being a parent, of loving a child who had no one, and of helping her to grow and discover who she was. I had read all the books, and I knew all the theories. I knew it wouldn't always be a smooth road, but I also knew it was the right road for me. I could cope with a few potholes.

I thought about adopting infants, but there were too many reasons to adopt older children. I knew they would all come with the "baggage" that books on adoption mentioned, but I didn't worry about missing the diaper stages and daycare costs. I wanted to adopt children who needed me, and for whom there weren't other parents waiting.

And so I adopted four "older" girls.

**Alicia Yupin** was a beautiful four-year-old from Thailand. She had lived in a workhouse, where children were rented out for manual labor, and she didn't know what a mother was. Her temper tantrums lasted hours each day of the first years she was with me, and she had night terrors. After a year I took her to a renowned child psychiatrist who specialized in children with inter-cultural adjustments. He said she was fine. No one had heard of early childhood trauma disorders in 1978. I loved her, hugged her, reassured her, and knew it would all get better soon.

**Carolyn Yoon Kyung** became Alicia's big sister eighteen months later. She was three years older than Alicia, Korean, almost nine, and had lived with an alcoholic and abusive father and an illiterate but loving mother until her father died. Her mother, unable to support both Caroline and her brother, relinquished Caroline for adoption. For several months after she arrived Caroline was in mourning for her family and culture, and she didn't talk. When the mourning ended, the anger began, although she had trouble letting it out. But she learned that hugs didn't hurt, and eventually her migraine headaches came less often.

**Rebecca Siu Kuen** had grown up in a series of Hong Kong orphanages after being deserted in an amusement park when she was two. When she was seven she was placed with a Chinese-American family who could not cope with the heavy demands of her emotional or physical needs. When she was eight she came to live with us. She and Alicia were close to the same age, and immediately became competitors. Becky was immature, hyperactive, and stubborn. She would run into trees and not feel the pain. Her voice was the loudest one wherever we went, from football stadiums to church sanctuaries. When Becky touched something, it broke. When Becky was hungry, she ate until she was sick. When Becky wanted something, she bullied. When Becky needed to urinate, she wet her pants. I child-proofed the house and stopped taking the kids to restaurants and other public places, certain that time and love would make things better.

**Elizabeth Purnima** was at least ten when she joined us, although her papers said she was eight. By that time Caroline was 15, Alicia was 13, and Becky, 12. Elizabeth had lost her family in a railroad station in Calcutta when she was four, and since then had supported herself by caring for sick and dying babies in missions and orphanages. She had never been to school, so no one knew her capability for learning. She was deeply scared of making a mistake, or of offending anyone. And she had trouble learning to read. But she could draw, and build elaborate cardboard houses, and she loved to help around the house. She was going to be all right.

I believed. I believed nurture was stronger than nature. I believed I could make a major difference in my children's lives. I believed I knew what I was doing. And I did whatever I could to help my children see the possibilities in their lives, and to make these possibilities realities.

Alicia and Becky, my active daughters, joined gymnastics teams and competed statewide and nationally. Channel the energy! Caroline's and Elizabeth's self-esteem and knack with crafts were encouraged by Girl Scouts and church activities.

We were culturally aware--Korean Culture Camp, Bengali Festivals, Chinese New Year, Thai food. Everyone had counseling--individual or family, depending on the situation and year. We were doing all right. We weren't a perfect family, but the good days outnumbered the bad. I helped found a single-adoptive parent support group that backed us up, and ensured that both the girls and I knew other families like ours. We went to picnics and Korean art exhibits and Chinese restaurants and American barbecues together. And in after-bedtime telephone calls I compared notes with other adoptive parents, and laughed over our shared day-to-day traumas.

The girls got along as well as most sisters--chaos and tears alternating with hugs and laughter. We all sang off-key. We all loved the coast of Maine, where we visited my mother for two weeks each summer. We stir-fried everything, from potatoes to snow peas to popcorn.

Christmas became their favorite time of year, too, and we started decorating our house the day after Thanksgiving. We laughed a lot, ate the Christmas cookies my mother made because I never had time, and wrapped up everything from underwear and socks to the books I wrote for each of the girls each year. That was the most writing I ever seemed to manage. I gave up trying to find the time to finish my dissertation. Instead, I edited an adoptive-parent newsletter.

I parented on my own. Except for Alicia, who attended day care for the first two years she was home, my girls went straight into elementary school. After school there were Brownie meetings, basketball, gymnastics, and painting lessons. And, from Thanksgiving until Christmas . . . and then January . . and then until early spring, as the years went by, my mother visited us from Maine, so she could avoid the coldest part of winter, and she would be there to keep an eye on the kids after school, and to get dinner for us during the week.

My job changed from department to department, but at the same large company. I had to refuse two jobs because they required too much traveling, but I was still rated highly. One supervisor did counsel me not to volunteer any information about my children ("If anyone knew you had chosen to adopt four children they'd never believe you were serious about your career,") and another advised me not to have pictures of the kids in my office ("They raise too many questions.") I kept the pictures, but small ones, and I tried not to talk about the kids, but it was hard. When I wasn't in the office, they had become my life.

Dating? Well, there was the guy who invited me and my (then two) children to go to the Bronx Zoo and was surprised they didn't wear "oriental robes and things, like they should." And the guy who said he'd always wanted a mother like me. And the one who asked me (in his first phone call) whether I was still fertile, because he wanted to have some "real" kids.

And then, of course, there were the girls. They worked together in wondrous ways to influence

103

my social life. "Oh, who are you? Will you be my daddy?" changed to "Hey Mom! There's a weird looking guy downstairs to see you," over the years, but the men beat the same hasty retreat. Most of them I didn't miss.

And then there was Bob, a man I'd known and loved off and on for many years, through various jobs, relocations, marriages (his and mine), and crises. We kept ending up together, and decided there must be a reason for that. Even though he had never wanted children, he was willing to get to know mine. He became a semi-permanent fixture at weekend gymnastic meets and barbecues.

Life seemed to be going the way I'd planned. Sure, I was tired, and the kids had day-to-day problems. And I wasn't doing much writing except on my job. But I had four beautiful children, a house, a successful career, a special man--there was nothing I couldn't handle.

And then adolescence hit.

I've read that although adolescence is a time of emotional highs and lows for all children, for children who have unresolved, deep-seated issues, those highs and lows can become precarious heights and depths.

My family hit both. Many times.

**Caroline:**
The first blow came when Caroline's best friend--also adopted from Korea at age nine by a single parent--stayed home from school one day and turned on the car ignition in a closed garage. She was sixteen, and no one had any warning. She was doing well in school, had many friends, had been in counseling, and had a bright future ahead of her.

Caroline, always quiet and easily depressed, felt that if this friend had been unable to cope, then certainly she couldn't. She stopped studying or going out with friends, closed herself to emotional contacts, and started sleeping most of the time she was at home. Her guidance counselor called to say she'd been talking about ways to kill herself.

Counseling helped, but it was only a beginning. Caroline was very fragile emotionally, and the slightest disappointment or setback became a major problem. She talked very little to her family or friends but, luckily, she did talk to her counselor and to her co-workers at a local supermarket. Not much, but enough to keep her going.

When she went away to the small women's college of her choice, things fell apart again. Always shy, she had trouble making friends, and trouble coping with decisions she had to make on campus about drugs, sex, and alcohol.

Caroline wanted so much, and trusted too easily. She was hurt and scared. She got counseling at school, she tried, but at the end of her freshman year she came home and announced she wasn't going back.

Living at home, Caroline worked several jobs concurrently, went to more counseling and then, at twenty-one, surprised everyone by enlisting in the United States Army. "I need a world where there is structure," she explained. She believed the Army would help her to "Be All That She Could Be."

Caroline's five years in the Army were not easy, but she faced the challenges of racial issues, chronic depression, and constantly having to make new friends. Physically, she had never been strong; in the Army she picked up every infection she came in contact with in her job as a medical technician.

But Caroline fought the specters of loneliness and depression that had always haunted her and, at 25, she married a man she had met in the Army. (Adding to our family's diversity, Caroline's husband is African-American.) They have both now completed their tours of duty and are back in civilian life and planning to start a family of their own soon. They are creating a life that is right for them.

**Alicia:**
Alicia had never had a strong self-image; she knew she was pretty, but she believed deeply that she wasn't smart, despite IQ tests to the contrary. And if she had friends and boyfriends to love her, then why want anything else? Alicia could never focus on the future, or on the long-term consequences of her decisions.

Abusive boyfriends. Alcohol. Disappearing for days and nights. Telling her friends I beat her. Accused of stealing. Lying. Keeping suitcases in her room packed with cosmetics and stuffed animals. Screaming obscenities at me, or at anyone else who tried to get her to focus on what was happening to her life.

I took her to Planned Parenthood. I found a series of counselors--none of whom she would talk to. I cried myself to sleep. I worried that the child welfare authorities would find her on the streets and believe I had beaten her. I worried that no one would find her on the streets.

On Valentine's Day of her senior year in high school Alicia had a fight with her latest boyfriend, and called several friends to tell them she would never see them again. That night I had her hospitalized. After she was released, on medication, life seemed calmer. But two months later, when I was hospitalized for emergency surgery, she ran away again. This time for a week. This time she got pregnant.

Being a mother has taught me many things. One is that the problem you anticipate may not be the problem you get. Another is that miracles come in strange places and at strange times.

Alicia was 18 when she gave birth to my first grandchild on December 29, 1990. I was with her in the delivery room, holding her feet, telling her to push, and was the second person, after the obstetrician, to see her daughter. As the ironies of life continue I, who adopted "special needs" children, now have a "special needs" grandchild.

Victoria Louise, now known to the neighborhood as Tori, was born with Down Syndrome and a severe heart abnormality. When she finally weighed five pounds, at four months old, she had open heart surgery. Her mother and I stayed with her at Columbia Presbyterian Hospital in New York, where we shared both pain, as we saw her suffering, and laughter, as doctors and nurses tried to figure out our family relationships. (The most popular conclusion? I must be Alicia's mother-in-law, since I obviously wasn't Asian, and so couldn't be Alicia's mother.)

Tori's heart is fine now. As I'm writing this she is six years old, and, developmentally, about four. She spends half of each school day in a mainstream kindergarten program, and half in a program to prepare developmentally delayed children for full-time mainstreaming. She is a self-confident and affectionate young lady who loves singing, dancing, and people.

Alicia has had highs and lows during those six years. She has held four administrative jobs, but was fired from three. She was married, but came back home after the honeymoon and did not join her husband in the state where his job had taken him. She has moved away from home twice but, for financial reasons, has had to move back both times. She has taken several college courses, and has done well in them, but has not been able to focus enough to make college a priority.

Alicia is still dealing with issues related to self-esteem and relationships which, I feel, are directly related to separation and loss issues she faced as a child. But during the past several months she has agreed that counseling would help her to break the pattern of sabotaging her life when it is going well and has started counseling with someone who specializes in helping people cope with traumatic stress disorders. The expense is high--but the rewards could be very great. I'm hoping.

In the meantime, Alicia and Tori live at home, and I encourage Alicia to make decisions about her daughter's future and her own, but am there to back them both up when plans or decisions fall through. Tori loves living in a household full of people, and Alicia, although she frequently talks about moving out, also voices concerns about the day when I retire and move to Maine--as I have been planning for years.

As long as downsizing doesn't hit me, that won't be for five to seven years. I'm hoping that Alicia will have broken her self-defeating patterns by then, and be living on her own. I'm doing everything I can do to encourage her to be able to focus her life, and plan for her future, and that of her daughter.

**Becky:**
Becky planned to go to college, and her grades had always been high, but during her last two years of high school her old problems with hyperactivity came back, worse than ever. Her grades plummeted as she found it impossible to focus on studying or on planning for her future. Her behavior was close to manic, and the closer to graduation (and the possibility of separation from the stability of home) the worse it got.

Her expectations were higher than her grades and SATs so, afraid to fail, she began to be afraid to try. She started smoking, experimenting with beer and marijuana, and "hanging out" with kids whose only future plans were for the weekend. She got to school late on days she got there at all. She was antagonistic, and she screamed a lot. As with my other girls at her age, she "hated" me. (Counselors say it is displacement--that the girls really hate their birth mothers, but I'm the mother who is available to yell at. The yelling hurts anyway.)

In the fall of Becky's senior year she was diagnosed with Attention Deficit Disorder, but she found the prescribed medication "changed her personality," so she refused to take it.

Three weeks before graduation she left home and moved in with a girlfriend's family, where they would "let me have my freedom." I knew that if she cut English one more time she would lose credit for it, and not meet state requirements for graduation. I attended her graduation not knowing if she'd be there. Becky cuts things close--but she usually gets where she wants to go. She graduated with her class.

I told her that she was only welcome to come home when she agreed to take her medication, go to counseling, and do her share of family chores. A month later, she was ready to try. It wasn't easy--and a month after that she and a girlfriend borrowed a car and drove to Arizona to "make a new start," with dreams, but no plans, contacts, or money.

During the next four months Becky hit bottom. She held a series of unskilled jobs--one of which disappeared when the company she worked for was indicted for illegal activities. I sent her cartons of food, but refused to send her money. She got involved with some young people who were heavily into drugs, and she experimented with them. At least once she gave blood to help get money for rent.

In December she called home, and asked me to pay her airfare home for Christmas. I said I would—if she was ready to pull her life together.

In her few weeks at home Becky found a neurologist specializing in ADD, made an appointment with him, and got medication. She was accepted by a university in Arizona.

Returning to Arizona, she pulled her life together. She found a better job, and a new apartment, near campus. She registered for two courses. She took her medication.

She stayed in Arizona for 18 months. I paid her tuition, but she worked to pay for her living expenses. After a year and a half she decided to move closer to home on the East Coast, and applied to colleges here.

It is now two years later. At age 23, Becky has only two semesters left before she graduates from college. She has a summer internship at a major corporation. And she knows where she is heading. She takes her medication during work or

school or study hours, but not when she is partying with friends. Her ADD is still an issue, but she has learned to live with it, and to focus her life when she needs to. She will graduate from college with a high average and a degree in English before she is 25, with a goal of working in marketing or public relations.

Becky has found a purpose in life, and her goals are within reach.

**Elizabeth:**

When Elizabeth graduated from eighth grade, at age fifteen, she couldn't read above a fourth-grade level, although she studied hard, had an average IQ, and had no identifiable learning disabilities. Our school system suggested vocational high school, but because Elizabeth was very shy and socially immature, and our vocational high school was full of young people whose lifestyles were the opposite of hers, I wanted her to have other options.

An educational counselor helped us find a special American high school in Italy that taught both art and academics, and specialized in helping teenagers who had survived dysfunctional childhoods to deal with their pasts and take responsibility for their futures. The head of the school suggested that perhaps Elizabeth was so strongly bonded to her birth family that unconsciously she wasn't allowing herself to learn English or grow up emotionally, because she had to stay the little girl they had lost ten years before. They offered her a full scholarship for a year. Elizabeth was discouraged about public school, our home life was chaotic (Alicia and Becky were in high school at that time), and Italy seemed the perfect solution.

I went with Elizabeth to Italy to enroll her, and after a few hours at the school flew back to the United States.

Because many of their students had drug or alcohol problems or had acted out sexually and the school considered itself "therapeutic," I could only speak to Elizabeth for a few minutes every two weeks, with someone from the school present. Elizabeth's disabilities prevented her from writing.

Although it seemed harsh, Elizabeth did not complain, and enjoyed her art classes. Her counselors told me that she was not really participating in their group therapy sessions, but that they were sure she would soon. Distracted by issues at home, I was just glad Elizabeth was getting the attention I thought would help her.

I visited her in six months, and although the school seemed uncomfortably communal, Elizabeth did have friends there, and she was better able to verbalize some of her emotions. When she had been there a year, I visited again. This time she had been "on punishment" for several months because she refused to participate in some of the therapeutic activities. I was very concerned about the answers to a number of my questions, but since the school had extended the scholarship to 18 months, looked forward to bringing Elizabeth home soon. They then offered to keep her there for all of her high school years. Because the school was not accredited in the United States--something the school administration had not been clear about before--I wasn't enthusiastic about that, but I left it up to Elizabeth. She said she'd stay.

Two days after I returned home she changed her mind. I started getting a series of frantic telephone calls from the school. Elizabeth, who had never fought back in any way, had gone on a hunger strike. She refused to talk to school officials. Finally, she ran away. When found by local Italian police, she still wouldn't return to the school--and school officials said they didn't want her back anyway. They packed her things and arranged to have her escorted to the Rome airport, where I made sure there was a ticket back to the United States waiting for her.

Elizabeth had surpassed my expectations: She had made two major decisions--one, that the school she was attending was not the right one for her, and two, that she wanted to live at home.

During the next year I found out more and more about the school itself--which closed, as a result of legal actions, about 18 months after Elizabeth left. Officials there had lied about the credentials of many of their staff members, the "therapeutic" techniques they were using in many instances were closely related to brainwashing; and one of their primary assumptions was that their students' families had created their problems and, therefore, that the young people had to separate themselves, physically and emotionally, from those families forever.

The more I learned, the more I realized just how strong Elizabeth, despite her shyness and inability to do much introspection, was. She had resisted all of the pressures of the school community, and had trusted me instead.

After surviving that year, Elizabeth easily survived public high school. Taking some developmental courses, using a tutor, and having accommo-

dations in other classes, Elizabeth graduated from high school with her class, winning senior awards for art, and for "most diligent" in mathematics.

Elizabeth is still socially immature, and finds change and taking on new responsibilities very intimidating, but in the last year she has successfully worked full-time as a cashier at a local supermarket, opened a checking account, passed her driver's test, and bought her first car. She attended community college for one semester, but found it impossible to balance the needs of school, work, and her first attempts at her own social life.

She is buying dishes and pans in hopes of having her own apartment some day. Elizabeth is persistent. When she has a goal, she works slowly and steadily toward achieving it. I'll be behind her every step of whichever way she chooses to go.

*        *        *        *        *

So--we're all doing all right. It took years of emotional exhaustion to get here, and there are still unresolved issues to confront--and financial drains I never anticipated--but I know now we're going to make it.

What happened to me during those years? In thinking about our children's needs, we often forget to factor in our own. During the past ten years I've had to struggle with my own realities.

My mother aged during those years, and became even more of an integral part of our family, as her medical problems increased. She now lives with us for ten months of the year. We are four generations of women living together, and I'm the textbook example of the "sandwich generation." And, as my mother's challenges have increased, so have conflicts between her needs and views and those of my daughters and me.

Bob said he loved me, and tried to cope with the continuing day-to-day crises, but couldn't. He left.

Since Bob left I haven't dated anyone. In the first few years I was too emotionally exhausted from dealing with my family to find the energy for another relationship. And there weren't many men looking for a woman who came with troubled teenagers as part of the package! My girls are now in their twenties, and I feel ready to begin again--but I'm older and finding that "right person" doesn't get easier with age! And now I'm responsible for my mother as well. So--maybe someday. In the meantime, I'm concentrating on issues I have more control over.

Beginning when my children were in high school, I lost touch with many of my adoptive parent friends. Those who also had teenagers were coping with their own issues. And the parents of teenagers don't have the freedom and privacy of "after bed-time" to chat with friends and compare notes. The telephone is in constant use--teenagers often stay up later than parents--and there is never privacy to talk about your own feelings, or about the problems you're dealing with.

I have one close friend (also a single adoptive mother) with whom I share traumas and occasional dinners out, and I am consciously trying to do more of the things I need to and want to do for myself.

I take one evening "out" a week--even if it just means quietly reading at the library--and when I travel on business I don't call home as frequently as I used to. I am more involved now in a family antiques business that I have always owned, but that has been managed by someone else. I am writing more.

Counseling has helped. I began talking with someone once a week when Caroline first needed help, and I continue doing it today. At minimum, it gives me one hour a week that is mine: To complain, to cry, sometimes to get valuable advice and, often most important, to be assured that I am still sane; that I am doing the best I can.

My job? There have been some rough times there too. Although I managed my time well, the emotional drain of my children's problems, especially during their high school years, affected my concentration. I was clinically depressed for at least two years, but I kept functioning. Sometimes I had to leave my office to deal with emergencies that couldn't wait until after-hours. In a corporate environment of increasing workloads and down-sizing, that was a liability.

One supervisor explained that, obviously, I wasn't capable of managing my family (at that time I was dealing with running away and suicide threats), and if a woman couldn't even manage her family, how could she possibly manage a demanding job? I was taken off the "fast track."

I finally accepted that my career would not go any further, and counted myself lucky to have stayed employed through difficult corporate times. Four years ago I took a "low profile' job and decided to find fulfillment elsewhere. Ironically, that "low prorile" job has increased considerably in corporte stature since then. And in the last few years, as the emotional drains of my family have decreased, I've been able to put more energy into my job, and have again enjoyed the challenges of meeting the needs of both people reporting to me, and those I report to. I have regained the sense of competence I lost when my children were in the midst of crises.

What have I learned?

I've learned that my daughters need me to hang in, no matter what happens, and to be there for them, no matter what they say out loud, or how they treat me--or what the rest of the world thinks. If I hadn't done that, I don't think we all would have made it through to where we are now.

I've learned that even if you do everything that can possibly be done, it may not be enough. I've learned that if your children fail, it's not your fault. Ultimately, a parent can only point the way. Each child has to choose his or her own road--and live with the consequences of those choices.

I've learned how it feels not to want to go home because home is a battlefield, not a sanctuary. How it feels to devote all your emotional strength to one problem, knowing there are other volcanoes activating. How it feels to wait alone all night for a child who doesn't come home.

I've learned that, despite their mature appearance, most teenagers are not ready to give emotional support to others; they think of everything in terms of themselves:

If you have to travel on business, it is because "You don't care about my basketball game!"

If you are sick it's because "You always have an excuse not to help me with algebra!"

If you don't understand chemistry, it's because "You never loved me. You helped my sister with English!"

I've learned that parents have to have very strong egos.

I've learned to take each small victory for what it is: a victory. And to celebrate it!

I'm still learning that it's not selfish for a parent to take time away from the family: It's that time that gives the energy to cope with the next crisis.

I've learned to roll with the punches. I've learned to smile in the face of seeming disasters, if not to laugh; to know there are other parents, of adopted or nonadopted children, who have coped with the same problems I have. Or worse.

I still believe in nurture, but I know nature and early nurturing experiences also have major influences on my children. I believe I am making a major difference in my children's lives. But I now believe it will take a lifetime--not a few years--to see that difference.

Caroline is chronically depressed; Alicia has a trauma disorder. Becky has attention deficit disorder; Elizabeth is severely learning-disabled. None of those things will change, although the girls' acceptance of them, and the way they deal with them, have changed over the years, and will continue to change as they are faced with adult responsibilities and decisions.

My girls will continue to need more love and understanding and structure and patience than other children. They will continue testing the stability of my love for years beyond the "adjustment period" cited in books on older child adoption. They will be children longer than other children.

No, it hasn't been the way I planned. But, despite detours along the way, my family is succeeding. Every day my children have more perspectives on their lives and relationships, more ability to focus on their goals, and more confidence in taking responsibility for themselves.

I have learned that being a parent requires all of your emotional strength.

That adoption is a lifelong process, not an event.

But, since the beginning, I've remained sure about one thing: Adoption was the right road for me. I do believe that my girls will all soon be self-supporting, sane, and maybe even sensible, adults. And that, when they are, we will still be speaking to each other.

It is just taking longer to get there than I expected.

And, despite it all, I wouldn't have missed the last twenty years: gymnastic ribbons, first words in English, proms, midnight discussions about the past and the future, memories of homemade doughnuts at slumber parties, blurs of Christmases, weddings, and even a birth.

No; despite the tears, the decision to become a single adoptive parent was the right one for me. it was the decision to become the woman I am today.

Lea Wait lives in Maine, on the Sheepscot River, where she writes and cares for her mother. In earlier years she was co-founder of Adoptive Single Parents of New Jersey, and often spoke and wrote about adoption of older children. Her first novel will be published in the fall of 2001. Lea has a B.A. from Chatham College, and advanced degrees from New York University. As achild Lea dreamed of adopting children, of living in Maine, and of writing books. "I'm still living my dreams," she says. "After all, dreams should last a lifetime."

## Addendum to my article:

I wrote this essay four years ago. Since then, in a major reversal, my own life's changes, not my children's, have had the most effect on our family during the past two years.

Four years ago, as I wrote above, I anticipated retiring in five to seven years. But two years ago AT&T offered an unanticipated early-retirement buyout package, and I decided it was the right time to leave corporate life. I sold my home in New Jersey and moved to my family home in Maine. That decision had major ramifications for everyone in my family.

Perhaps the least affected was Caroline. She and her husband had settled in Virginia, where they were living with his mother. Caroline called rarely, and we saw her only about once a year, although I wrote to her several times a month, so she knew what was happening with the rest of us. To Caroline, my retirement only meant that she and her husband had to collect the belongings they had stored at my home. Since I have moved to Maine Caroline has returned to college part-time, on the GI bill, in hopes of someday getting her teaching certificate. She and her husband have bought their own home. And, most exciting, she has given birth to her long-anticipated first child. My granddaughter Vanessa was born in 2000, and is a happy, healthy baby, with loving parents. During her pregnancy Caroline began to increase her contacts with me and with her sisters, and I am hoping these contacts will continue in coming years.

While I was still living in New Jersey Alicia and Tori moved in with Alicia's boyfriend. After living together for two years she and her friend were married, and they have just purchased their first home. She is talking about having a second child. (Tori is still mainstreamed, and is now in the third grade.) Like Caroline, Alicia is continuing to work during the day, but has returned to school at night and hopes to complete her degree. Alicia stays in touch with me---I hear from her via telephone or email two or three times a week---and Tori spends some of her vacations visiting Maine.

Becky and Elizabeth, still living at home, were the two most affected by my retirement and move. Becky had decided to change majors at college, delaying her graduation until after I had left New Jersey. That meant she was not able to live at home while she looked for and started her first job. She bitterly resented that, although my sister did offer her space to live in for her first few months after gradua-

tion. Becky is now 27, has her own apartment, and is working in New York City, but has not yet found a "career" job, and many of her belongings are still in storage. She is still very angry because I "deserted" and "abandoned" her. Heavily laden words from someone who was adopted. Becky and I are in touch, but I finally told her that I didn't need to hear her anger any more. Now she doesn't yell at me as much. But Becky has yet to claim an adult life that she has chosen and is passionate about.

Elizabeth was also caught unprepared when I moved. Only 21, she was not ready to be on her own. I invited her to come with me (an opportunity also offered to Becky), but Elizabeth did not want to live where there would be few people her age, and few people of color. Elizabeth moved in with a boyfriend who turned out to be abusive. It was a painful introduction to the adult world. After she got out of that relationship she moved in with a co-worker. Her apartment-mate is considerably older than she is, and provides a pseudo-parental relationship which has worked for both of them for over a year now. (Ironically, many years ago her friend relinquished a child for adoption.) Elizabeth and I are in touch by telephone perhaps once or twice a month, and I see her, as I see Alicia, whenever I visit New Jersey.

What am I doing in Maine? One of the things I've wanted to do for years. I am writing. My first middle reader (ages 8-12) chapter book will be published by Simon & Schuster's Margaret K. McElderry Books. *Stopping to Home* takes place in a seaport town in Maine in 1806. In it, two orphaned children find a new "parent" in a young widow and form an extended-family unit. (Early single parent adoption?)

My goal is at least one book each year.

I am also operating my antique print business, which takes me to antique shows in several states; and caring for my mother, whose health is slowly deteriorating. I am enjoying the river view from my bedroom window and concentrating on getting my new life in order. There are guest bedrooms in my home. My girls are always welcome here, and I am welcome at their homes.

Despite Becky's concerns, I have not abandoned them. I have just moved on to another stage of my life, as they have moved on to other stages of theirs. My children are now aged 23 to 30. I am 53. I hope we have many years ahead in which we can all live our dreams, both separately and together.

And I already have two wonderful grandchildren. I'm still reading Dr. Seuss.

# MY THREE SONS
## ---Adopting Older Children

by Paula J. McDermott

*Despite [my son's] many adjustment problems, . . . I really didn't personally find it an adjustment becoming a parent except perhaps in a positive sense. I constantly reminded myself with a foolish grin, "I have a son of my own. I am a mom. I have my own beautiful child."*

I never could have imagined when I was waiting to take the law school admission test 14 years ago that that day would lead to my becoming not only a lawyer but also a single adoptive parent of three beautiful sons. I stood waiting in line compulsively reading everything on the bulletin board. A flyer caught my eye which said, "Have a child, not a baby." Further on the flyer read, "You don't have to be married, and you don't have to have a lot of money to give a child a home." This got my attention since I was both single and poor. I wrote down the name of Tressler Lutheran Services in York, Pennsylvania, and filed it for future reference. Several years later, when I had graduated from law school and had my first decent job, I contacted Tressler and enrolled in their program to adopt a special needs child. I really knew nothing about adoption. I only knew that I wanted to be a parent and that for me a child who was older would be best because of my frenzied schedule as a lawyer.

I was fortunate to be spared some of the logistical issues that confront would-be single parent adoptors since I live with my dad, who is a widower. We discussed the issue of adoption thoroughly, and my father encouraged me to go forward. He also very generously volunteered to do whatever child care was necessary. I really don't think, especially when the boys were younger, that I could have managed at all without his assistance, given my hectic schedule. He has been completely involved in every stage of the adoptions and has a major role in my children's life as their grandfather and in effect their father.

Tressler requires its prospective adoptive parents to take nine weeks of classes which offer suggestions on how to deal with special-needs adoptive children. During those weeks the Tressler staff and panels of adoptive parents give a realistic picture of the difficulties and problems encountered by adoptive parents. Also, during that period adoptive parents are afforded an opportunity to consider what type of children might be available to single parents.

Unfortunately, many prospective parents come to the special needs adoption route by default. They are often infertile couples who discover that healthy Caucasian infants are unattainable and that it costs tens of thousands of dollars to adopt from abroad. When they learn of the comically low fees charged to adopt special needs children, they see it as a short cut. Usually, they aren't at all interested in dealing with any type of problem and are looking to satisfy a need within themselves for the child whom, for whatever reason, they cannot have. When asked what sort of child they are looking for, they say "a young child with very few problems." Someone with this attitude will not do well with a child who has a problem of any kind, however minor, and it is just as well that they learn this through the realistic scenarios depicted in the classes.

In my home study I had indicated that I thought that I could deal with one or two children from ages three to thirteen. I did not care about gender, but I really thought that I would get girls because of being a single woman. What I didn't realize then was that the real need was for families for older boys. I went through about a four-month waiting period while the agency sent my study out to children in whom I was interested.

Tragically, there does still appear to be some bias against single parent adoptions. I find this humorous for many reasons. Something like 51% of marriages end in divorce. I wonder what makes these agency professionals think that a child going through a divorce with an adoptive family would be in a more stable environment than a single parent could provide. I have also been startled by the fact

111

that although we could all agree that every child should have a mom and a dad, certainly when the choice is single parent or no family at all, the preference really should be for the single parent. This simple logic, however, seems to escape many social workers.

## The Information Provided on the Child

When you are adopting, or trying to adopt an older child, you will receive a stack of information many inches thick relating to the child who has been passed along through the foster care system. Every Tom, Dick, and Harriet who interacts with the child, however briefly, will entrust his or her opinions of the child to paper. The information that one receives on any of these "system" children is frequently characterized by gross misrepresentations, inaccuracies and baseless judgments founded upon incomplete observation of the child. People should also be aware that in any situation that arises between a child and an adult in the foster care system, the adult is assumed to be in the right and the child is assumed to be in the wrong.

In the fall of 1988, I received information from the State of Mississippi on a little boy of nine years old who was supposed to be so emotionally disturbed that he could never function in a home. The information on him was voluminous, all of it negative. As a six-year-old in a foster home he was supposed to have attempted to poison the family dog. I subsequently learned that the truth of this episode was that he had seen the foster parents give the dog heartworm medicine. On the theory that if one pill is good, ten pills must be better, he then gave the dog ten pills. Certainly, it was no attempt to poison. This is the sort of unfair comment that characterizes much information that one receives from an agency.

The legal definition of "hearsay" is an out-of-court statement which is offered for the truth of the matter asserted. The reason such testimony is not allowed in court is because it is a basic and constitutional right in America to cross-examine witnesses against the accused. The information contained in the studies of children in the foster care system is complete, unexpurgated hearsay. You have no opportunity to cross-examine the person making those statements, so you have no way of knowing whether this person has values which are in any way similar to your own, or whether conduct that would horrify this person would also horrify you.

My oldest son had a social worker at the group home in which he lived who did not like to be touched. Here you have a person who is working in an orphanage for children without parents, and she doesn't like to be touched. Of course, this woman regarded any attempt by a homeless child to seek affection from an adult as a horrifying intrusion upon her personal space. It is pretty obvious that she was the one with the problem, but it certainly would not be obvious reading the reports that she would generate.

## A chance that paid off

Fortunately, for my son's sake and especially for mine, the social worker believed in him and explained to me the episode with the pet. She was candid with me but really thought that my son could adjust to a home and have a normal life. She even told me she thought he had potential to go to college. His life had been a nightmare: He had had ten placements including a ruptured adoption. The ruptured adoption had occurred because the Missisippi agency misguidedly placed him with infertile parents who had hoped to get an infant. Their agency told the couple that they would consider them for an infant only if they took my six-year-old son. When I think about these people and their selfishness, my blood boils. They had my son for a year and a half, adopted him officially and then returned him.

I agreed to take a chance on my son, and I have never regretted it for a moment. From the first time that we met, we bonded. He came and sat on my lap and hung on to me for dear life. (He'd still like to sit in my lap, but he is now 6'1" and 175 pounds.) I was to spend the entire weekend with him at his group home. On the first day, he asked if we couldn't leave for Pennsylvania that day. The poor child was frantic with fear that something would happen to ruin his chance of having a family. He had made himself physically ill prior to our arrival worrying if we would change our minds. While we visited with my son at his group home, he wrote me countless notes with hearts on them stating plaintively, "Thank you for adopting me. I love you."

When we got home, I put my son in a private school, which was a difficult adjustment for both him and the school. They were kindly people, though, who recognized that he was a lovable, extremely immature child. It was really like adopting a child from the third world. He had never been in a grocery store. He didn't know what a check was. He didn't understand that he lived in the United States.

He thought cartoons were real. The abuse and neglect that he had suffered had caused him to tune out the world around him, and it has been a process getting him willing to deal with reality.

## Adjustments

Despite the many adjustment problems my oldest son had, I really didn't personally find it an adjustment becoming a parent except perhaps in a positive sense. I constantly reminded myself with a foolish grin, "I have a son of my own. I am a mom. I have my own beautiful child." During the first year I had my oldest child, I was thrilled when I was asked if I had children so that I would get an opportunity to tell everyone about my beautiful son. (Actually, as all of my friends will readily attest, I'm still only too ready to regale people endlessly with tales of my children.)

My oldest son had difficulty realizing that this placement, after his ten previous ones, was permanent. This led him to test us in various ways to see if we would keep him. He would state to me many times a day, "You're mine forever?" To this I would respond, "Forever." He would rejoin, "No matter what?" I would reply, "No matter what." He seemed to need to hear this 20 or 30 times a day. It must have sunk in eventually because he finally stopped saying it a couple of years ago.

My oldest son and I had some struggles as we got to know each other, and as he got to learn who was in charge in our house. He has always been a warm and affectionate child, and we soon discovered that he is also extremely musically gifted, very intelligent and highly coordinated. Gradually, he has caught up in school and has gotten himself to the point where he enjoys a normal social life. He is now 17 and a junior in high school. He is driving, is one of the top-ranked racquetball players in his age group in the state, plays on the varsity tennis team at school, and plays clarinet and keyboards in the marching and concert bands in high school. I could be happier with his academic performance, but he is in college prep. I don't know too many mothers of teenage sons who are completely satisfied with their sons' academic performance.

## Adopting Again

At his urging we adopted my second son, when he was eight years old and my older son was thirteen. My second son was supposed to be seriously emotionally disturbed with attention deficit disorder and low average intelligence. Fortunately, for him as for my older son, he had a dedicated social worker who liked him and believed in him, and she

tempered some of the information we received about him. Nonetheless he, too, like my older son, was supposed to be so seriously disturbed that it was doubtful whether he could function in a household.

From the first time I met him, I began to question whether the information we had on him was any more accurate than the information we had on my older son. The child was obviously very bright, and it turned out that he reads constantly. Whereas my older son escaped from abusive circumstances by withdrawing into his own universe, my second son escaped into books. When he arrived as an eight-year-old he was reading Mark Twain, and his taste for reading continues to be a delight.

As with my older son, we received no positive information whatsoever from the agency about my second son. It was a joyous process with him, also, discovering his hidden talents and abilities. While he has Attention Deficit Disorder (ADD), which has presented many problems with school, he is extremely bright with a well-above-average to genius IQ. Now at age 12, he reads light adult fiction and has spent the summer learning classical Greek. He wishes to learn Greek because of his love for the Iliad and the Odyssey. He also is extremely musically gifted with a beautiful singing voice. He plays violin, tuba, and keyboards. He also plays racquetball and tennis.

As with his older brother, we have our struggles with school. One problem is that he is often bored there. This, combined with the ADD, makes his behavior unstable. It is a rare week that I don't get a call from some irate or disappointed authority figure at school. The principal has been very understanding, and when my son has an entire week when his behavior has been good, the principal will play chess with him as reward.

## Handling Conduct Problems

I have had to be creative in learning to reward and punish both of my older boys. A child who has been abused is impervious to most conventional forms of punishment. After all, they have had many worse experiences which you would not be able, nor would you want, to duplicate. One time, I got very exasperated with my oldest son for making $2,000 worth of calls to the 900 sex lines when he was about 13. I didn't know when I received the three-inch-thick phone bill that I did not have to pay for these charges. Fortunately, I didn't. Nonetheless, to punish my son for his conduct, I initiated a program of arising at 5:00 a.m. and learning Latin, doing extra math, and running laps. My theory was, as I told my son, that he would be so busy he wouldn't have time to get in trouble. These punishments completely backfired. He loved the Latin and math, and he buried me at running on the track. At any rate, we discovered some new common interests.

My middle son is even harder to punish or reward. He is so arrogant that he regards any praise as only his due, and he will very dismissively acknowledge it. His counselor says that he is "narcissistic." He, too, is very philosophical about punishment, and when confined to quarters will simply read, draw, or build something.

**Adopting the Third Time**

Just last summer, as a family, we started thinking about adopting another child. This time we had no choice about getting a boy since two of the kids would have to share a bedroom. My third son arrived at the age of nine just in time for Thanksgiving, 1995. It was very difficult to get him since the private, for-profit agency that had him in foster care was very reluctant to let him go. Considering that they were receiving $2,500 a month for his care, it is perhaps not too cynical to speculate that the reasons for this were largely mercenary.

My youngest son also had a two-inch stack of information, all of it negative. No one develops the talents of children in foster care. My boys had never taken a lesson or been on a sports team prior to coming to our home. My youngest son came from a severely dysfunctional family. Since he was the oldest, it was assumed that he would be the most dysfunctional; to the contrary, we have discovered that he is a sweet, loving, socially well-adjusted boy. He went right into Catholic school with no problems or disruptions whatsoever. Indeed, he only got one detention for the whole school year, a new McDermott family record. We are still in the process of discovering what his talents are, but he has started playing the flute and played on a Little League team this summer. This fall, he will be playing soccer. He is very bright and did well academically last year, especially considering everything he had to deal with--new city, new family, new school, new religion.

It has been a big adjustment for me to be a parent. With my schedule as a busy trial attorney, it is difficult for me to fit in meetings with teachers. It is also difficult for me to devote every evening to my job as tutor/jailer to make sure that all homework is conscientiously done. Fortunately, my father is home when the children arrive from school, and takes care of them with love, snacks, and encouragement. Additionally, he is a wonderful and loving male role-model for the children. I do try to spend as much time as I can with the boys, but I have learned that I am not able to attend every activity they have and maintain any type of life for myself. I have found it important to continue to play racquetball and engage in some other recreational activities by myself and for myself. I also integrate the children into my professional life to the extent that I can. Both of my older two boys love to come to my office and spend the day. They read and draw, and we have lunch together. I have taken both of them to court appearances as well, which they seem to find quite fascinating.

Taking children on, especially children with special needs, is a ferociously expensive proposition. It costs very little to adopt them--perhaps $1,500 to $2,000, and most of this money is refunded. On an ongoing basis, however, there are counseling fees, lessons, dental braces; all of the normal expenses of childhood. Luckily older children such as mine are generally eligible for subsidies and medical cards. I have never used those medical cards, but it is good to know they exist. I didn't accept any subsidy on my first son, but do gratefully accept a subsidy to help with the expenses of my younger children.

I can honestly say that even in my worst moments, when I have been called by teachers, principals, irate neighbors, I have never for one minute regretted adopting any of my darling boys. They are great kids. All they needed in this world was a chance.

# Adopting Gwen from China

## by Cheryl Vichness

*By Christmas she could crawl and by Valentine's day she was walking. By her second birthday she was declared "all caught up" with her peers. . . Over time she has blossomed into an extremely bright, confident child.*

The decision to adopt my daughter, Gwendolyn Lee, was hands-down the best decision of my life. It has not been the easiest of projects, but--- oh! the joys of raising this little angel!

When I was approximately 35 years old I ended a relationship that had no future and I remember promising myself that I would wait only a few more years before taking some concrete steps toward having a child. The notion of adopting a baby seemed completely logical and natural to me with hardly any need for serious soul-searching. I'd always adopted pets from the animal shelter and had always loved my friends' children without reservation.

The decision was really only about getting it together to actually begin the process. Get a real steady grown-up job, get a house, get my finances in shape, get started on the process. Working all those things through took about four years. When everything seemed right and I was looking at my 40th birthday, I made my first calls, starting with the State of Maryland.

They required that I take an introductory class in adoption. The teacher spoke highly of the China program as a good option for single people looking to adopt healthy infants, and also suggested an agency with particularly good ties to China. Because of his strong recommendation I didn't really agency-shop. I called them and the paper chase began.

Daunting packets of material arrived in the mail from the agency. Form after form to fill out. Send money to the agency. Begin building a dossier: references, financial records, the home study (several visits with a social worker--more money), a criminal and child abuse check (a little more money), a special birth certificate--a little more money, a doctor's statement. All these things kept me pretty busy through the next several months.

But the China program was closed during this time anyway due to reorganization and central-ization of the foreign adoption process within China. No one knew when or if the China program would reopen, though the agency was ever-optimistic. Of course, at that point I had sent the agency thousands of dollars and there were nagging suspicions (voiced especially by cautious friends) that the agency was being so reassuring in order not to jeopardize business. There were some uncomfortable times.

I spent the time doing things I knew I wouldn't be able to do once I was a mom. Traveling, going to concerts, a little wildness, some mountain climbing, some indulgences.

And then--approximately 11 months after I began actually getting my dossier together--I got a letter from the agency that the China program had reopened. Another four months after that I got THE CALL. It was a long wait. In total, about 18 months from when I decided to actively pursue adoption to the day I left for China. When the call finally came, of course, everything changed: now the task was at hand.

It was not all happy anticipation. The baby that had been chosen for me was over 11 months old and had been in the orphanage since 3 weeks of age. I had wanted a younger infant, feeling that a shorter orphanage stay would be important. But after waiting so long, there was no turning back now. We had been promised a month's notice before the trip, but we got only two weeks. Lists and lists of things to bring came in the mail--major shopping. I had superstitiously refused to prepare the baby's room in advance, so I had to paint and furnish the nursery. I was faxed a copy of my daughter's medical report with a postage-stamp sized photo; she looked like a little monkey. Hardly the Asian princess I had visualized. Again, a little disappointment but no turning back. Travel arrangements had to be final-ized along with last-minute documentation from U.S.

Immigration and Naturalization. It was an anxious, hectic time.

The day of departure arrived and it was off to L.A. where I met up with the others in my group-- four couples and seven other single women from all over the country. We were the largest group the agency had sent. The next day we flew to Hong Kong, arriving at the very nice airport hotel at about 9 p.m. local time. We took a whirlwind, three-hour taxi tour of the city--highly recommended--and then fell into bed. The next day we flew to Shanghai where we met our guide and interpreter (the only English-speaking Chinese we met until we were at the end of our trip) and then, later that same day, we flew on to Hefei, a smallish city (population about 1 million) where, the next day, we would meet our babies. It was unbelievably hot and humid (this was in August) and in Hefei the air was so polluted it always smelled like cinders. We stayed at a very nice hotel, however, all of us alone on one floor--like a dormitory.

The next day the babies came. Our names were called and one by one we were handed our babies by a nanny from the orphanage. We took them to our rooms and were given about twenty minutes to spend with them before we had to return them to the nannies and decide if we would accept the placement. Then the paperwork and interview with the Chinese officials began--this was the actual adoption. These were some of the most agonizing moments of my life. Some of the babies were real charmers from the start. Some were terrified and hysterical. And some were withdrawn and de-pressed.

Gwennie was **extremely** withdrawn, and I feared that she had been seriously damaged by her year-long stay in the orphanage. Luckily we had a doctor in our group who agreed to look Gwennie over and give his opinion on whether she was OK. He could find nothing physically wrong with her and, hysterical with exhaustion, nerves and worry, I decided to accept the placement. Later that after-noon they brought the babies back and demon-strated how to mix their food--all in Chinese of course!--and left them in our care. I was a mommy!

We didn't see the orphanage itself since it was some six hours away by car, but from what we could gather it wasn't a showplace and it wasn't a hell-hole either; just a place with too many babies, not enough staff, not enough money, no toys, no color: a baby warehouse. Many of the babies had rashes from lying in pools of sweat and many were skinny and had never been out of their box-like cribs.

Some had been tethered hand and foot to the cribs for their safety since they were left unsupervised so often.

We spent the next ten days in the hotel getting to know these little people and each other and just hanging out. It really was in a strange way like freshman year in college. We drifted in and out of each others' rooms at all hours of the day and night, we developed cliques, we experienced the instant intimacy you feel with people when sharing an intense life-changing activity. The food was mediocre, but once I discovered that the hotel gift shop carried dried fruit and ramen noodle soup, I was happy. Some members of the group got an awful stomach bug, but I was religious about taking my Pepto-Bismol before every meal and never had any difficulty.

Gwennie's only problem was constipation which I treated by adding applesauce to her rice cereal and formula. Her depression also lifted after about three days. When she finally smiled and reached for me, words can't describe how I felt. I ran into the hall exclaiming "She laughed!!" There were general congratulations since many in the group had shared my concern over Gwennie's emotional state. From then on she and I were a team. Although she remained pretty reserved, I knew she knew me and liked me best.

The ten days in the hotel seemed to stretch out endlessly. There was really not much to do but walk around our floor and the lobby. It was too hot and dirty to go outside other than at dawn. Some people went for walks at that early hour and were rewarded with seeing groups practising their morn-ing T'ai Chi in the park.

Then suddenly the wait was over: Our paperwork came back from Beijing with the adoption decrees and the babies' passports. We now faced the ordeal of traveling with these little ones. We flew to Ghuang Chou (Canton) where we spent two days getting the babies' medical examinations (at a Chinese clinic--what an ordeal), having their visa photos taken and being interviewed at the U.S. consulate. This was a logistical nightmare. Ghuang Chou is a beautiful city (in a faded sort of way) and we stayed at an absolutely gorgeous hotel--totally luxurious--but unfortunately we couldn't really enjoy it since we had so much to get done in so little time.

There was wonderful shopping in the hotel's shopping arcade and some of our group spent time and money scooping up treasures, but others were too frenzied to look for bargains. Of course, now that we're home I think it would have been nice to have brought back a lot of souvenirs, and I did manage to get a few nice objects, but it was taking almost all my concentration to hold it together as we neared the end of our journey.

Suddenly, it was time to go home. Back to Hong Kong and then the challenge of the long flight to L.A. The flight was completely full--not an empty seat. No stretching out; no real relief. But we made it. The noisy, frenetic L.A. airport and waiting around in lines to clear customs and immigration after all that time on the plane and no real sleep and dealing with miserable babies and all their stuff--well, it's all a blur now but it was certainly no fun.

Amazingly enough, many of our group flew straight home from L.A., but Gwennie and I spent the night in an L.A. motel before flying home to Balti-more--which I really recommend. It wasn't a restful night, but I ordered-in what turned out to be the best pizza I've ever had and watched TV while Gwennie rolled around on the king-size bed as if it was the middle of the day which, to her, it was.

And then we were home, and real life began. The readjustment period is another blurry time, but my friends say I wore a glazed, happy-but-kind-of-grim expression for about a week. It took a few unpleasant days to get Gwennie on the new time schedule, but luckily she was a pretty good sleeper, and we actually had a wonderful month before I had to go back to work.

There were lots of things to deal with, of course. I found excellent day care and then took time to slowly get her used to going there and saying good bye to Mommy. I had her evaluated by Maryland's child development agency which found her significantly delayed in several areas. She was referred for physical therapy, speech therapy, eye examination, and the eating clinic. The evaluation and all the therapy sessions were free and very high quality--a wonderful surprise; I had no idea such a comprehensive resource was available.

In those first few months, it seemed as if I was always taking her to one appointment or an-other: the pediatrician, one of her therapies, postplacement interviews (the agency required five of these and each cost $200; I had not anticipated those fees). I had budgeted $20,000 for the adop-tion, and I **just** made it with travel expenses and post-placement fees. I never thought twice about the money, although it pretty much used up my entire life savings. What better investment could I possibly have made?

Gwennie's progress has been steady and extremely gratifying for me and for all who have worked with her. She couldn't even sit up when we came home from China. By Christmas she could crawl and by Valentine's day she was walking. Over time she has blossomed into an extremely bright, confident child. By her second birthday she was declared "all caught up" with her peers and released from her therapies. Now, at three and a half, she is in pre-school, which she loves, and she speaks beautifully with an extensive vocabulary and grasp of abstract concepts. Her memory and ability to make connections constantly amaze me. She is a whiz at the computer and would absolutely run our house-hold if I only let her.

Most importantly Gwennie is a happy, outgoing, loving, delightful child. She is always playing adorable and occasionally hilarious imagina-tive games with her stuffed animals. I often get choked up when she gives me an unexpected decla-ration of love with hugs and kisses and snuggles. She has filled my life. Our first years together have been nothing short of amazing. There's been stress: some high fevers (scary) and the "juggling" of Gwennie-care and a full-time job (something often has to give, and it's almost always housework and personal correspondence and hobbies and sometimes work). All in all, though, it's been even more wonderful than I imagined. Yes, it is a challenge taking care of this active, inquisitive, determined little person--the most rewarding challenge of my life.

Cheryl Vichness is the client services and office manager for a small but very active human resources consulting firm in Baltimore, Maryland.

# Adopting the Physically-Challenged Child

**by Jim Forderer**

*Most important, there is the child who becomes a member of the family,
a person who needs love and who has much love to give in return.
What may be apparent as a disability on the outside quickly fades into
a routine, and what one is most aware of is the person who is the child.*

There are many children today in need of families, and some of these children have various disabilities which make their management different from that of a normal child. Most single people, like most couples, are interested first in adopting a "normal, healthy infant," but discover that such children are not available to them, at least in the United States. Agencies that will not place so-called normal children with single people will place "waiting children" with unmarried women and men. I would like to suggest that there are some good reasons to consider adopting a child with physical limitations.

I would first like to share with you some of my own experiences in adoption so that you might understand better where my thoughts and feelings are coming from. As I write this article I am now 57 years old. I adopted my first child at the age of 29 as a single parent. Scott is now 39 years old, and is both an emergency medical technician and a family and drug counselor. Scott came to me as an emotionally disturbed 11-year old who had been in nine other placements before being placed with me. He was an interesting as well as difficult child to parent and I am thankful that we both survived the experience.

After that time I adopted eight more children as a single parent and parented seven foster children--all boys. All of the children that I adopted since Scott were severely physically disabled. Three of the foster children are also disabled. In 1985 I married Marian Aiken who was the single parent of four physically- and multi-handicapped children. Since our marriage we have added 14 children to the family, all of whom have significant disabilities. My oldest child is now 43 years old and the youngest is seven. Fifteen of our children are currently living at home, five have passed away, and the other older children are either living on their own or in a group home for young adults. One of them lives in a college dormitory and comes home on many weekends. Seven of our children were born in Russia and the rest were born in the United States.

The following describes the fifteen children living at home now: Six of the boys have Cerebral Palsy and multiple disabilities (seven cannot speak orally, though three use computers with speech output devices and two use sign language). One is fed through a stomach tube. We also have children with missing arms, legs and two without any limbs at all. We have a child with severe arthrogryposis, and one with Rubinstein-Tabey Syndrome. Three of our sons are dwarfs, two are deaf, and a number are mentally retarded (some severely, some mildly). We also have children with clubbed hands, missing fingers, and heart conditions (Holt-Oran Syndrome). Thirteen of our children go to school and two to a social, vocational program. Ten of the children use wheelchairs for their mobility; some are able to use electric wheelchairs. Most of the boys require assistance meeting their daily needs of dressing, toileting, feeding, etc. All of the children we have adopted have been boys, as the logistics of the family makes this the only sensible thing to do at this point. We have a person who comes in five days a week to help out with the care of the children.

My older children are now grown and have lives of their own. John, who is deaf, works for Target stores and helps out with our younger children two evenings a week for extra pay. He has his own apartment in the rear of our property. David is now living at San Francisco State University where he will graduate with a degree in Government and Foreign Affairs later this year. Tom, 31, and Tim, 21, have their own apartments nearby, where they live on their own, and Sean and Rusty, both 21, live in a group home. Jay is now 37 years old. He is a dwarf who is also quadriplegic due to a spinal injury. He has his own apartment, drives a van, and holds a good job as an office manager for a legal firm. He has had several other jobs that he did not like as well, and took some time getting his act together, but is now doing quite well and feeling good about his life. All of these young men keep in close contact with the family, as do many of my other sons, both foster and adopted.

As a family we are quite active, though not as active as when we were a smaller group. We like to swim, horseback ride, sightsee, go on picnics, go to sporting events and do many other things. We are always able to find a way to do the things we want. We live in a single-story house that we have completely adapted to our needs, and drive two vans so that all the wheelchairs can fit inside. Being in a wheelchair is the normal condition in this household, so the boys feel that they are in the mainstream. We really lead a very normal life in most respects and are generally a happy, active family.

## Why Adopt a Special-Needs Child?

There are many misconceptions about handicapped individuals. Most people view them as tragic and pity them; many people are repelled by their presence. Most people feel that they could not cope with the management of their problems and the emotional strain it would create. These, however, are usually people who have not had any direct close personal contact with handicapped individuals.

Handicapped people and handicapped children, in particular, are not people to pity. They are people, like everyone else, who are trying to lead their lives in the best way they know how. They do not need pity, they need acceptance. They generally do not pity themselves unless they have been taught to do so and, in most cases, they do not consider themselves as handicapped, but rather as individuals who have to find different ways of doing the things that others do, or different ways of satisfying the same needs that we all have.

Young children, particularly, do not have the concept that they are different from other people, and are most willing to accept their condition as the way things are and go on from there, if they can get some support in doing this. They need to experience love and acceptance like all children. They need encouragement to try new things and discipline to learn to conform to a normal society and to respect authority. They need to be given responsibility whenever possible and as much initiative in planning their own activities as is reasonable for the situation.

## How Will the Parent's Life Change?

Families adopting handicapped children do not have to change their life styles. In fact, it would be very wrong to attempt to do so, as it would create resentment in the parents and guilt in the child. Families must, however, be flexible, patient, and creative in figuring out new ways to do the things that they have always done. It sometimes takes a little longer to get things done, or the way in which an activity is done might be somewhat altered, but the experience can be the same and the enjoyment just as great (usually, with handicapped children, the enjoyment is greater because so much pride and excitement comes with accomplishing new activities),

Parenting a child with a special need does take more involvement on the part of the parent. There are agencies to deal with, doctors to talk to, information to learn, special programs for the child, and decisions on how best to cope with it all. To be most effective in doing this, a parent must become an "expert" in the field of the child's disability. The professionals are there to help, but often it is the parent, alone, who really understands just what the needs of the child are, and what effect each new program or procedure will have on his entire life. This demands enough self-confidence on the part of the parent to be able to meet with doctors, therapists and educators on an equal basis, knowing that the final decision as to the best treatment for his chilld rests with the parent.

For the involved parent there will be the opportunity to meet a lot of new and interesting people, and to get a broader education. One may also learn to become more assertive in dealing with people, and in advocating for the rights of children. He will also gain an increased awareness and dignity of all people and to the basic sameness that we all possess. Most important, there is the child who becomes a member of the family, a person who needs love and who has much love to give in return. What may be apparent as a disability on the outside quickly fades into a routine, and what one is most aware of is the person who is the child.

As a parent, I find myself more involved in the educational process of my more handicapped children than I am in that of my other children. This is not to say that I am not involved with the education of my other children or that I spend more time with my more handicapped children, but rather that it takes more specialized and individualized planning to meet the needs of a child with a major disability.

Cerebral palsy is a condition affecting the brain and is often accompanied by perceptual difficulties which can cause learning disorders. Staying on top of the school program is a must if a parent is to insure that his/her child will receive the best possible education. With the passage of Public Law 94-142, which mandates a free, appropriate public education, in the least restrictive environment, for all handicapped children, parents are now part of the planning team and must participate in every step of the planning for their child's educational program.

There are other areas that may need attention that do not occur with a nonhandicapped child. There may be physical therapy, occupational therapy, or speech therapy. These programs may take place in the school or in clinics, but often exercises must be done at home as well. There will be doctors' appointments and sometimes hospitalization to correct physical defects or to improve the functioning of the body. Helping a child deal with a disability can become a family project and the child's gains can be a source of pride to the entire family.

Having a physically challenged child in the family will have a positive as well as negative impact on all other children in the family. Families adding a child with special needs can anticipate a few problem situations, but they can minimize the problems if they anticipate them and handle them in a positive manner.

One situation is jealousy, caused by the parent giving more time to the child with special needs than to the other children. There are two positive ways to deal with this problem: One is to explain to the other children that it simply takes more time for the challenged sibling to accomplish some activities, but that the added time you spend with that child does not mean you love that child more. The open line of communication between parent and child is what is important here.

But just talking about a situation is not enough: The parent should also plan to spend individual time with each member of the family, so that each child feels s/he has the undivided attention of the parent for a specified amount of time. I like to take one child out to dinner alone each week, so that he has a special time to be with his father. The kids really look forward to their turn to go out to dinner, and it is a pleasant time for me as well.

Another problem can occur if other children in the family do not feel comfortable with their peers because of their disabled brother or sister. Going to the same school can sometimes be a problem for the non-disabled child if he feels that other kids in the school pick on him, or just single him out, because he has a brother or sister who is different. Again, with the right kind of understanding for all concerned, these situations can usually be worked out in a positive way.

There are some positive effects to having a physically-challenged child in the family. Siblings are exposed to a greater variety of human situations and often develop a sensitivity toward others that would not have grown without the exposure to their disabled sibling. There can be great joy in sharing experiences of childhood for every sibling in a family.

With all that the raising of a physically challenged child entails, why would anyone want to consider adopting one? The adopting parent who knows that the child has a disability before the adoption is spared the very painful and often damaging grief, guilt, and disappointment that is often felt by biological parents of a baby who turns out to be handicapped. No guilt is associated with adopting a handicapped child, no grieving for the child who might have been. The adopting parent meets the child knowing full well what the situation is, and can be prepared ahead ot time for many of the conditions surrounding the upbringing of that child.

### Benefits Associated with Special Needs Adoption

There are a number of positive aspects to the parenting of a physically-challenged child, that make the decision to adopt a child with special needs more attractive to the prospective adopting parent. Some of these programs can benefit the entire family and some can be passed on to the child when he/she becomes an adult. Such things as SSI, and Medicaid that can go with it, become entitlements to the child when that child becomes an adult, under the current laws.

All states have adoption subsidy programs for families adopting special needs children. These incentives include waiving of adoption fees, medical aid to meet the existing and future medical needs of the child, and a monthly allowance to help meet the financial costs that such a child might bring to a family. Federally-supported and state-legislated programs such as Adoption Assistance Programs (AAP), Supplemental Security Income (SSI), In-home Support Services, Medicaid and special agreements for services such as nursing care or respite care can be worked out. One-time payment for non-recurring costs associated with the adoption (such as travel expenses) can also be worked out with a public agency before placement so that these services follow the child into his new home.

Other public laws also favor disabled individuals. The whole educational experience is at least more carefully thought out for the child with special educational needs than is the program for regular education students. That is not to say that the quality of their educational experience is necessarily better, but rather that the parent is at least better informed and has more of an opportunity to have an impact on the educational program than with a normal education.

Other areas get consideration as well. There are programs for special recreation, homemaker services, respite care, special transportation services and lower-cost electrical bills. There are special parking and gas-buying privileges in some areas. Counseling may be available, and also job placement services such as those that the department of vocational rehabilitation offers to some disabled people. There are also tax breaks associated with the costs of raising a disabled child.

### Managing Psychological and Social Needs:

Parenting a child who is physically challenged creates some extra responsibilities that need to be pointed out in advance. These conditions are not necessarily different from the responsibilities of any parent but, because of the special ways in which the parent-child relationship might develop, they must be kept in mind.

One of the biggest pitfalls in parenting a child who is limited in some way is that of being overprotective. Because the child may not be able to do some things or may depend on the parent for assistance in some areas, parents tend to keep their child more dependent on them than they would a normal child. Children must be encouraged to be as independent as possible, allowed to take risks, allowed to fail when the situation is appropriate, and allowed to find their own way at their own rate. This may be a hard thing for a parent to do for any child, and it is particularly hard for the parent of a disabled child. It is a tremendous disservice to the child, however, not to let him grow up, mature, and find his own way. Life is filled with adversities, and the physically challenged child must be helped to learn how to cope with them.

Another area of concern is helping the child to develop a sense of responsibility. In order to develop a positive self-image, a child must feel competent in performing some tasks. These tasks should be at a level that the child can accomplish, and that gives the child the feeling that he is contributing to the wellbeing of the whole family. Allowing the child to be on his own, when appropriate, is another way to instill a sense of responsibility and a positive self-image. These attitudes must be developed fairly early or the child may develop patterns of overdependency on his parents that will be hard to break as he gets older.

Social development for the physically challenged child will tend to be slower, due to lack of interaction with his non-handicapped peers. Here again, a parent can take steps to minimize this problem. Most adults, as well as other children, tend to treat dependent children as younger than they are. This is seen in the way people talk to or about disabled children, as well as the way in which people in authority delegate responsibility to the disabled. I have often observed people talking down to my boys because they are in wheelchairs--even to my then-sixteen year-old son!

This attitude demeans the individual and makes him feel less competent than he really is. Parents must be watchful that they do not treat their own children in this manner, and try to steer other people away from this as well. Such things as talking about a child in his presence as if he weren't there, or answering questions for the child that he could be answering himself, are examples of how disabled kids are sometimes put down. When I am asked in front of one of my boys how old he is, what is his name, or why he is in a wheel chair, I always redirect the question to the child and, in a friendly way, let the person know that the child can answer these questions himself.

Parenting a physically challenged child requires the parent to be an advocate for the rights of his child. Parents must be prepared to do more than just deal with the here and now. Some services are just not being provided. Parents are the most effective advocates in compelling agencies to provide needed services.

Social attitudes toward the acceptance of disabled individuals into the main stream of society are another area in which a parent can be an effective advocate. The parent becomes, in effect, a public educator. There will be many times when talking to people in the community will improve understanding of the needs of disabled individuals. Public schools, recreation departments, churches, and business establishments are becoming more and more aware that they must include all people in their service planning, but they still need help in learning how best to deliver their services to disabled individuals.

### Finding Your Special-Needs Child:

Finding a baby who has medical problems or is at high risk of developing problems is not so difficult for the single person. Today, many babies are born whose mothers have been exposed to drugs or alcohol (or both) while pregnant. Not only do the babies often exhibit medical problems at birth, but the mothers are often unable to care properly for these babies because of their own addiction. Usually an effort is made to help the mother get off the substance she is abusing and reunite the family, but these efforts are not always successful, and the children do enter the adoption system. If you are interested in parenting such a baby you should become familiar with the ramifications of raising a child with these types of problems. Sometimes they do not seem too difficult for the younger child, but manifest themselves more strongly as the child grows older. Here the word "risk" becomes very real, as it is often impossible to tell at an early age which children will be able to overcome their difficult beginnings and which will not.

Another type of special-needs child that can be available to a single person is the baby born with AIDS or who tests positive for the HIV virus. There are many more of these children now than in years past, and they have a very difficult time finding homes. For persons willing to take on the challenges that these children present, the supply of these children is in favor of the single adopting parent.

Babies with other types of severe medical conditions are likely to be made available to single persons. Children with Down Syndrome, Spina Bifida, Cerebral Palsy, Bronchial Pulmonary Dysplasia (BPD), congenital deformities, and multiple birth defects might be placed with a single person.

If a person is interested in a child such as this he/she can often find one. Going to a large hospital and asking if there are any "boarder babies" might uncover a child who has been in the hospital since birth, abandoned by its parents. They often stay in the hospital for many months, particularly if there is a medical condition involved. These children often are not brought to the attention of the social welfare departments or adoption agencies, but the social workers in the hospital know of these children and are usually anxious to find resources for them. it is helpful if you know a nurse or other staff person in a hospital to keep an eye out for you for such a child.

For the older, school-aged children the places to look are a little different, again depending on the type of child you are looking for. If you are working with an agency, ask them to allow you to look at whatever exchange books they might have available. Each state or region usually has a listing of its hard-to-place children, to which licensed adoption agencies usually have access. Additionally there are regional and national exchanges that publish books or have computer-based data networks that can help in finding a child. [A list of such exchanges appears at the end of Chapter II.]

Joining a parent support group can be good from many standpoints. They can be very supportive to a waiting parent, they can steer you to sources of waiting children, and they can help you find resources to handle special needs. There are groups for many different interests: Single adoptive parents, parents adopting children from abroad, parents adopting transracially, parents with special characteristics who are interested in adopting like children (such as Little People of America); and parent groups specializing in children with Down Syndrome, quadriplegia, learning disabilities, or many other kinds of handicaps.

Volunteering your time with organizations that help children can also be a way of locating children in need of adoptive families. This will also prepare you to be more experienced as a parent, by exposing you to children in different settings. One very good program to become associated with is the Court Designated Child Advocacy Program. This exists in many parts of the country, and pairs a child advocate with a child who is usually a ward of the court. The advocate follows the child's case and presents to the court an overview of all the different agencies and people who are acting on behalf of the child, so that the court has a better understanding of what is really in the best interest of the child. Because the Advocate is not connected with any agency or special interest group, he/she is not influenced in his/her opinion of what is in the best interest of that child by political or psychological leanings.

This experience also brings the advocate in contact with children who are in out-of-home placement and whose long range planning may include adoption. It also brings them in contact with agencies and workers who know the system and the children in the system and who may be of help in locating a child or making contacts. It also (and perhaps most importantly) performs a very valuable service to a child who is in a vulnerable position.

Another resource for the prospective parent is the regional center. If you would consider adopting a developmentally-delayed child, these agencies are involved with the long range planning for these children. Because these children are not covered by the regulations set forth in P.L. 96-272, the Child and Family Protection Act of 1980, they are often not brought to the attention of adoption agencies and are sometimes placed in community-based facilities where they will never get the chance to develop their potential. This is also a very expensive option for the state, and an adoptive placement serves the needs of both the child and the state much better. The problem is finding out about these children and getting them out of the system before they become lost in the files.

For the child who does not have exceptional needs, the services mentioned under **Benefits**, above, may not be available. However, if the child is from a minority ethnic background, is a member of a sibling group being placed together, or is over the age of ten (this varies from state to state), these services may be obtained. For children coming in from foreign countries, these services are not available.

To sum up, if you are looking for a child to adopt, figure out what type of child you feel you can handle. Make your intentions to adopt known to as many people as possible, and be prepared to do your own search. Since personal contacts are often the best way to find a child, tell everyone you know that you are looking. Ask that nurse you know if he/she knows of any children in the hospital who might be available for adoption, and have them ask around to the doctors and nurses, social workers, etc.

Let your agency know that you want to assist in the search for your own child. Then, as you hear about possible available children, try to make a personal contact with the child's worker. It is always better if the child's worker knows you personally rather than just as a case number on a piece of paper. This can go a long way toward dispelling negative attitudes about single parents.

Assisting in your own search will also open the field to the possibilities that may be available to you. It is difficult to put down on paper exactly the type of child you would consider adopting. You may find that while the general concept of a particular type of child might not be what you had in mind, when you find out about a specific child you are moved by something else that you had not explained to your social worker. This might be the child for you, but if it is left up to the worker who is going by your initial indication that this is not the sort of child you would be interested in, you might not even be told about that one.

Be friendly, be persistent, be flexible and open-minded, be knowledgeable about the resources for waiting children and the ramifications of taking a child with a particular set of conditions or risks. Your child is out there waiting for you to find. Hang in there and you will succeed.

**The Future of a Special-Needs Child:**

Finding resources for older disabled children and young adults is one of the biggest challenges for their parents. Once their school days are over, they need some type of program to move into. This is not so much a problem for individuals who are able to go into competitive employment and to meet their own physical needs, but it is more of a challenge to people who must rely on others to meet all or part of their daily needs. Planning well in advance can help bridge the gap between childhood and adult living situations.

When a young person reaches age eighteen, he (or she) is considered an independent person by the Social Security Administration and can qualify for SSI benefits regardless of the family income if he meets the qualifications of disability. He also might become eligible to receive services from the state department of vocational rehabilitation, Goodwill Industries, and other adult organizations. These and other state and local programs might allow a person to move into a more independent living situation.

Parents need to begin looking into these programs when their children are young, so that the services will be available when a young person needs them. At the present time far more people need vocational, housing, and attendent care services than there are agencies to fill the need. Working with the schools and other independent living organizations will help alleviate the problem of what to do when the school program is finished.

There are no guarantees for the future of physically challenged children. There are no guarantees for the future of any child. We, as parents, can only give our children as rich an experience as our family can provide. Our children will learn and grow from their exposure to family life and the value system of their parents. What they choose to do with this experience as adults is a choice that they must make for themselves. Handicapped children are no different in this respect. They may not be able to lead totally independent lives, but they can lead lives that do not depend on their parents. If they are dependent as adults there are government programs that might help with their support, and private programs where handicapped adults live together and help each other to the extent that each is able to contribute.

I do not know what sort of situation will be best for each of our sons as they become adults and choose their own life styles. I do know that we will provide them with all the love and support that we can, to help them become as independent as possible. I will continue to offer my support and love, as any parent would to his adult children, but I do not intend to provide our children with constant care for the rest of our lives. Their lives will be theirs for the living, and their choices will be theirs to make. My goal now is to give them the confidence, skills and responsibility to make these decisions for themselves when the time comes.

I do have hope for a brighter future. Public attitudes have changed greatly toward the needs of disabled individuals. There is still a long way to go but at least one can be confident that progress is being made to end job discrimination, provide public accessibility to buildings and better transportation; and generally to be more open and accepting of all individuals regardless of their situation. There is also great progress in the fields of medicine and technology. Better treatments as well as devices to make life more manageable are constantly being developed, so that the gap between the able-bodied and the disabled is steadily narrowing. As the parent of a physically challenged child, you could look forward to your child having a better quality life in the future than has been possible in the past.

# ADOPTING *TRANSRACIALLY*

## By Betsy Burch

*I am a strong proponent of transracial adoption as a means of placement for children who are in need of families . . . Race, [however,] is a fact of life that cannot and should not be ignored.*

I am a single parent who has adopted transracially. I am a strong proponent of transracial adoption as a means of placement for children who are in need of families. Those who oppose placing waiting children in good, caring families seem to be blind to the needs of the children who are waiting for families and permanence TODAY. I believe that it is our responsibility, all of us, to encourage adoption for all children and to encourage all families to consider adopting. And when the day comes that we have enough families for all the waiting children, we can match them up in many ways. We do not live in that world now, so now we do the best we can--and the results are actually quite wonderful. I have known dozens of families who have adopted transracially. Only a handful of these should not have done so, and I believe that the agencies who placed their children did not do a very good job of screening.

Most of the adoptive families I know are willing and able to raise their Black children in a caring and responsible way--to raise them to be proud, healthy, loving adults who are aware of the joys, and problems, of the world and are ready to embrace the good and to deal capably with the bad. Race is a fact of life that cannot and should not be ignored. We need to let our children know how beautiful and wonderful they are, what impressive lives Black men and women have led who came before them, what special things they are capable of doing in their lives. Our society is certainly not "colorblind." Anyone who forms a family transracially needs to understand, as much as possible, what the issues are that will, in all probability, present themselves to our children and to our families. Indeed, you will need to prepare yourself and your children for a lot of negative behavior, if you adopt transracially. However, I feel that there is nothing in this life that I could have done that would have been as joyful, as fulfilling, as extraordinary as forming my family in this way.

I have been a single adoptive parent for 28 years. I have four children, currently ranging in age from fifteen to thirty-five. When I became a parent my whole family was forever changed--not only in the "usual" ways that families are changed when a new child is added, but in a wonderful and different way. My family will forever be, at least in part, African-American. Transracial adoption affects not only the parent and child(ren), but extended family--grandparents, aunts, uncles, and cousins in the immediate and, in the long run, generations to come.

I have spoken with hundreds of single people over the last twenty years who were considering adoption. Some people, who identified themselves as White, said that they were not open to adopting transracially, which used to bother me. I realized, however, that they were absolutely correct--if they were not completely comfortable parenting a child of a race different from their own, it would not be in anyone's best interest (especially a child's) to try to talk them into it. I am more concerned with those who wish to adopt "not a Black child, but mixed race would be okay." These are people who obviously do not have a clue about race issues in America today, who do not understand that a child who is "part Black" is a Black child to most people.

When I began the adoption process, I had very little support and even less information.

1971: I was 25 years old, living in my own apartment, teaching sixth grade in the Boston Public Schools. I had my Master's degree, a feeling of stability, and no plans for major life changes--just go with the flow.

Then I started thinking about adoption, about being a mother--not many years later, but then. Adoption runs in my family: my mother was adopted as an "older child"; her adoption occurred when her birth mother placed an ad in a national newspaper and had Mom, at age six, choose her new family from the responses. Mom chose well and had a wonderful life after those first six difficult years.

In 1971 just a few single parent adoptions were being made by agencies on the East and West coasts. Most of these adopters were single, White, professional women in their 30's and 40's adopting young, Black girls. At that time most of my experience was with Black children--I was teaching in an all-Black school, and my students were "my children." I began noticing ads (very new at that time) showing pictures of children available for adoption and asking interested families to consider adoption.

I decided there was no reason that I should not be a single adoptive parent. Two Boston agencies however, decided that I couldn't adopt unless I lived near my "extended family." My parents and siblings were in upstate New York; I took the agencies at their word, picked up my life, and moved back to New York. I took a job teaching in a small school in the hills of upstate and settled into an old farmhouse I found to rent. I started talking with new friends and co-workers about my adoption plans and was told about a little girl in the first grade of the school in which I was teaching. Lorrie had been free for adoption since birth and had been in three different foster homes. I called her social worker just to find out about her, and seven weeks later she moved in with me. I was a Mother; she was my daughter.

My daughter was six-and-a-half and beautiful. I wish that I had known other adoptive families at that time; I think I would have been smarter about the feelings she must have had. She must have been really scared; she was moving in with a stranger. She had no idea if I would take care of her or abandon her. What were the rules in THIS house? I felt excited and scared--and guilty, because I did not fall in love immediately. I'd never known anyone who had adopted an older child, and it took me a while to realize that I was in the process of knowing and loving her, but that she was a person who came with her own set of feelings, experiences, likes and dislikes, and our relationship had to develop.

In the midst of these huge life changes, for both of us, was the fact that Lorrie is Black and I am White. In some ways this was not a major adjustment for her: She had always lived in White foster families and actually knew only one Black family, so she thought any Black person she encountered must be a Pritchard. When we first went to Syracuse, the largest city nearby with diverse population, Lorrie was amazed, saying, "Mommy, look at how many Pritchards there are!"

Her social worker, earlier agency dogma to the contrary, agreed that we should move back to the Boston area where our family could be part of a more diverse population. So we did. Our neighborhood was not as diverse as I would have liked, however (something that would be an absolute priority for me if I were in the same position again), and I asked the school system to transport Lorrie to a different elementary school that was more diverse than our neighborhood school. A school psychologist told me that I was "looking for problems where none existed" and that Lorrie's race should not be a consideration. I explained that Lorrie was very much a Black child, that she was beginning not only to be aware of that but to feel very good about herself and that, new as I was to being part of a Black family, I was trying to encourage her in every way to know and understand differences in people and to feel good about them. So began my education of the public schools. I say this not arrogantly but, as any parent would say who has a child who is adopted, has a "special" education need, or is of a different race or background from the school's usual population--we learn to teach the educators.

When I thought about adding a child or children to our family, there was never any question in my mind about race: It was clear that my children are African-American, that they would all be African-American, that they would share their pride, their problems, their dealings with a world not always welcoming to them. Travis came to me at age seven (Lorrie was thirteen by then); three years later Benjamin arrived at age three-and-a-half and, to my surprise, Jamie joined us three years after Ben, at age four months! The only additions to my family now are grandchildren.

As my family grew, the consciousness of the country was being raised about issues of racism. Some things changed for the better, some did not. Although there have been many incidents of people staring at our family, some nasty name-calling, and a few really vile racist confrontations, I didn't realize the full force of racism in this country until my sons got older. The African-American male is feared, disrespected, hated, and blamed for many of the wrongs in the world. It is heartbreaking to see your son, your child, treated horribly by ignorant people who prejudge him simply by his skin tone.

I wish I could tell you that I have figured out a way for my children and myself to overcome this, but I haven't. What we do, and what every interracial family has to do, is to prepare our children as much as possible for the racism that they will surely experience, and to let them know that we will be there, beside them, emotionally if not physically, when they deal with it.

So, if it's this difficult, this much heartache, why become the parent of African-American children? First, 99% of the time life in a family like mine is the same as life in other families--school, work, play, shop, do the laundry--lots of laundry. I stressed some of the more difficult things in this article because I think it's important to bring people back a bit toward center from that pre-adoption glow of thinking it's going to be like running through a meadow on a Spring day.

Second, to answer more fully, please indulge me while I speak directly to my children.

Lorrie, Travis, Ben, and Jamie: You have opened my world. I have met people, gone places, and done things that I never would have done without you. You have taught me so much about strength, courage, and facing things head on. We have laughed, a lot (but please, not at the dinner table with your mouth full). We have had and continue to have, great times. You have given me beautiful grandchildren, and I'm sure there are more to come. We are different; we are the same. We have been, we are, we always will be, a family. Thank you for letting me be your Mom. I love you.

### Pre-Adoption Considerations

Some things to think about and discuss with others (friends, family, social worker, support group members, etc.):
o How does your family feel about changing the family tree forever?
o How welcoming will your community, family, friends be to a Black child?
o Do you have a preconceived idea of how "black" your child should be?
o Do you know, or are you willing to learn, how to care properly for your child's skin and hair? (Do Black people need to use sunscreen?)
o How multicultural is your life right now?
o Are the issues of the Black community important to you?
o Will your child have other children of color with whom to spend time regularly? How about Black adults?
o Would you be comfortable with people assuming that your spouse is Black?
o Do you know how it feels to be in the minority?
o Have you ever been the only White person in a gathering?
o Do you acknowledge and confront racism, even in your workplace or among family or friends?
o Are you prepared to deal with those who feel that you have "settled" for second best because you "weren't able" to adopt a White child?
o How do you feel about being white?

### Post-Adoption Strategies

o Find and consistently attend support groups--both for you and your child. Single adoptive parent group; interracial family group, etc.
o Live in a diverse community.
o Reach out to families of color; find common interests.
o Let your Black friends know that you are open to advice about bringing up your Black child. Ask specific questions—about racism, about schoolteachers, about hair care. Keep the dialogue going.
o Be aware of places, situations, communities into which you take your child and yourself. Don't think that because you are an interracial family that you can go anywhere; probably the opposite is true. Be aware and be smart.
o When your child tells you about racial name-calling, let him know that name-calling is not acceptable and that you will intervene to make sure that the adults (school personnel, parents, etc.) are aware of the problem and are reacting appropriately. As your child becomes older s/he will learn to handle most situations on her/his own, but will continue to need your support.
o Always remember that you are your child's parent; no one cares about her more, loves him more, or is THERE for him, like you are. Don't let anyone intimidate you or try to make you feel that you are not the Right parent for your child. You are the best parent for your child, and she knows that.

Betsy Burch, MA, is the mother of four adopted children and the grandmother of three. She works as a mediator for the Massachusetts Department of Education, mediating disputes between parents and schools over their children's special education. She is the Executive Drector of SPACE ----Single Parents For Adoption of Children Everywhere, a single adoptive parent support group founded in 1974, which sponsors the biennial national conference for single adoptive parents. In 1991 she was honored as one of the national leaders in adoption issues at a ceremony in the White House.

# Adopting Privately in the United States

by Mary Ellen Payne

*Life has never been so good [as it has been] since I became a mother. Every moment of angst (even the fall-through) was worth it since without them I would not have Cait and Mike.*

When I adopted Caitlin in 1991 from Romania, there was never a doubt in my mind that she would have a sibling. I just was not sure of how or when I would do it. While private domestic adoption was plausible, as a single parent it did not seem probable. The prospect of going overseas with an extended absence from Caitlin was too painful to contemplate.

My first adoption involved a lot of data collection and so did my second. I attended, among many other seminars, the Families for Private Adoption class. There I learned a key fact:

> Approximately half of all non-familial private adoptions comes from word of mouth and the other half comes from some form of promotion.

Once you are a parent through adoption, it is much easier to speak openly about your desire to adopt again. So, given the opportunity, I would mention my interest in adopting another child.

One of the families I met in Romania called and told me that their 17-year-old daughter was pregnant and thinking about adoption . . . was I interested? They were not sure of her commitment but she had asked her parents' help in making an adoption plan. After speaking with her and indicating my interest, she agreed. However, she expressed her desire for me to direct all ongoing inquiries to her parents, not to her. Her mother warned me that their daughter was given to whim and might change her mind. I assured her as well as myself that it would be okay if she did change her mind. I understood the risk and would not have my hopes too high. I busied myself with updating my home study.

I thought I had remained distant from this potential adoption by not buying the first piece of infant paraphernalia until the baby was born. In reality, I was very emotionally connected to this baby-to-be. When the call came of her arrival and news that I

should be in Texas in the morning to bring her home, my heart soared. The six-hour shopping spree that followed took me to an incredible high. A high that came crashing down when the phone rang, just as I was walking out the door for the airport, to tell me that "she is too cute to give up."

It took six months before I could even walk into the room where all the baby's things were piled. While I admitted publicly to still wanting a sibling for Caitlin, I seriously doubted whether I could go through the roller coaster again.

However, the analytical part of me continued to collect data. I focused on countries that required only a short or no in-country stay, monitored the Romanian situation and immersed myself in being Caitlin's mom. I tried to convince myself that maybe it would be okay to have only one child. Perhaps eleven first cousins would be good enough for Cait. Yet, I continued to tell interested friends that I wanted more children, only I was not sure when.

Then the call came. A colleague from my office told me that her daughters were friends with an individual whose girlfriend was pregnant and was considering adoption. Her daughters thought I was a good Mom to Caitlin and wanted to know if I were interested in speaking to the birth mother. I was frightened by the prospect and overwhelmed by the painful renewal of those feelings of loss.

I convinced myself that meeting her was not a commitment, that she was only just looking into the possibility. I could decide that this was not an arrangement for us and with a home study that was still valid, what was the risk?

The following week I met her--a very together freshman in college. Not only did she have a plan, but a complete set of questions! While I was not sure I could go through this again, the competitor in me did not want to lose the interview. It is very awkward attempting to convince a nineteen-year-old that you have what it takes to be a good mother while sitting in a bustling fast food restaurant. At the end of the meeting, she asked me if I wanted feedback. She told me I had two things working against me--neither of which was that I was single! She was raised primarily by her father and believed that children could be raised successfully in a single parent home. Her issues:

> 1. I already had a child. She believed that since it is difficult to find children available for adoption, she would prefer to place her baby where there was none.

> 2. I was Catholic. She had recently embraced a non-Christian/Judeo philosophy and would prefer to find a family with a similar orientation.

Since neither of these objections could be surmounted, I wished her the best with her search and her pregnancy. A week later she called and asked me to be the mother of her child. While she had not found her "ideal" situation, she had initially selected a family that she had interviewed via their 800 telephone number. However, when she asked to meet them in person, they refused and told her that they only wanted contact to be made through their attorney.

I told her that I was thrilled but asked her to promise me that if she began to change her mind to please be honest with me. I shared with her how deeply hurt I was by my previous experience and that the sooner I knew of a change of heart, the better. She promised.

I then asked her what her parents thought of her plan. She told me they did not know. She claimed that they would never know of her pregnancy since the baby was due in June and she was away at college. Since she had a part time job, her parents knew that she could not come home on weekends. She would only see them at Christmas and she was not showing yet. I panicked. Another key learning from the many seminars screamed in my head:

> There is a strong correlation between birth grandmother support for an adoption plan and a successful adoption.

I urged her to speak with her parents about her plans. If this adoption was not going to work out, I wanted it to end now, not after the baby came. She appeared to have tremendous resolve to place her baby for adoption, and did not want to be dissuaded. She was intent on continuing her education.

So I focused on getting the adoption under way.

In Virginia, you need three attorneys--one for the adoptive mother, one for the birth parents, and one for the baby. I consulted the many seminar documents I had acquired and began to contact the many attorneys listed. I called their offices and inquired about the hourly rate, estimated price range for an "easy" placement, inquired about their experience with the Interstate Compact for the Placement of Children and what other services they offered. I learned that most attorneys charge a flat rate to be the baby's counsel. I asked how they billed--in what increments--ten or fifteen minutes. Did they charge for a discussion over a billing discrepancy? Since your attorney is one of the most expensive aspects of the adoption, it is key to have a good grasp of expected expenses. If cost containment is a goal, be sure to use your attorney only for legal advice, not moral support. Lawyers charge for the time they work for their clients, whether in person, on the telephone, or by any other medium.

I did not ask for references--but I would if I were to do it over again. I set up appointments with four different firms. Most do charge for the initial consultation even if you do not hire them. I hired my team: three attorneys from different firms.

I accompanied the birth mother on her first trip to the obstetrician. I requested that the birth mother have the array of STD tests available and she agreed. I met with the office manager while the birth mother had her appointment. Bills were to be sent to me. While your attorney could handle the bills it does cost you more. My attorney provided me with a list of average costs for a private adoption **in Virginia** [see end of article], a state that is probably on the high end for costs in the U.S.

I met with my attorney and he advised me of what I could pay:

> All related medical and psychological costs
> Transportation to and from the appointments.
> All adoption-related legal fees.
> Housing and food

He advised me to contact her regularly. Perhaps have dinner with the birth father and her from time to time. I called her every three weeks and had dinner with the two of them every eight weeks. I was anxious before each encounter. She gave me updates on the pregnancy and shared her hopes and dreams. They shared their family histories and medical issues. I really started to care about them.

I set up appointments with their attorney and urged the attorney to discuss the merits of telling her family about her plan.

I arranged an appointment with my home study agency to conduct the joint counseling session, required by the state of Virginia.

At this point, the birth mother was only four months pregnant. We had a long way to go. I told only a few trusted friends and family--I was so afraid of being hurt again. The birth mother and I discussed the merits of an open adoption, and we decided against it. I promised to supply information to her, should she want to know how he was doing (she has not made inquiry). Both promised to be available if a medical need warranted. They also promised to meet him should he want that to happen but they would not instigate a meeting. While the birth parents were no longer in a relationship, the birth father promised to be, and was, fully cooperative: He gave up all rights to the baby in writing, joined the birth mother in counseling sessions, and came to court with her for the provisional adoption.

Her due date came and went. Finally, at 3 a.m. on July 2, the birth mother called to tell me that she was on her way to the hospital. At 4:30 a.m., the birth father called and stated that if I was going to participate, I had better get there quick. Never had we discussed my presence at the birth. Not only were the birth parents placing the greatest gift, their baby, with me, they let me participate in his birth. At 6:54 a.m. a beautiful 8-lb. healthy boy arrived. What a miracle birth is! I was awed by his perfection. I was humbled by the strength of this young woman when asked, minutes after the birth by the obstetrician, if she was still planning an adoption and she said "yes."

After holding him as long as I could in the delivery room, (only birth parents are allowed in the nursery at this hospital), I adored him through the window of the nursery. I inquired whether I could get the birth mother anything--only a candy bar. I left to tell the world. While I could not contain my joy, I secretly prayed that she would not change her mind. In Virginia, the birth parents cannot relinquish their rights sooner than ten days after the birth of a child. On July 12, hampered only by poor directions given by their attorney which caused an hour's delay with the judge, John Michael McGillen Payne was probationally mine. The birth parents had fifteen days to change their minds. On July 27 at 5 pm. (that's when the courts close), there was quite a celebration in the Payne household!

Virginia further requires three follow-up visits with a social worker before the adoption is ultimately finalized. Life has never been so good since I became a mother. Every moment of angst (even the fall through), was worth it since without them I would not have Cait and Mike. They are happy and healthy children, and I can not imagine a life without them.

If a private domestic adoption is the method that you believe to be the best approach for you, do it. Do not let the naysayers, or the statistics, undermine you.

Mary Ellen Payne is the Vice President-Marketing for Bell Atlantic. She is a single mother of two children--Caitlin, adopted from Romania at the age of 20 months, and John Michael, adopted domestically and privately at birth.

*Average Private Adoption Budget in Virginia:*
(as of September 2000)

| | |
|---|---|
| Agency fees for home study, counseling and court report, and postplacement supervision: | $ 3,000 |
| Legal fees for separate attorneys for the adopters, birth parent, and guardian ad litem: | 4,500 |
| (Add $750-$1,000 for out of state attorneys) | |
| Advertisements--newspaper, flyers | 2,000 |
| Separate telephone line installation, monthly charges | 200 |
| Medical expenses for birth mother and baby | 1,500 |
| Living expenses for birthmother--food, housing, maternity clothes | 800 |

Average range, $12,000-$18,000

# Chapter VI
## Studies of Single-Person Adoption

# Single Parent Adoption

by William Feigelman and Arnold R. Silverman

*These findings confirm earlier studies on the success of the overwhelming
majority of single parent placements and suggest that single parents are
as viable a resource for adoptive placements as couples.*

Adoption by single individuals represents a relatively unprecedented phenomenon in the field of American social services.  In the past such a policy would have been considered "unthinkable" by most agency workers.  Earlier viewpoints assumed that only couples possessed the necessary role models and resources that could offer children psychologically supportive experiences.  Today, however, child care professionals and social workers are increasingly aware of the large number of children who are permanently estranged from their families.  These professionals are intimately acquainted with the fates of children whose early lives consist of passage through a series of foster and institutional residences.  Ultimately, these children are likely to be disproportionately overrepresented in reformatories, prisons, and mental institutions.  Agency personnel have become increasingly receptive to new alternatives that could offer children permanency in a familial context.

Child care professionals have also become aware of the changing nature of American family life: increasing divorce, and the large numbers of children growing up in the absence of close association with both parents.  As American family lifestyles have become varied and as single parenting has become a relatively commonplace experience, agency personnel have begun to consider placing children in one-parent homes, especially in cases where institutionalization or long-term foster care would be the only other likely alternative.

Perhaps the earliest relatively large scale effort at single parent placements was undertaken by the Los Angeles Department of Adoptions, when forty children were placed in single-parent homes during 1966 and 1967.[1] More recently, the Los Angeles Department of Adoptions reports that 379 children have been placed in single parent homes.[2] Across the country the number of single parent placements slowly and steadily continues to mount. Single parent adoptions have been made in a number of American cities, including Washington, D.C.; Chicago; New York City; Portland, Oregon; Minneapolis; Indianapolis; and Bridgeport, Ct.[3]  Nationwide, approximately between 1,000 and 2,000 single parent adoptions have been effected [Editor's note: This study was published in 1977].

Alfred Kadushin's research has been particularly influential in stimulating single parent placements. Reviewing the research evidence of children reared in "fatherless" families in the areas of mental health, emotional adjustments, suicide, delinquency, and sexual identification he found no compelling evidence that single parent family life is inherently or necessarily pathogenic. He states:

> Research seems to indicate that children
> are able to surmount the lack of a father and
> some of the real shortcomings of a single
> parent home . . . the material suggests a
> greater appreciation of the variety of different
> kinds of contexts in which children can
> be reared without damage.[4]

Yet,  the philosophy governing single parent adoptions has viewed these placements as less desirable and the single prospective adopter is perceived as an adoptive parent of last resort. In most situations, single parents have been assigned older, minority, and handicapped children--the least preferred kinds of children, whose emotional, physical, and social needs are considerable, often exceeding those of most other children. Although consistent with the laws of supply and demand and the child welfare perspective, these placements appear paradoxical: Those who are felt to possess the least resources to parent have been assigned the children who would seem to require the most demanding kinds of care.

Questions arise regarding the success of these adoptions. How well do children adjust in single parent homes? How well do their adjustments compare with children reared in two-parent adoptive homes? Moreover, what are the common social characteristics among single parent adopters? How do these characteristics compare with those of other adoptive couples? In selecting prospective single adoptive parents, agencies generally insist that applicants have close relationships with their extended families to aid with the many demanding tasks of child rearing. How essential are extended family involvements for facilitating children's adjustments? Are there other sources of support which single parents utilize to meet the demands of child rearing?

## A Review of the Research

The limited research done to date indicates wholly positive results for the children adopted by single individuals. The earliest published study, based upon eight adoptive placements, undertaken by the Los Angeles Department of Adoptions, came to the following conclusion:

Our experience with single-parent adoptive placements has, to date, been very promising. In no instance have we observed regression on the part of any of these children. There has been steady progress in the development of the child as a person in his adoptive home, and in several instances, the development has been truly dramatic.[5]

A later study, also conducted under the auspices of the Los Angeles Department of Adoptions, was based on thirty-six single parent placements.[6] This study found that of thirty-six single parent adoptors, thirty-five were women. Blacks were overrepresented (almost 66 percent). Although the sample varied in its educational achievements, sample members tended to be more highly educated than most; half had completed at least

some college. Most had close relationships with extended family members; 66 percent of the women were formerly married. Most sample members were employed and income ranged from $3,000 to $13,000. Although this research was primarily descriptive it was noted that "these thirty-six case records strongly suggest that the children involved have found true 'familiness'."[7]

More recently, Joan Shireman and Penny Johnson[8] completed a study of thirty-one single parent adoptions of black infants in the Chicago area between 1970 and 1972. Eighteen of these families were reinterviewed three years later.

Like the Ethel Branham study most single parents were women; most were black; most had been married before. Although educational backgrounds, occupations, and incomes varied, comparable trands were noted with this sample: The Chicago group was somewhat high in occupational status; half the sample were engaged in professional occupations, with low to moderate incomes; the median income was only $9,000. The group also appeared to be extended-family oriented.

Although initial adjustments of the children tended to be somewhat negative, two months later their adjustments were reported to be problem-free by 81 percent of the parents. Trained interviewers substantially confirmed parental assessments. A followup study conducted three years later showed only two of the eighteen children in the reinterviewed families to have emotional adjustment problems.

Many questions, however, remain unanswered. Almost no information has been acquired on the smaller but growing number of male single adoptive parents.

Because these three studies have been completed with clients served by two agencies--the Los Angeles Department of Adoptions and the Chicago Child Care Society--it is unclear whether the social characteristics of these single parents accurately reflect the single parent population; whether they represent selection criteria of the agencies, local features, or some combination of all three factors. A survey drawing single parents from a diversity of sources and localities would offer a better base to form a general picture of single adoptive parents.

Further, in discussing adjustments of adopted children in single parent homes, studies should be designed that offer some kind of control population; for example, comparisons with other children who were not placed in single parent homes. In the present survey the authors have attempted to address these matters.

## Method and Sample

This study[9] was based upon a mailed questionnaire taken from a nationwide sample of adoptive parents. This work is part of a larger, now ongoing study of adoption. The data were collected between November 1974 and March 1976.

The sample of adoptive couples tended to overrepresent those who had adopted minority children. The typical adoptive couple in the sample consisted of white, native American parents who adopted a foreign-born child, most often from Asia. In selecting parent organizations to cooperate with the research, efforts were made to enlist the participation of parent groups whose memberships were acknowledged to include members who had completed transracial and transnational adoptions.

Attempts were also made to ensure the inclusion of at least several constituencies that represented in-country, in-race adopting families. Participating executive officers of the various organizations were asked to provide the names and addresses of any individuals they may have known who had adopted children but who did not belong to their organizations. Seven hundred thirteen questionnaires were returned in the samples of adoptive parents; a response rate of 60 percent.

A comparison of the characteristics of these respondents with those of other adoption studies reveals that the sub-samples of white native-born parents adopting domestically and abroad do not differ in any significant way from those respondents found in similar studies.[10]

## Findings

Of the fifty-eight single adoptive parents in the sample, fifteen were males and forty-three were females. As a group they were much more likely to live in urban areas; couples, on the other hand, were much more likely to be suburbanites.[11] Only 16 percent of the couples lived in urban places, compared to 51 percent of single parents. Seventy percent of the couples lived in suburban areas, compared to 35 percent among single parents. These urban residence patterns of single adoptive parents probably reflect the residential patterns of single individuals, the higher levels of tolerance for unconventional lifestyles found in cities, and the wider availability of services such as clinics, day care centers, special schools, and medical facilities sought by single parents.

Single adoptive parents tended to be more highly educated than their adoptive couple counterparts. Seventy-five percent of the male and female single parents had completed some graduate study beyond the bachelor's degree level, compared with 47 percent of the married fathers and 33 percent of the married mothers. This relationship was statistically significant for the women, and approached significance for the men. Also, single parents generally held higher status occupations; yet, their incomes tended to trail behind those of couples. Only 22 percent of the single parents had annual incomes that exceeded $25,000, compared with 40 percent among the couples.

There are a number of reasons why the incomes of the single parents generally were below those of the couples. First, couples possess dual earning power. Second, women are overrepresented among the single parents, and it is widely known that women in nearly every occupational category earn less than men performing similar functions. Also, women are more likely to pursue their occupations on a part-time basis. Virtually all the single parent women in the sample were employed; 87 percent were working full time, 11 percent part time, and only one was unemployed.

Other minority members are similarly subject to discrimination. Minority members were far more common among the single parents of the sample. While only 2 percent of the married couples was nonwhite, 14 percent of the single parents was nonwhite.

Further, the single parents were concentrated primarily in two fields: Education and social work. Typical occupations included a social worker, a professor of social work, a coordinator for a school-based drug prevention program, an elementary school teacher, a special education teacher, a university professor, a teacher of Asian studies, and a school psychologist. It is probable that those choosing careers in human services initially are more likely to be receptive to single parent adoption. Moreover, occupational experiences with children and the needy tend to support and sustain motivations toward single parent adoption. Also, service professionals are more likely to be knowledgeable about children who might be available for adoption.

In terms of religious preferences no differences were noted between single parents and the married adoptive parents. Similarly, no differences were observed in the frequency of religious participation between the two groups. Single parents were somewhat more likely to describe their political viewpoints as liberal. Fifty-eight percent of the female single parents called themselves liberal compared with 45 percent among the wives of the sample; this finding was significant at the .05 level. A similar trend prevailed among the men. Fifty-four percent of the single parent men were self-described liberals and only 38 percent of the husbands; these differences approached, but did not achieve, statistical significance. The liberal perspectives of single parents may well reflect the occupational ideologies of educational and social service professionals.

While the literature would suggest that single parents are more likely to be closely affiliated with their extended families than married couples, the opposite trend was noted. Sixty-three percent of the adoptive couples saw their extended family members once a month or more often, compared with 55 percent among the single adoptive parents. Although the meaning of these findings is not certain, it is possible that the urban living patterns of the single parents may impose time and interest barriers against more frequent visiting with their usually suburban-based kin. Otherwise, in interaction with friends and organizational involvements, both groups showed similar patterns.

One other difference between the two groups was their relative ages. Although single fathers and husbands showed similarities in age, single mothers tended on the average to be older. Twenty-five percent were forty-five years of age or older, compared with only 11 percent of the wives. Fifty-six percent of the wives were less than thirty-four years of age, compared with only 38 percent of single mothers. These differences may reflect the greater period of time required to achieve sufficient resources, maturity, and the desire to adopt a child as a single parent. And in turn, may correspond to agency requirements for prospective single adoptive parents.

## Adoptive experiences of single parents and couples

Fifty-seven percent of the single adoptive parents were first time adopters. Single parents tended to adopt children of the same sex; 80 percent of the fathers adopted boys and 75 percent of the mothers adopted girls.

As one might have expected, single parents tended to have more difficulties in completing their adoptions. Thirty-nine percent had made three or more previous attempts to adopt, compared with only 18 percent among the couples. Also, experiences with adoption professionals were more often reported by single parents to be negative. Eighteen percent found adoption agencies to be uncooperative, compared with only 6 percent among couples. Fifty-five percent found the Immigration and Naturalization Service to be uncooperative, compared with only 19 percent among couples. Recent changes in immigration laws should reduce frustrating experiences with the Immigration and Naturalization Service for single parents.

There was a slight trend toward more single parents reporting uncooperative responses from regional social service departments, which fell short of statistical significance. Among each of the specified care-takers--adoption agencies and immigration social service departments--male single parent adoptors tended to report more uncooperative responses. Also, the data revealed that courts are less likely to be helpful to single parents. While 59 percent of the couples found the courts helpful, only 36 percent of single parents described courts this way.

Single parents showed substantially greater willingness to adopt hard-to-place children and these attitudes were reflected in the kinds of children they actually adopted. Seventy-nine percent would accept an older child, compared with 60 percent among adopting couples; 82 percent were willing to adopt a black child, compared with 56 percent among couples; 51 percent were willing to adopt a slightly retarded child, compared with 32 percent of couples; 40 percent were willing to adopt a handicapped child, compared with only 35 percent among couples. Although substantially similar trends in attitude were noted for both single fathers and mothers, men showed a greater tendency to actually adopt various hard-to-place children. Approximately 60 percent of the men adopted children six years of age or older, compared with 23 percent of the single mothers and 9 percent of the couples. Men also were more likely to adopt black children. Forty-seven percent had actually adopted blacks, compared with 30 percent among single mothers and 10 percent among couples. These patterns probably reflect the unwillingness of agencies to place children with male single parents.

As a group, the single parent adopters tended to adopt children who were older. Thirty-three percent adopted children between the ages of three and five, and 45 percent adopted children under three years of age. Couples, on the other hand, were much more likely to adopt infants; only 9 percent adopted children over six and 74 percent adopted children under three years of age.

Several major areas where parents normally confront problems in raising children were also investigated. Three areas were surveyed: Physical health, emotional adjustments, and growth or development problems. Parents were asked to evaluate whether their children had problems in these areas-- often, sometimes, rarely, or never. Parents were also asked whether their adopted children had received any extensive medical care in the past year. The responses given by the single parents paralleled those given by adopting couples. No statistically significant differences were noted, except in one case where making adjustments was difficult.

Male and female single parents reported substantially similar responses in their appraisals of the four problem areas. Single parents reported significantly more emotional adjustment problems than were true for couples. Forty-three percent reported problems sometimes or often, compared with 33 percent among the couples. Many earlier studies of adoption[12] have noted that older child adoptions generally present more adjustment difficulties because the child's personality development is already well underway before joining his adoptive family. Therefore, the authors attempted to control the age factor.

When age was controlled they found that the relationships between single parenting and poorer emotional adjustments disappeared for younger children but still persisted among children six years or older. Among seventy-nine cases adopting children six years or older, 77 percent of single parents reported emotional adjustment problems sometimes or often, compared with only 52 percent among couples. This difference was statistically significant with chi square at the .02 level. It is the authors' belief that these trends reflect existing placement realities. Single parents, as the agencies' adoptive parents of last resort, are more often obliged to accept children whose earlier experiences of deprivation, instability, and abuse have led to substantially more emotional adjustment problems. In addition, the professional experiences of these parents may lead them to recognize such problems more readily than other parents.

Children's adjustments are salient for their parents' own sense of ego integrity and well-being. Therefore, the authors include two indirect measurements of adjustment. Parents were asked how long it took for the child to be considered "their own." Responses were divided into two groups; those taking place within a month of less, and those taking place within longer time periods. Single parents took longer to consider their children as their own. While 36 percent of the single parents required more than a month to feel that the child was their own, only 26 percent of the couples required this much time. This difference fell a fraction short of the .05 level of significance.

Again, the authors believed it advisable to control for the child's age at adoption. With age controlled, both groups required substantially similar time periods to fully accept their adopted children.

Examining gender differences among single parents on adjustment, it was found that males required more time to fully accept their adopted children than females. While only 32 percent of female single parents took more than a month for the child to be regarded as their own, 53 percent of the single fathers took this long. Yet, when the age of the child was adjusted for, these differences disappeared.

The other indirect measure of adjustment used was response to the following question: On the basis of your own experience would you encourage others to adopt as you have adopted? Yes; Yes, with some reservation; No. Eighty-six percent of the adoptive couples responded with unreserved affirmation, compared with only 72 percent among single mothers and 67 percent among single fathers. This difference was statistically significant. Yet, when the authors compared single adopting parents with other couples adopting children of similar ages, the statistically significant association between these two variables again dissolved. Apparently, when the authors adjusted for differences in the ages of the child adopted, single parents and couples show substantially alike responses in recommending adoption to others. This factor would seem consistent with the interpretation that the older, more problematic nature of the children adopted by single parents is the source of much of the difference between their experience and that of the couples.

Agency workers frequently stress the importance of extended families in helping provide aid and support to the single adoptive parent with the many responsibilities of child rearing. In fact, most agencies engaged in single parent placements insist that prospective applicants possess extended family resources before they will be approved. An attempt was made to test this assumption that extended family affiliations are associated with children's adjustment. Seventy percent of the single adoptive respondents who saw kin at least monthly reported well-adjusted children compared with 63 percent among those seeing kin less often. Thus, the data show no significant association between the frequency of interaction with kin and adjustment of adopted children. On investigating the two indirect measures of adjustment--the time it takes to regard the child as a member of the family, and the willingness to recommend adoption to others--those who saw kin less often were no more likely to indicate adjustment difficulties than those seeing kin more frequently.

Yet, when the responses of extended families to the adoptions were investigated, it was found that when parents reacted positively it correlated with better adjustment. Eighty percent of single parents whose parents responded positively to their adoptions had children judged to have excellent adjustments, compared with only 40 percent among those whose parents responded with indifference, mixed reactions, or negatively. This difference was significant at the .02 level. Similar trends were also noted with our indirect measures of adjustment.

Those whose parents responded positively tended to feel that their child became their own sooner. This difference also was statistically significant. They were also more likely to urge others to adopt; this association approached but did not achieve statistical significance. The patterns which were observed among the single parents were also noted among the adoptive couples. Thus, positive extended family support facilitates adoptive adjustments not only among single parents but among all adoptive parents.

Apparently, friends also play an analogous supportive role in the adoptive process. Seventy-two percent of single parents whose close friends responded positively felt their children were well-adjusted compared with only 46 percent among those whose close friends responded with indifference, mixed feelings, or negatively. This difference fell a fraction short of significance at the .05 level among the single parents but was significant among the couples. Those whose close friends responded positively were also more likely to urge others to adopt; this difference was significant. The response of close friends, however, is apparently unrelated to the time it takes for the child to become a member of the family.

Another area that was potentially important was society's response to the single adoptive parent. Does the community generally approve of or reject the single adoptive parent? The authors investigated what reactions adopting parents experienced from their parents, other extended kin, close friends, and neighbors. Respondents were asked whether reactions had been positive, mixed, indifferent, or negative. On the whole, the experiences of our single parents were comparable to those of the adopting couples. Single adoptive parents reported substantially similar responses from their parents, other relatives, and neighbors as were reported by the adoptive couples; no statistically significant differences were noted between the two groups. Positive responses ranged from a high of 74 percent among mothers' parents to a low of 64 percent among fathers' parents. Friends of single parents, however, were less likely to respond positively. While 89 percent of couples encountered positive responses by close friends, only 77 percent of the friends of single parents responded similarly. Male single parents were somewhat more likely to report their friends' disapproval, although this relationship fell short of statistical significance.

## Summary

The data documented some trends that are probably well-known to many single adoptive parents. Namely, that single parents are much more likely to encounter resistance from the various social agencies with whom they must deal in completing their adoptions; they are more likely to be turned away and discouraged in the adoptive process. Once they adopt, they are more likely to be subject to disapproval by their close friends than is true among other adoptors. This uniformly discouraging response on the part of the community seems to be slightly more intense toward male single adoptive parents. Yet, these negative evaluations appear to be without foundation when one considers the outcomes of these adoptions. With few exceptions, both male and female single parents report substantially similar experiences to adoptive couples in raising adopted children.

The results obtained in this research offer positive support for the new and growing practice of single parent adoption. With the one exception of emotional adjustment problems, it was found that single adoptive parents report substantially similar information on the variety and severity of problems encountered in raising their children as is reported by other adoptive couples. When controlling for the age of the children adopted, both direct and indirect assessments of children's overall adjustments show fundamentally corresponding patterns among single parent placements and suggest that single parents are as viable a resource for adoptive placements as couples. In fact, given the present discrimination against single parents in the adoption process, the absence of spouse supports and their more limited economic resources, these positive findings suggest that single adoptive parents possess unusually high commitments to parenting.

Before being entirely confident that single parents offer similar benefits to waiting children as are found in two-parent homes, additional studies will be necessary. Future research should examine more objective indicators of adjustment such as school records, psychological adjustment test scores, and so forth, among comparable groups of children, in single-parent and in two-parent homes.

If future studies confirm the present results, then there would be a need for reconceptualization of a great many theories of child development. Numerous viewpoints of child development maintain that two-parent families are indispensable to successfully resolve the Oedipus complex, to offer role modeling opportunities, and to insure the inter-generational transmission of cultural values and conforming behavior patterns. Most of the theories positing the inherent need for the two-parent family were conceived, however, during the early and mid-twentieth century, at a time when sex roles were far more differentiated and segregated than is true today.

Today, with married women participating in the labor force and pursuing careers in formerly male-dominated occupations in ever increasing numbers, with household and child-rearing tasks increasingly becoming shared by both men and women alike, with formal educational experiences of both sexes more nearly convergent, there is considerable commingling of sex roles. No longer are men the exclusive task specialists and women the providers of nurturance they were in earlier times. With the increasing flexibility of contemporary sex roles, culturally appropriate role learning can be acquired from either parent as well as from both parents.

The findings outlined here also point to a need for reconsideration of the role of extended families in aiding and supporting the single adoptive parent. The mere availability of extended families, whether through living in the same community or frequent mutual visitations, has little to do with contributing to the success of single parent adoptions. A core of positively responding intimates, composed of kin or close friends--rather than availability of kin per se--would seem to offer a good prognosis for adoption success.

William Feigelman is Chairman and Associate Professor, and Arnold R. Silverman is Assistant Professor, Department of Sociology, Nassau Community College, Garden City, New York. This report appeared in Social Casework (July 1977), pp. 418-425.

Endnotes:

1. Ethel Branham, One Parent Adoptions, Children, 17:103-107 (May-June 1970).
2. Personal communication, September 21,1976.
3. Alfred Kadushin, Single Parent Adoptions: An Overview and Some Relevant Research, Social Service Review 44:263-74 (September 1970).
4. Ibid., p. 271.
5. Velma Jordan and William Little, Early Comments on Single Parent Adoptive Homes, Child Welfare, 45:536-38
6. Branham, One Parent Adoptions, pp. 103-107.
8. Joan Shireman and Penny Johnson, Single Persons as Adoptive Parents, Social Service Review, 50:103-116 (March 1976).
9. This research was supported by the Research Foundation of the State University of New York (Grant Nos. 082-.7105A and 082-7106A) and the National Institute of Mental Health. (Mar. 1976).
9. This research was supported by the Research Foundation of the State University of New York (Grant Nos. 082-.7105A and 082-7106A) and the National Institute of Mental Health.
10. Lawrence Falk, A Comparative Study of Transracial and Inracial Adoptions, Child Welfare, 49:82-88 (February 1970); Lucille J. Grow and Deborah Shapiro, Black Children: White Parents (New York: Child Welfare League of America, 1974); Elizabeth Lawder et al., A Follow Up Study of Adoptions; Postplacement Functioning of Adoptive Families (New York; Child Welfare League of America, 1969); and Thomas Nutt and John Snyder, Transracial Adoption, February 1973, Department of Urban and Regional Planning, Massachusetts Institute of Technology,
11. All tests of significance employed in this article were calculated from contingency tables employing chi square as a test of significance. Unless indicated other wise, all associations mentioned in this section achieved statistical significance at the .05 level of significance or higher.
12. Alfred Kadushin, Adopting Older Children (New York: Columbia University Press, 1970).

# Single Parents and Their Adopted Children
## A Psychosocial Analysis

Victor K. Groze and James A. Rosenthal

*Children in single-parent homes experienced fewer emotional and behavioral problems than did children in two-parent homes . . . Recruitment and adoption policies should target non-traditional families such as single parents in their efforts to secure permanent homes for children.*

Single-parent adoption is defined for the purpose of this article as adoption of a child by a single person; couples who adopt and later divorce are not characterized as single parents. This distinction is important because the former made a conscious decision to become a single parent, whereas the latter became a single parent as a result of life circumstances.

Special-needs children commonly include older children, physically handicapped children, children of mixed or minority ethnicity, children who are members of a sibling group, and children with emotional or behavioral problems, although these definitions vary slightly from state to state. Adoption of special-needs children is a relatively new phenomenon. The initiative to place special-needs children permanently with adoptive families when they cannot be returned to their biological family is consistent with the intent of the Adoption Assistance and Child Welfare Act of 1980 (see Maluccio & Fein, 1983). Although this law (Public Law 96-272) mandated adoptive placement of special-needs children, it left the definition of "special needs" to individual states. The definition of a special-needs child used here reflects the definition used by the states from which the data were collected. It excludes healthy children adopted from countries other than the United States (cross-cultural adoptions).

In the following sections, single- and dual-parent families who have adopted a special-needs child are described and compared. Previous research on single-parent adoption is reviewed, and adoptive family functioning is described in the context of a psychosocial model. The following areas of functioning for the adopted child or family are examined:

emotional, behavioral, educational, and ecological. Issues of relevance to practitioners working with single-parent adoptive families are addressed.

## Literature Review

Few studies have focused specifically on the experiences of single adoptive parents. Jordan and Little (1966) examined eight placements with single adoptive mothers, concluding that the mothers possessed an "above-average child orientation" and developed healthy mother-child relationships.

Branham (1970) examined 36 single-parent placements and concluded that children and parents had formed viable and healthy relationships, recommending single-parent families as a resource for special-needs children waiting adoptive placement.

Feigelman and Silverman (1977) compared children adopted by two-parent and single-parent families via a mailed survey of a national sample of adoptive parents. No significant differences were observed regarding the children's physical or emotional health or social development. They discovered a significant relationship between single parents' ratings of their children's social adjustment and the support given by extended family and friends. Single parents whose friends and parents responded positively to the adoptions were much more likely to judge that their adopted child had made an excellent adjustment. Feigelman and Silverman (1983) recontacted 60% of the single-parent respondents from their earlier study. Six years after the initial study, the adjustment of children raised by single parents remained similar to that of children raised by adoptive couples.

Dougherty (1978) obtained a 67% response rate in a mailed survey to 131 single women who had adopted a child. Two-thirds of the children were labeled difficult-to-place children. The adoptive mothers were personally mature, had viable social support systems, and were aware of their own needs as well as the needs of their children. Dougherty's conclusion, like those of previous researchers, was decidedly supportive of placement of children with single parents.

Shireman and Johnson (1976, 1985) and Shireman (1988) conducted a longitudinal study of adoptive single parents. The initial sample included 31 predominantly black single parents who had adopted children younger than three years old. When the children were four years old, researchers noted concerns about the extreme isolation of some parents and the highly intense relationships between parents and children (Shireman & Johnson, 1976). Four years later the experiences of this group of children were compared with those of black children in transracial placements and in two-parent intraracial placements (Shireman & Johnson, 1985, 1986). The isolation of the single parents was lessened when the children entered school. Overall, children in all three types of placement were doing well and were accomplishing the major developmental tasks appropriate to their age.

Shireman (1988) interviewed these same children when they were in early adolescence. Only 15 adoptive single parents could be located. They were compared with single birth parents, traditional adoptive families, two-parent birth families, and transracial adoptive families. The adopted adolescents continued to do well. No significant differences in adjustment were observed among adopted and nonadopted children of single, traditional, two-parent, or transracial adoptions.

Although the extant research demonstrates good outcomes for single-parent adoptions, no studies of single-parent adoptions have focused on special-needs children. The current study addresses child and single-parent functioning following the legalization of a special-needs adoption.

## Methods

This study reports on the responses of 799 families from three midwestern states who had finalized their adoption of a special-needs child before September 1988. A 15-page questionnaire was mailed to adoptive homes in 1988 ($N = 1,413$). Included in the questionnaire was a standardized instrument--the Child Behavior Checklist--that examined child behavior (Achenbach & Edelbrock, 1983). Achenbach and Edelbrock present test-retest reliability, interrater agreement, longer-term stability, content validity, construct validity, and criterion-related validity for this instrument. All intraclass correlations for individual items and scale scores were .90 or higher. The median Pearson correlation between mother's and father's ratings was .66. Test-retest correlations for inpatients' scores over a three-month period averaged .74 for parents' ratings and .73 for child-care workers' ratings; the correlations with other behavior-rating scales and diagnoses of disorders provide evidence of construct validity. With referral for mental health services as a criterion, evidence for criterion-related validity was presented in terms of significant differences between demographically matched referred and nonreferred children for all sex and age groups.

In the present study, children had been in their adoptive homes a minimum of six months. Only children living in the home were included. Children who had reached their 18th birthday at the time of the mailing were excluded. The response rate for successfully contacted families ($N = 1,328$) was approximately 60%, which is similar to the other studies using this method (Feigelman & Silverman, 1977; Dougherty, 1978). All data presented represent the adoptive parents' responses to the questionnaire.

Five parents who were single at adoption subsequently married. These families were still considered single-parent families for the purposes of this study. The sample included 122 single-parent (15%) and 651 two-parent (85%) families. Status of the adoption at the time of the survey could not be determined for 26 families; these families were not included in the analysis. The following analyses are based on the responses of 773 families.

### Representativeness of Sample

The representativeness of a sample of nonrespondents can be assessed by comparing demographic characteristics for respondents and nonrespondents or by comparing the sample with the population from which it was drawn. Selected characteristics of respondents for each state were compared with the characteristics of nonrespondents or the population by means of the difference of differences or proportions test (Blalock, 1979). Results suggest that the sample of respondents is largely representative of the population for most variables examined, including child's age, percent female, and race.

Sampling procedures differed across sites. The necessity of using different sampling methods in various states may have affected some study findings. However, the majority of relationships observed in

TABLE 1. Demographic description of adopted child.

| | Single-parent family | | Two-parent family | | |
|---|---|---|---|---|---|
| | % | Frequency | % | Frequency | $X^2$ |
| *Gender* | | | | | 8.54[a] |
| Male | 40.0 | 48 | 55.0 | 358 | |
| Female | 60.0 | 72 | 45.0 | 293 | |
| *Age at time of survey* | | | | | 10.88[b] |
| 0-2 | .8 | 1 | 1.7 | 11 | |
| 3-5 | 5.0 | 6 | 10.6 | 69 | |
| 6-8 | 17.6 | 21 | 20.4 | 132 | |
| 9-11 | 23.5 | 28 | 28.7 | 186 | |
| 12-14 | 31.9 | 38 | 25.3 | 164 | |
| 15-17 | 21.0 | 25 | 13.3 | 86 | |
| *Ethnicity* | | | | | 82.02[a] |
| White | 31.1 | 37 | 69.3 | 449 | |
| Black | 49.6 | 59 | 15.3 | 99 | |
| Native American | 5.9 | 7 | 4.5 | 29 | |
| Hispanic | 5.9 | 7 | 3.9 | 25 | |
| Asian | .8 | 1 | .8 | 5 | |
| Other | 6.7 | 8 | 6.3 | 41 | |
| *Handicaps* | | | | | |
| Blind or vision impaired | 1.6 | 2 | .8 | 5 | .87 |
| Deaf or hearing impaired | 1.6 | 2 | 4.1 | 27 | 1.79 |
| Physical handicap | 9.8 | 12 | 7.8 | 51 | .55 |
| Mental retardation | 16.4 | 20 | 9.4 | 61 | 5.40[b] |
| Chronic medical problem (not life threatening) | 6.6 | 8 | 5.8 | 38 | .10 |
| Chronic medical problem (life threatening) | 4.1 | 5 | 1.5 | 10 | 3.54 |
| Other handicap | .8 | 1 | .2 | 1 | .00 |
| Learning disabilities | 27.9 | 34 | 29.2 | 190 | .87 |

*[a]p<01; [b]p<.05*

the full samples were also observed in the reports prepared for each state. Thus, the sampling methodology does not appear to distort the essential findings. A complete description of the sampling methodology and the comparison analysis of sample and population characteristics are available from the authors.

**Results and Discussion**

*Demographic Description*

Overall, approximately 15% of adoptions were single parent adoptions. Table 1 presents the demographic description of the adopted children for one- and two-parent families. Statistically significant relationships between family structure and the child's race, age, and handicap status were evident. Single parents were more likely to have older children, non-white children, and mentally retarded children in their care. They were also more likely to adopt girls. The finding that older children often reside in one-parent homes compared with two-parent homes is consistent with other studies (Barth, Berry, Yashikama, Goodfield, & Carson, 1988; Barth & Berry, 1988; Reid, Kagan, Kaminsky, & Helmer, 1987), although the finding that single parents more often adopt girls contrasts with previous reports (Barth et al, 1988; Barth & Berry, 1988). This finding should be considered in the context that most single parents (84%) are women and that single parents tend to adopt children of the same sex as themselves (Shireman & Johnson, 1976; Feigelman & Silverman, 1977). In this sample, 106 single mothers adopted

**TABLE 2. Demographic description of parents.**

| | Single parent | | Two parent | |
| | Mother (n = 108) | Father (n = 21) | Mother (n = 639) | Father (n = 611) |
|---|---|---|---|---|
| **Age (years)** | | | | |
| Mean | 48.04[a] | 43.95 | 41.46[a] | 43.77 |
| SD | 10.38 | 11.15 | 8.38 | 8.91 |
| **Ethnicity (%)[a]** | | | | |
| White | 38.0 | 57.1 | 79.7 | 78.5 |
| Black | 55.6 | 33.3 | 15.0 | 15.3 |
| Native American | 2.8 | 0.0 | 2.2 | 3.4 |
| Hispanic | 2.8 | 0.0 | 1.4 | 1.9 |
| Other | .9 | 4.8 | 1.7 | 1.0 |
| **Education (%)** | | | | |
| < High school | 26.2[a] | 20.0 | 10.0[a] | 11.8 |
| High school diploma/GED | 23.4 | 20.0 | 26.9 | 25.5 |
| Some college | 22.4 | 5.0 | 34.9 | 28.2 |
| College graduate | 11.2 | 30.0 | 17.7 | 20.0 |
| Master's or above | 16.8 | 25.0 | 10.5 | 14.5 |
| **Family income[a]** | | | | |
| Mean | $21,322 | | $38,378 | |
| SD | $ 11,328 | | $ 22,680 | |

[a] $p < .01$

36 boys (34% and 70 girls(66%), whereas 14 single fathers adopted 12 boys (86%) and 2 girls (14%).

Table 2 presents demographic information on the adoptive parents. A statistically significant difference in the ages of adoptive mothers was noted. Single adoptive mothers were approximately 6.5 years older than were adoptive mothers in a two-parent family. Adoptive fathers were about the same age in both one-parent and two-parent families.

Ethnic differences between single- and dual-parent families were noted. Most single mothers were black, and a substantial minority of single fathers were black. In contrast, most couples were white.

Differences in educational achievement between singles and couples were also evident. The modal educational achievement for single mothers was less than a high school education; for single fathers, college graduate; for both mothers and fathers in two-parent families, some college. However, the differences in educational attainment were not statistically significant except in one instance: single adoptive mothers were more likely to have finished high school than were their counterparts in two-parent families.

Single parents had lower incomes than did two-parent families. On average, they earned approximately $21,000 per year, whereas couples earned approximately $38,000. This finding is consistent with other investigations (Shireman & Johnson, 1976; Feigelman & Silverman, 1977; Shireman, 1988).

**Children's Emotional and Behavioral Functioning**

Ratings of children's behavior were obtained by means of the list of 113 behavior problems in the Child Behavior Checklist (CBC) (Achenbach & Edelbrock, 1993). The CBC elicits parents' descriptions of their children's behavior in a standardized format. To reflect age and gender differences, Achenbach and Edelbrock created specific subscales. Behavior scores for the adoption sample were compared with the scores of clinical and nonclinical normative groups as presented by Achenbach and Edelbrock. The clinical group consisted of children receiving mental health services, whereas the nonclinical group consisted of "typical" children identified via representative sampling. The percentage of adopted children who scored in the clinical range on each scale was compared with the corre-

TABLE 3. Comparison of adoption sample with clinical and nonclinical samples on selected scales of the Child Behavior Checklist

| Behavior problem | Normative groups | | | | Adoption Sample | | | |
| | Clinical sample | | Nonclinical sample | | Single-parent family | | Two-parent family | |
| | Boys | Girls | Boys | Girls | Boys | Girls | Boys | Girls |
|---|---|---|---|---|---|---|---|---|
| *Age 4-5 years* | | | | | (*n* = 1) | (*n* = 2) | (*n* = 25) | (*n* = 24) |
| Internalizing | 59 | 68 | 11 | 9 | 0 | 0 | 12 | 17 |
| Externalizing | 62 | 42 | 10 | 6 | 0 | 0 | 16 | 21 |
| Total problems | 74 | 73 | 14 | 12 | 0 | 0 | 16 | 25 |
| | | | | | (*n* = 18) | (*n* = 28) | (*n* = 155) | (*n* = 153) |
| *Age 6-11* | | | | | | | | |
| Internalizing | 68 | 69 | 10 | 9 | 22 | 18 | 28 | 27 |
| Externalizing | 70 | 72 | 8 | 9 | 17 | 39 | 38 | 42 |
| Total problems | 77 | 75 | 9 | 10 | 17 | 39 | 43 | 44 |
| | | | | | (*n* = 20) | (*n* - 38) | (*n* = 138) | (*n* = 87) |
| *Age 12-16* | | | | | | | | |
| Internalizing | 62 | 58 | 10 | 5 | 40 | 18 | 42 | 26 |
| Externalizing | 66 | 52 | 9 | 4 | 25 | 21 | 41 | 26 |
| Total problems | 71 | 74 | 10 | 10 | 45 | 36 | 46 | 47 |

*Note:* All figures represent percentages scoring in clinical (problem) range)

sponding percentage in the normative groups. For the three scales, the clinical range represents approximately the upper 10% of the nonclinical groups; hence, such a score in the clinical range conveys that a child has more serious behavioral problems than does 90% of his or her peers (Table 3). Externalizing refers to acting-out behavior while internalizing refers to inhibited and withdrawn behavior.

As a total group, the percentage of adopted children in the clinical range in both single- and two-parent families exceeded the corresponding percentage for the nonclinical sample. This finding suggests that many special-needs adopted children exhibit serious behavioral difficulties. Differences between the special-needs sample and the nonclinical sample were modest among 4- to- 5-year-old children but much more pronounced among the 6-11 and 12-16 age groups.

Comparisons of single-parent and two-parent adoptions showed that children in single-parent families experienced fewer problems. For boys and girls in all three age groups, the percentage of scores in the clinical range was lower in single-parent families. This finding holds for all three scales. Among latency-age and adolescent boys, internalizing problems seemed to predominate in single-parent families. Among boys in two-parent families, internalizing and externalizing problems were equally common.

### Educational Functioning

Table 4 presents data on the adopted child's educational functioning. Among children ages 6 to 17 years old at the time of the survey, only 1% were not attending school. With the exception that children in two-parent families were more often taking speech and language classes, the percentages of children in various specialized classes did not vary according to family status. No significant differences between single-parent and two-parent families were found regarding attendance, grades, or enjoyment of school. Most children performed well in school and, according to parents' reports, enjoyed school.

### Ecological Functioning

This final area of functioning examined the adoptive family in the context of their life space by focusing on the service-delivery system. The service resources available to the family and the parents' perception of those resources were examined.

Table 5 presents data on agency services, focusing on home visits and the provision of information about the adopted child. Statistically significant differences in the number of in-person meetings with the social workers between one- and two-parent families were noted. Single parents reported fewer visits after placement than did two-parent families.

TABLE 4. Educational Functioning of Adopted Child

| | Single-parent family (%) | Two-parent family (%) | $X^2$ |
|---|---|---|---|
| *School attendance* | | | .25 |
| Attending | 97.3 | 99.1 | |
| Not attending | 2.7 | 0.9 | |
| | | | |
| *Most recent grades* | | | .94 |
| Mostly As | 10.5 | 13.5 | |
| Mostly Bs | 40.0 | 30.4 | |
| Mostly Cs | 36.8 | 35.1 | |
| Mostly Ds | 10.5 | 10.5 | |
| Mostly Fs | 2.1 | 1.5 | |
| *Feelings about school* | | | .75 |
| Enjoys school | 70.2 | 66.0 | |
| Neutral | 25.4 | 28.9 | |
| Dislikes school | 4.4 | 5.1 | |
| | | | |
| *Special education school information* | | | |
| Learning disability class | 18.1 | 20.4 | .19 |
| Speech & language class | 7.8 | 17.8 | 6.52[a] |
| Class for emotionally disturbed | 6.9 | 8.0 | .04 |
| Class for mentally handicapped | 9.5 | 8.7 | .01 |
| Deaf or hearing impaired | 0.9 | 1.0 | .00 |
| Blind or vision impaired | 1.7 | 0.8 | .13 |
| Class for physical disabilities | 3.4 | 2.5 | .050 |
| Other special education | 6.0 | 6.5 | .00 |

[a] $p < .05$

Surprisingly, more than 40% of single parents reported no visits after placement compared with 27% of two-parent families; most families (more than 70%) reported no visits since finalization of adoption. Of families who met with a worker, most families were visited one to three times after placement. However, comparisons between one-parent and two-parent families were influenced by the sampling method. Families were visited least often in the state with the highest percentage of single-parent families. The lower visiting level in this state is itself a sampling artifact related to the specific sampling frame. Hence, the results on visitation must be viewed with caution.

No statistically significant differences were found between single-parent and two-parent families in their evaluation of the appropriateness of the number of visits with the social worker, the amount of information provided, the accuracy of the information, or the evaluation of the helpfulness of services. Most families indicated that the number of visits was appropriate. Approximately one-fifth of single-parent and two-parent families indicated that they had not received enough visits. A substantial majority of families (more than 80%) reported that the social services provided by the agency were helpful. Of families who received information, most indicated that they were given enough information and that the information was accurate.

Table 6 presents data on services received since adoptive placement. Different patterns of post-placement services for one- and two-parent families were noted. Approximately one-third of single parents and one-fourth of two-parent families were involved in family therapy, and one-fourth of single parents and approximately one-third of two-parent families were in contact with other families adopting a special-needs child. The helpfulness of these services was evaluated differently. Whereas both single- and two-parent families evaluated parent support groups and contact with other special-needs families as being more helpful than was individual or family therapy, single-parent families were much more likely than were two-parent families to report that parent support groups had been very helpful (72% of single-parent families compared with 44% of two-parent families).

### Summary

This study noted differences in the characteristics of children adopted by single- and two-parent families. Single parents, most of whom were women, tended to adopt girls, older children, nonwhite children, and mentally retarded children. Single mothers tended to be older and to have finished high school. Single parents tended to be nonwhite and to have lower incomes. Children in single-parent homes experienced fewer emotional and behavioral problems than did children in two-parent homes, although both groups of adopted children showed serious emotional and behavioral difficulties. Perhaps the intensity of relating to two adults on an intimate basis results in more difficulties after placement than does having to relate to one adult caretaker. Given that the older children--who often have more severe problems than younger children do--are adopted by single parents, it is unlikely that couples adopt more difficult children. There was no indication that the relationship between single parents and their children was closer compared with that of the adopted child and couples (Groze & Rosenthal, 1989a, 1989b, 1989c). Bourguignon (1989) suggests that although many single adoptive parents enjoy taking care of children, they do not themselves have high needs to be nurtured. Consequently, they may set up emotional boundaries between themselves and the children and

TABLE 5. Agency services

| Number of meetings with social worker | Single-parent family % | | Two-parent family % | |
|---|---|---|---|---|
| | Since placement[a] | Since finalized | Since placement[a] | Since finalized |
| None | 42.7 | 70.1 | 27.0 | 70.8 |
| 1-3 | 26.5 | 17.9 | 35.4 | 21.7 |
| 4-9 | 19.7 | 6.8 | 24.2 | 4.8 |
| 10-19 | 5.1 | 3.4 | 8.3 | 1.4 |
| 20 or more | 6.0 | 1.7 | 5.1 | 1.3 |

| | Single-parent family (%) | Two-parent family (%) | $x^2$ |
|---|---|---|---|
| *Since placement, would you say you had:* | | | 0.91 |
| More visits than necessary? | 3.9 | 2.6 | |
| *Did the social worker provide:* | | | 0.69 |
| Too much information on the child's background and problems? | .9 | .8 | |
| About the right amount of information? | 60.4 | 64.6 | |
| Not enough information? | 38.7 | 34.6 | |
| *Was the information:* | | | 1.85 |
| Accurate? | 51.1 | 58.4 | |
| Mostly accurate? | 37.4 | 30.8 | |
| Mostly inaccurate? | 11.1 | 10.8 | |
| *Thinking about the services provided, were these services helpful?* | | | 1.86 |
| Yes, very much so. | 58.6 | 53.0 | |
| Yes, somewhat. | 30.6 | 31.7 | |
| No, not really | 10.8 | 15.3 | |

[a]$p < .05\%$

in so doing provide a safe environment for the child who has previously experienced failure in close emotional relationships with adults. The decrease in intimacy may result in reduced behavioral difficulties with the child and fewer unmet needs for the parent. Fewer behavior problems reported in single--parent homes may be associated with fewer visits with a social worker after placement.

Regarding educational functioning, no differences between children in single-or dual-parent homes were noted.

Finally, differences in ecological functioning were noted. Single parents reported that parent support groups were very helpful more often than did couples. This implies that single parents, who do not have another adult in the home to rely upon for support, may use support groups in the community to make up for lack of partner support. The findings also suggest that traditional mental health services may not be adoption-sensitive, which consequently may lead to less involvement of adoptive families in traditional therapeutic services.

Table 7 presents the parents' perceptions of adoption smoothness and overall impact of the adoption. Although differences were noted in the child's emotional and behavioral functioning, and in the social and ecological functioning of one- and two-parent families, no differences were found in their evaluation of adoption smoothness. A statistically significant relationship exists between family structure and the impact of the adoption on the family. Single-parent families were more likely than were two-parent families to evaluate the adoption's impact as being very positive. Clearly, however, these findings speak to the affirmative perception of both single- and two-parent families regarding their adoption of special-needs children.

In an exploratory analysis, we searched for characteristics of children for whom single-parent adoption might be more advantageous than two-parent adoption. Factors such as foster-parent adoption, sibling placement, relative placement, handicap status of the child, age of the child, gender of the respondent, out-of-home placement history,

TABLE 6. Services since adoptive placement

| | Single-parent family | | Two-parent family | |
|---|---|---|---|---|
| | % | Frequency | % | Frequency |
| Individual therapy for child | 35.0 | 41 | 36.9 | 236 |
| Family therapy | 31.6 | 37 | 25.0 | 161 |
| Parent support group | 18.3 | 21 | 19.5 | 126 |
| Contact with other special-needs adoption families | 26.3 | 31 | 31.7 | 204 |

| | Helpfulness of services for single-parent families | | | | | |
|---|---|---|---|---|---|---|
| | Very helpful | | Somewhat helpful | | Not helpful | |
| | % | Frequency | % | Frequency | % | Frequency |
| Individual therapy for child | 40.0 | 16 | 35.0 | 14 | 25.0 | 10 |
| Family therapy | 44.4 | 16 | 38.9 | 14 | 16.7 | 6 |
| Parent support group | 72.2 | 13 | 27.8 | 5 | 0 | 0 |
| Contact with other special-needs adoption families | 50.0 | 13 | 50.0 | 13 | 0 | 0 |

| | Helpfulness of services for two-parent families | | | | | |
|---|---|---|---|---|---|---|
| | Very helpful | | Somewhat helpful | | Not helpful | |
| | % | Frequency | % | Frequency | % | Frequency |
| Individual therapy for child | 35.1 | 79 | 51.1 | 115 | 13.8 | 31 |
| Family therapy | 36.2 | 55 | 50.0 | 76 | 13.8 | 21 |
| Parent support group | 43.6 | 51 | 47.9 | 56 | 8.5 | 10 |
| Contact with other special-needs adoption families | 51.3 | 96 | 41.2 | 77 | 7.5 | 14 |

and sexual-abuse history were examined. Only one potentially important factor was identified.

Children who had experienced group-home or psychiatric placement prior to adoption managed particularly well in single-parent adoptions. The mean score on the family-impact question provides a global measure of outcome from the parents' perspective. The highest possible response (very positive) was scored as 5, the next highest as 4, and so on; the lowest response (very negative) was scored as 1. For single-parent adoptions, mean scores for impact of adoption on children who had and those who had not experienced group home or psychiatric placement were approximately equal. These scores were as follows: placement group, mean = 4.23, $SD$ = 1.30, $n$ = 9; nonplacement group, mean = 4.36, $SD$ = .88, $n$ = 67. In contrast, in two-parent families, children who had experienced prior placement fared much worse: Placement group, mean = 3.56, $SD$ = 1.18, $n$ = 54; nonplacement group, mean = 4.30, $SD$ = .81, $n$ = 347. A $t$-test of the difference in means reached significance for two-parent adoptions ($t$ = 4.49, $p$ < .01, separate variance estimate), whereas this test was not significant in single-parent adoptions ($t$ = .30, $p$ > .05).

To conclude our analyses, multiple regression of selected variables on the family-impact response was conducted (Table 8) Cohen and Cohen (1983) describe the interpretation of interaction terms in multiple regression. A variable for one of the states was included so that variation due to differential sampling methodology could be controlled. Questions on prior placement and sexual abuse history were asked in only two of the three states. Hence, sample size is smaller than in other analyses.

The coefficient for single-parent adoption does not reach significance ($p$ = .70). Thus, among children who have not experienced group-home placement, single-parent versus two-parent home is not predictive of outcome. The interaction of single-parent placement with previous group-home or psychiatric placement is significant ($p$ = .05, beta = .109). This indicates that single-parent placement may be particularly effective for children with prior group-home or psychiatric placement. Other significant predictors included age of child at time of survey ($p$ < .01, beta = .26) and prior placement

## TABLE 7. Respondent's perceptions of the adoption experience.

| | Single-parent family (%) (n = 122) | Two-parent family (%) (n - 651) | $X^2$ |
|---|---|---|---|
| *Overall smoothness of the Adoption* | | | 2.19 |
| Smoother than expected | 31.7 | 31.9 | |
| About as expected | 40.0 | 33.8 | |
| More ups and downs than expected | 28.3 | 34.3 | |
| *Overall impact of the adoption* | | | 11.99[a] |
| Very positive | 58.9 | 44.1 | |
| Mostly positive | 21.4 | 29.6 | |
| Mixed | 16.1 | 22.0 | |
| Mostly negative | .9 | 3.3 | |
| Very negative | 2.7 | 1.1 | |

[a]$p < .05$

## TABLE 8. Regression of selected variables on impact of adoption on family.

| Variable | Beta | p |
|---|---|---|
| Single-parent adoption | .021 | .70 |
| Group home or psychiatric placement prior to adoption | -.210 | .00 |
| Interaction of single-parent and group home or psychiatric placement prior to adoption | .109 | .05 |
| Adoption by foster parents | .051 | .35 |
| Minority or mixed ethnicity (at least one adoptive parent) | .100 | .08 |
| Age when entered home | -.177 | .33 |
| Age when entered home (curvilinear term)[a] | .239 | .14 |
| Age at survey | -.260 | .00 |
| Respondent is female | .062 | .22 |
| Subsidized adoption | .039 | .53 |
| Sibling placement | .092 | .08 |
| Relative adoption | .014 | .79 |
| Child is handicapped | -.040 | .46 |
| Family income (in thousands of $) | -.075 | .19 |
| Mean level parental education | -.046 | .43 |
| Sexual abuse prior to adoption (actual or suspected) | -.113 | .06 |
| State 3 placement[b] | .065 | .36 |

*Note.* All dichotomous variables are coded as 1 if characteristic is present and 0 (zero) if it is not. $N = 362$; $R^2 = 19$. adjusted $R^2 = .15$.
[a]Term formed by squaring child's age in years at entry.
[b]Dummy variable for one state to control for difference in sampling procedures.

history ($p < .01$, beta = .21). Sexual abuse history and sibling placement approached significance.

## Conclusion

These findings suggest that flexibility is critically important in the assessment process and in the development of recruitment strategies. Recruitment and adoption policies should target nontraditional families such as single parents in their efforts to secure permanent homes for children. Single-parent adoption emerges as a good plan for children.

In addition to this data on postfinalization functioning of adoption, most studies (Boyne, Denby, Kettenring, & Wheeler, 1984; Urban Systems Research and Engineering, 1985; Festinger, 1986; Kagan & Reid, 1986; Barth & Berry, 1988; Barth et al., 1988) found that single parents were equally represented in disrupted and intact adoptions. The pattern indicates that marital status has little, if any, effect on risk of disruption.

Singles make up a significant portion of the population and a number of single people are raising children on their own. Single adoptive parents are not only a feasible but an untapped resource to provide homes for children with special needs, a recommendation made two decades ago by Kadushin

Practitioners may find this psychosocial analysis helpful in their work with adoptive families. Using the psychosocial model as a guide, they can assess adoptive families and their special-needs children along the same dimensions as discussed here and thus be able to determine what is normative for other families who have adopted special-needs children. Such comparison may be useful in case planning for these families by indicating differences between the family requesting services and the typical experiences of other special-needs adoptive families. The results may also help identify the most appropriate types of services for adoptive families. The findings suggest that parent support groups and adoption-sensitive mental health services may be most helpful, particularly for single parents.

This article appeared in Families in Society: The Journal of Contemporary Human Services., February 1991. It was copyright in 1991 by Family Services America, and is reprinted with permission from the publisher, Manticore Publishers.

# References

Achenbach, T.M., & Edelbrock, C.S. (1983). *Manual for the child behavior checklist and revised child behavior profile.* Burlington, VT: Department of Psychiatry, University of Vermont.

Barth, R.P. & Berry, M. (1988). *Adoption and disruption: Rates, risks, and response.* New York: Aldine de Gruyter.

Barth, R.P., Berry, M. Yoshikami, R., Goodfield, R.K., & Carson, M.L. (1988). Predicting adoption disruption. *Social Work,* 33, 227-233.

Blalock, H.M. (1979) *Social statistics* (rev., 2nd ed.). St. Louis: McGraw-Hill.

Bourguignon, J-P (1989, May-June). *Single parent adoptions.* Workshop presented at Sustaining Adoption National Conference, Charleston, SC.

Boyne, J., Denby, L., Kettenring, J.R. & Wheeler, W. (1984) *The shadow of success: A statistical analysis of outcomes of adoptions of hard-to-place children.* Westfield, NJ: Spaulding for Children.

Branham, E. (1970). One parent adoptions. *Children,* 17(3) 103-107.

Cohen, J. & Cohen, P. (1983) *Applied multiple regression/correlation analysis for the behavioral sciences.* Hillsdale, NJ: Lawrence Erlbaum.

Dougherty, S. (1978). Single adoptive parents and their children. *Social Work,* 23, 311-314.

Feigelman, W., & Silverman, A.R. (1977). Single parent adoptions. *Social Casework,* 58, 418-425.

Feigelman, W., & Silverman, A.R. (1983). Chosen children: *New patterns of adoptive relationships.* New York: Praeger.

Festinger, T. (1986). *Necessary risk: A study of adoptions and disrupted adoptive placements.* New York, Child Welfare League of America.

Groze, V., & Rosenthal, J.A. (1989a). *Special-needs adoption survey: an analysis of Oklahoma's intact adoptive families and children.* Monograph prepared for the Oklahoma Department of Human Services, Oklahoma city, OK.

Groze, V., & Rosenthal, J.A. (1989b). *Kansas intact families and their adopted children: A survey analysis of special needs adoptions.* Monograph prepared for the Kansas Department of Social and Rehabilitative Services, Topeka, KS.

Groze, V., & Rosenthal, J.A. (2989c). *Subsidized adoptions in Illinois: A survey of special needs children and their intact families.* Monograph prepared for the State of Illinois, Department of Children and Family Services, Springfield, IL.

Jordan, F., & Little, W. (1966). Early comments on single-parent adoptive homes. *Child Welfare,* 45, 536-538.

Kadushin, A. (1970). Single-parent adoptions: An overview and some relevant research. *Social Service Review,* 44, 263-274.

Kagan, R.M. & Reid, W.J. (1986). Critical factors in the adoption of emotionally disturbed youths. *Child Welfare,* 65, 63-73.

Maluccio, A.N., & Fein, E. (1983). Permanancy planning: A redefinition. *Child Welfare,* 62, 195-201.

Reid, W.J., Kagan, R.M., Kaminsky, A., & Helmer, K. (1987). Adoption of older institutionalized youth. *Social Casework,* 68, 140-149.

Shireman, J.F. (1988). *Growing up adopted: An examination of some major issues.* Chicago: Chicago Child Care Society.

Shireman, J., & Johnson, P. (1976). Single persons as adoptive parents. *Social Service Review,* 50, 103-116.

Shireman, J., & Johnson, P., (1985). Single-parent adoptions: A longitudinal study. *Children and Youth Services Review,* 7, 321-334.

Shireman, J., & Johnson, P. (1986). A longitudinal study of black adoptions: Single parent, transracial, and traditional. *Social Work,* 31, 172-176.

Urban Systems Research and Engineering. 1985. *Evaluation of state activities with regard to adoption disruption.* Washington, DC: Urban Research and Engineering.

Victor K. Groze is Associate Professor of Academic Affairs, Mandel School of Applied Social Sciences, Case Western Reserve University, Cleveland, Ohio. James A. Rosenthal is Associate Professor, School of Social Work, University of Oklahoma, Norman, Oklahoma.